HUMANISM AND CULTURE

By the Same Author

★ The Social Criticism of Matthew Arnold (1996)

About the Author

Dr (Mrs.) Meera Panigrahi was awarded the M.Phil and Ph.D. degrees by the Utkal University in 1982 and 1994 respectively.

Earlier she published a book *The Social Criticism of Matthew Arnold* (1996) apart from contributing researched articles to different journals and books.

At present she is working as a Reader in English, B.J.B. College, Bhubaneswar.

HUMANISM AND CULTURE
Lionel Trilling and the Critical Tradition

MEERA PANIGRAHI

CONCEPT PUBLISHING COMPANY, NEW DELHI-110059

ISBN 81-7022-871-9

First Published 2001

Published and Printed by
Ashok Kumar Mittal
Concept Publishing Company
A/15-16, Commercial Block, Mohan Garden
NEW DELHI-110059 (India)

Phones: 5648039, 5649024
Fax: 091-11-5648053
Email: publishing@concept.com

To

The Memory of

Prof. Bidhubhusan Das

FOREWORD

This book highlights the humanistic critical tradition in literature and situates Lionel Trilling as a literary critic who made important contributions to the strengthening of that tradition. The tradition, which has its roots in the secular humanism of the age of Enlightenment, found its ardent followers in Samuel Johnson, Matthew Arnold, T.S. Eliot and F.R. Leavis. The New Humanists in America, Paul Elmer More and Irving Babbitt shared their basic assumptions, and tried to stem the tide of excessive Romanticism and Impressionism in literary criticism by bringing to bear on their writings the restraint and decorum of the classical spirit.

The role of criticism is to study the contextuality of literature seen as the product of an entire tradition. Few critics today would spare much effort to study the sociological basis of literature, or to study the human being as a complex of biological, psychological, social, political and cultural processes, his material and spiritual nature and his deep inexplicable psychic impulses. He is repeatedly subjected to a series of inquiries that subvert his innate human quality, making him out to be either a cultural subject (or, in David Reisman's words, other-directed) or only a literary construct, imprisoned in the "Prison-house of language", as Fredric Jameson would like to say.

Lionel Trilling enjoys an undisputed eminence in American literature and culture. The book establishes him as a true humanist in an age when scientism and positivism intruded into the realms of literary study deflecting it from its aims to propagate human values that can nourish and strengthen culture. It requires broad learning and disinterested preoccupation with man and culture to make it clear that literature was not just the product of an ephemeral imagination, but a chronicle of abiding human experiences, the pulse of an entire culture, its breath and finer spirit; Dr. Meera Panigrahi effectively shows that Trilling had it all.

The author has made a deep study of Trilling's works and ventilated the most important elements of the philosophy of humanism in his writings. She classifies Trilling's position as an apt critic of society, culture and literature and focuses on their interrelatedness. She maintains that the humanistic tradition in literary criticism examines the socio-historical matrix of literature and that the literary criticism of Lionel Trilling redefines the function of literature and criticism as a value shaping force in the modern world of alienation, atomisation and pervasive dehumanisation.

The book deserves special attention as it highlights Trilling's humanistic method which counters theories of quantification, structuralism semiotics and deconstruction originated by science and positivistic epistemology and linguistics. The fourth chapter "Trillings' Theory of Criticism, as A Moulder of Culture" makes it clear what the function of criticism is, the social consequences of bad art or anti-art, and the subversion of tradition and culture. The last point is the result of 'acculturation of anti-culture' and the legitimisation of amoral and asocial elements that find a glorified space in modernist thought and art.

In the context of humanism the book studies the implications of the self-reflexive model which isolates not only the texts, but the self as well from social existence.

The chapters on Trilling as a critic of poetry and novel, emphasize his humanistic intentions as he sets out to find what criticism can contribute to the advancement of culture in the way of defining purposes, values and ends.

The last chapter is an effective rendering of the theme of literature and humanism. More importantly it validates the position of the human being as existing in a middle state between the brute and the angel where choices are to be made heroically taking full responsibility for his actions and words. The choice is between living sincerely and living 'authentically'; between being true to one's own self; realised as being dialectically linked to culture, and the autonomous self, answerable to no other authority, but to its own inner volitions.

The book is an important addition to works on modern theories of literary criticism. It will encourage more research into the writings of other American literary intellectuals who have made significant contributions to the cause of literature, society and culture.

Professor of Philosophy
Utkal University
Bhubaneswar

P.K. MOHAPATRA

PREFACE

Lionel Trilling, teacher, intellectual and critic, enjoys an undisputed eminence in American literature and culture. He emerged as a major presence in American literary life in the mid-1940's with the publication of his essays in the *Partisan Review* and the *Kenyon Review*. His writings constitute one of the strongest and most permanent achievements of the American literary intelligence in the present time.

As a humanist interested in the pedagogical value of literature he made it clear that literature was not just the product of an ephemeral imagination, but a chronicle of abiding human experiences, the pulse of an entire culture, its breath and finer spirit.

This book is a study of the literary criticism of Lionel Trilling as the product of an eminent humanist who belonged to a line of thinkers and critics from the eighteenth century to the modern age. It establishes the fact that he belongs to the critical tradition of Samuel Johnson, Matthew Arnold, the New Humanists of America Irving Babbitt and Paul Elmore More, as also T.S. Eliot and F.R. Leavis. These critics endorsed the inclusion of truth and human values in literary criticism and their importance in the upgradation and sustenance of culture and society. Trilling's individual genius lies in his endeavour to justify criticism as a means of preserving and moulding culture by guiding the individual consciousness. The book, therefore, highlights Trilling's critical argument which is directed towards the authenticization of the self in the context of biological, sociological and political processes.

Trilling's theory of culture is an important alternative to the cultural theorists who adopt an anthropological attitude to depict culture as a relative and local concept representing a particular culture at a particular moment. Hence this book may be helpful to those scholars who are searching for holistic methods of cultural interpretation and are sceptical of the anti-humanist view that literature is nothing more than a self-reflexive aesthetic reality.

JF-6, Utkal University Campus
Vani Vihar, Bhubaneswar-751 004

MEERA PANIGRAHI

CONTENTS

Foreword 7
Preface 9
Introduction 13

Chapter 1
The European Humanistic Tradition: An Overview 19

Chapter 2
The Humanistic Tradition in the Literary Criticism of Lionel Trilling 41

Chapter 3
Lionel Trilling: Critic of the Intellect and Spirit 70

Chapter 4
Trilling's Theory of Criticism as a Moulder of Culture 83

Chapter 5
Lionel Trilling's Literary Criticism: Poetry 104

Chapter 6
Lionel Trilling's Criticism of the Novel 125

Chapter 7
Literature, Society and Culture with Special Reference to *The Middle of the Journey* 157

Conclusion 174
Bibliography 181
Index 191

INTRODUCTION

The present work is an attempt to study the literary criticism of Lionel Trilling who is one of the great disseminators of the humanistic tradition in English criticism. His literary and cultural criticism is of immense value not only to the student of literature but also to intellectuals of all disciplines who are seriously trying to imbibe a certain mental resilience to deal with the countless ideas, literary and non-literary, that the society today is flooded with owing to the rapid expansion of knowledge. He appears to be as much relevant today as he was to his times because the theories that he propounds in his essays spring from an organic view of life, a serious attempt to understand and define the human dilemma in a technological society, and a sense of history that is essential to sharpen the perceptual powers of a critic. When he is read against the background of the plethora of literary theories that the experimental ethos of modernism has generated, he appeals to us as a voice of sanity and balance that contains the power to re-vitalise the modern dessication and confusion of mind.

His works retain a link with traditional classical humanism in the way they make a conditioned existence meaningful for the individual in society, and in the way they exhort writers to follow some ideal, some centre of authority outside themselves in expressing themselves in their works. The ideal to be followed in literature is to be derived from a careful study of human emotions, manners, customs, class distinctions, moral ideas and a view of life which encompasses the material and the spiritual dimensions in a holistic frame.

Following the tradition of Arnoldian thought Trilling's concern has always been to understand the relation of literature with life and to make culture the chief concern of his business as a critic. Like a true humanist he felt that the most serious problem for the artist in the modern world is to recover permanent and universal values which have stood the test of time. His deep interest in humanism places him in line with the great moralists in literature, Dr. Samuel Johnson, Matthew Arnold, T.S. Eliot and F.R. Leavis. As a sociological critic, Trilling examines the validity of liberal or progressive ideas and assumptions in the organisation of social institutions. This is also reflected in the writings of Irving Babbitt and Paul Elmer More who were ardent followers of New Humanism in America, but their range was limited.

Trilling wrote at a time when humanism was being attacked by science, technology and positivism. His writings show that he criticised their dehumanising effects and stood up against the loss of self, alienation, atomisation and above all, the pervasive dehumanisation of the modern scientific, technological and utilitarian society. Literature as a centralising force, capable of resisting the destructive powers of modern civilisation was the major concern of Trilling. In this thesis I have attempted to show to what extent Trilling succeeded in achieving this goal in his criticism.

Chapter 1, contains a discussion of the European Humanistic Tradition from the Renaissance to the modern age. It highlights those landmarks in literary and social history that have affected humanistic ideas and have contributed to their decline. It focusses attention upon the process of disintegration in society that science and technology have accelerated and whose repurcussions are to be seen in the distorted view of human nature and the lack of objective assessment of reality that modern literature projects.

Chapter 2 examines the humanistic critical tradition in literary criticism, which can be traced back to the works of Dr. Johnson in the eighteenth century. He is of particular interest to the humanistic tradition as he followed the ideas of secular humanism as adumbrated in classical literature and the age of Enlightenment to determine his attitude to society, literature and moral questions. He advocates the depiction of the general, the universal and typical to make literature morally sustaining. Matthew Arnold is also a great literary critic and is relevant to the English as well as to the American literary context and he is at one with Dr. Johnson in linking literature with life. His social and cultural concerns make him study the literary, political and moral conditions of nineteenth century England. T.S. Eliot and F.R. Leavis have largely followed Arnold's concerns. They have in their own ways developed the idea of the individual and culture, and showed grave concern for a society governed by democratised ideas of politics, art and literature. All of them believed in a shared stable system of beliefs and values, as opposed to the modern tendency for individualism and repudiation of all inherited human values. In America the New Humanists, Irving Babbitt and Paul Elmer More protested against the effects of science and excessive romanticism in American culture. They exposed the deficiencies of intellectual liberalism that is relativistic and pragmatic regarding ethical, moral and aesthetic questions. Lionel Trilling belongs to this tradition which derives from Arnold, but goes a step further in doubting whether culture could be able to sustain the life of the mind in its highest capacities.

Chapter 3 attempts a general estimate of Trilling as a critic. It places him in his milieu and studies his methods in relation to the dominant critical theories of modern times. It also aims at bringing out Trilling's method of dialectical analysis by which he admits the powers of both the intellect and the imagination harmonised to serve the highest interests of literature and society. He is against pure intellectual inquiry that leads one into philistinism and against mere spirit which declares its freedom from the conditions imposed by culture and society, and as such he is a critic of the intellect and spirit.

In Chapter 4 there is a discussion of Trilling's theory of criticism to show that it aims at preserving and moulding culture by guiding the individual consciousness. The ideal position is to have the self exist in the proper relation to culture. The main thrust of Trilling's critical argument is directed towards the authenticization of the self by which he means the raising of the spirit to a high level of consciousness that can comprehend a selfhood that is both sentient and "sincere". He makes it imperative for the self in the modern age to hold on to the kind of sanity that was exhibited by Western humanism in its advocacy that man is neither brute nor angel, and in the eschewing of irrationalism as a legitimate form of alienation from a restrictive culture.

Chapter 5 is an analysis of Trilling's position as a critic of poetry. His critical essays on poets subvert the formalist's objective, analytic, linguistic and structural approaches that enjoy prestige in an age of science and technology. He justifies an organic approach which takes poetry to be the consummate expression of humanity, the essence of human experiences and of human nature. Keats' negative capability, Wordsworth's sentiment of being and Arnold's assertion that poetry is a criticism of life, find a justified acceptance in Trilling's study of poetry.

Trilling's position as a critic of the novel is discussed in Chapter 6. He points out the limitations of naturalism which regards man as the sum of biological, sociological and political processes. Trilling contends that a true depiction of the human personality is missing in modern literature and that the urge to cultivate the autonomy of the personal self of the novelists and their characters has been responsible for the disintegration of the paradigms of realism in modern fiction. The cultural viewpoint of reality which emerges from Trilling's interpretation of novels is one which is determined not only by social and economic forces, but also by the spirit of one's age and by the needs of one's psyche.

In Chapter 7, Trilling's treatment of literature, society and culture has been dealt with in the special context of his novel *Middle of the Journey*. Trilling realises the interrelatedness of literary, political and social ideas and their impact on culture. This is a novel which depicts the thought processes of intellectuals who are guided more by ideas than by direct experience of life. The rigid conventionalism of the liberal minded intellectuals leads them on to make erroneous assessment of human nature, and their stunted imagination becomes incapable of grasping complex moral issues which are beyond positivistic and reductive definitions. Literature makes it possible for individuals to live in the present with all its moral, political and social entanglements, to develop courage that permits us to deal with the conditioned and imperfect reality of ourselves and the world to which we are committed by the nature of our destiny. This in effect is the message of the novel which considers the middle position of man as between brute and angel, a truly heroic one.

If we look back to ponder upon the diverse critical opinions on Trilling we shall find that he has evoked a variety of critical responses which show that he was a force to reckon with. There are a number of articles written on Trilling before the 1980's. R.W.B. Lewis (1950-51) makes a very important point that has given us a deep insight into Trilling the critic in his review of *The Liberal Imagination* in which he discovers Trilling's centrist position and calls it "the new stoicism". Joseph Frank (1956) charges Trilling with passivity and social quietism, whereas W.M. Frohock (1960) thinks that Trilling's understanding of America was incomplete because of a narrow New York perspective. D.H. Hirsch (1964) criticises him for restricting the novel to the novel of manners, thus limiting the scope of reality. Tony Tanner (1966) concedes that Trilling asks profoundly important questions about self and culture but provides no possible answers. T.H. Adamowski (1975) complains that Trilling's treatment of modern literature errs by being too abstract. On the other hand W. Barrett (1982: 39) comments that Trilling was far ahead of his time. This remark he makes in connection with Trilling's criticism of the liberal attitude, whereas Frank (1956) had commented on Trilling's "conservative imagination".

Towards the 1980's there has been a definite shift in critical opinion in favour of Trilling. Robert Boyers (1977) focusses our attention upon

Trilling's "negative capability" and maintains that he avoids making reductive statements about literary and moral issues.

W.M. Chace (1978-79) admires Trilling's larger social concerns to which American liberalism would not give its concurrence. Chace published his book *Lionel Trilling: Criticism and Politics* in 1980 and in his introduction described him as a figure of "extraordinary influence" because "he made the life of the mind an exciting experience" and taught us to think. E.J. Shoben (1981) makes a detailed study of Trilling's works and assesses him as a critic of poetry and the novel. He points to the influence of Freud and Arnold in his appraisal of culture and society. Mark Krupnick (1986) also makes a perceptive study of Trilling's career and opinions and points to his ambivalent attitude to almost any literary question. S.L. Tanner's *Lionel Trilling* (1988) is an excellent study of Trilling's critical works. Daniel T. O'Hara (1988) calls him a "subversive patriarch" in his book *Lionel Trilling: The Work of Liberation.*

Most of these critics have seen affinities between Arnold and Trilling, particularly because Trilling's first critical venture was a book *Matthew Arnold* published in 1939, in which he declared that "Arnold was the most influential critic of his age" (191). Trilling remembers him as the great continuator and transmitter of the tradition of humanism (Trilling 1949: 3). It is my contention that the humanistic critical tradition that followed a secular trail can actually be traced back to Dr. Samuel Johnson who exhorted the critic to follow the "general and transcendental truths" and to rise above the prejudices of his age or country (*Rasselas*). My aim is to situate Trilling in this tradition and evaluate him as a critic who belongs to the humanistic tradition in literary criticism which is both British and American and to point out his contribution to the development and strengthening of that tradition.

WORKS CITED

Adamowski, T.H., 1975. "Lionel Trilling: Modern Literature and Its Discontents". *Dalhousie Review* 55: 83-92.

Barrett, W., 1982. "The Authentic Lionel Trilling", *Commentary*, 73: 36-47.

Boyers, R., 1977. *Lionel Trilling: Negative Capability and the Wisdom of Avoidance*, Columbia.

Chace, W.M., 1978-79. "Lionel Trilling: The Contrariness of Culture". *American Scholar* 48: 49-59.

————, 1980. *Lionel Trilling: Criticism and Politics*. Stanford: Stanford University Press.

Frank, J., 1956. "Lionel Trilling and the Conservative Imagination". *Sewanee Review* 64: 296-309.

Frohock, W.M., 1960. "Lionel Trilling and the American Reality". *Southwest Review* 45: 224-32.

Hirsch, D.H., 1964. "Reality, Manners and Mr. Trilling". *Sewanee Review* 72: 420-32.

Krupnick, M., 1986. *Lionel Trilling and the Fate of Cultural Criticism.* Evanston: Northwestern University Press.

Lewis, R.W.B., 1950-51. "Lionel Trilling and the New Stocism". *Hudson Review* 3: 313-17.

O'Hara, D.T., *Lionel Trilling: The Work of Liberation*. University of Wisconsin Press.

Shoben, E.J., 1981. *Lionel Trilling.* New. York: Ungar.

Tanner, S.L. 1988. *Lionel Trilling.* Boston: Birmingham, Young University Press.

Tanner, T., 1966. "Lionel Trilling's Uncertainties". *Encounter* 27: 72-77.

Trilling, L., 1982. *Matthew Arnold.* Oxford, Melbourne Oxford University Press 1st published 1939.

————, 1949 ed. *The Essential Matthew Arnold.* London: Chatto and Windus.

1

THE EUROPEAN HUMANISTIC TRADITION: AN OVERVIEW

> No more delirious spectacle has ever been witnessed than that of hundreds of millions of human beings using a vast machinery of scientific efficiency to turn life into a hell for one another. . . . The dissolution of civilisation with which we are threatened is likely to be worse in some respect than that of Greece or Rome in view of the success that has been attained in "perfecting the mystery of murder".
>
> — Irving Babbitt (*Rousseau and Romanticism*)

In the beginning of this study, it will be useful to trace the growth and decline of humanism in the thought of the West, and to attempt a definition of this term since Lionel Trilling, as a critic, subscribed to it. Today, the word is used in various contexts, all of them pointing towards the perfection of human life in a material sense, its progress, comfort and security.

This chapter attempts to give a definition of the term humanism as a philosophical concept aimed at developing the internal and external faculties of men. Secondly, it makes the point that the literature of the past two centuries has suffered due to the attack on humanism by scientific theories and materialistic concerns. In a technological age, literary criticism has fallen from its high aims of perfecting culture and civilisation, and by following the example of dry technique, has itself become arid, technical and limited. Thirdly, this chapter makes a survey of the European humanistic tradition from the Renaissance to the modern times, in order to study human values and changing moral concerns. Finally, the chapter argues for the reiteration of humanistic values in literature and criticism to counteract the disintegrative elements in modern and postmodern thought and literature.

Humanism is a philosophy that has influenced the thoughts of all great men who have felt the urge to improve the human condition. In literature it has been the moving force of great works that have withstood the test of time and the twists of changing tastes. It addresses itself to the general and the universal values of life, as distinct from the temporal and the local. Although it is impossible to fix the boundaries of humanism and to define and deduce its nature, goal and functions, some attempts can be made to understand it. Humanism stresses the importance of the individual human personality and its power to learn from suffering and to rise above circumstances and in the process it takes cognisance of the paradox that lies at the root of life—the individual is part and parcel of the cultural environment that shapes him, while the self is always in conflict with the culture that shapes him. Thus, it has a double task to perform. First, it aims at creating a cultural climate by perfecting the political, social, religious and artistic foundations of a society to suit the needs of the times, and secondly, to perfect the individual as a living, thinking, honest human being, sincere to himself and acting upon firm moral convictions. Following the example of the great classical, scholars and writers, the humanists aimed at the development of their emotions, intelligence, reason and instinct. As Irving Babbitt (1930) remarks, they "actually caught a glimpse of the fine proportionateness of the ancients at their best" (in Foerster 1930a: 26), and consequently attempted to bring about a harmonious development of all their faculties, "without one-sidedness or over-emphasis, whether of the ascetic or that of the specialist" (*ibid.*).

Humanism, we may say, makes the point, that men should live by great ideas which can be derived from any source—theology, science, politics or history; in fact all our knowledge should be derived from meaningful human experience. The imbibing of such ideas will help form the mind of the individual. A humanistic training will liberate the individual's powers of speculation, imagination and reason, so that there follows a right exercise of choice and will to countervail the disconcerting conditions in our culture. These conditions can annihilate his selfhood or destroy his inherited conceptions of value. Since the dignity of the individual rests on his power "to create and communicate . . . to speculate, imagine and reason" (Bullock 1985: 155), ideas go a long way towards the formation of character. But it should always be remembered that some ideas do outlive their utility, and therefore excessive and indiscriminate reliance on outmoded beliefs should be avoided at all costs. The purpose of humanism is to help cultivate a frame of mind that can evaluate, judge and analyse, so that the usable elements of culture are preserved or suitably modified to relate to changing social conditions. What is most essential for a humanistic approach is to relate ideas to society and history in order to see them in their proper perspective. Hence the development of the historic sense, or what Lionel Trilling calls "the sense of the past" or what H.J. Muller calls "the uses of the past" is essential to humanism. It helps us judge the efficacy of ideas, either to discard them or to revise them in the light of new ones as and when the situation demands. The historic sense binds us to those aspects of a tradition or belief that perfect the internal condition of man, making him morally committed to his society and culture.

In perfecting the environment, the humanist makes it a point to see that all social institutions, such as politics, philosophy, education, literature and art are aimed at developing the inner faculties of individuals. Both the material and the spiritual welfare become the object of intense consideration for the humanist. For doing so, the emphasis is not upon the materials that bring order, comfort, freedom, wealth and general well-being, but upon human values that guide his course in life and aid in affirming those universal truths that can transcend parochialism, narrow provincialism and uncritical nationalism.

In trying to understand and define humanistic assumptions it is best to remember that "no one has the right to say that his view of the humanist tradition is definitive, it can only be a personal one. . ." and that in judging ideas and assessing their value we should also bear in mind that "Any view which is deterministic or reductionist in its view of human life and consciousness, or which is authoritarian and intolerant" is non-humanistic (Bullock 1985: 155).

It is possible to sum up some basic tenets of humanism in the light of the formulations of Foerster in his book *Towards Standards* (1930). Humanism prescribes the application of a standard of values to life and literature, based on human experience and a harmonious blending of the rational, the imaginative and the ethical. Its assumptions are concerned with the universal and the central "not the eccentric and the idiosyncratic". It looks for sustenance towards the past, to Greece, Rome and Christian traditions that had seen great ages, seeking out those "constants" that should be "preserved" and allowed to influence the present, thus transcending "the specialism that limits all ages in the past as well as the present age". It uses reason for the process of discrimination but also "seeks to press beyond reason by the use of intuition or imagination" to grasp a higher reality inaccessible to science. "The anarchy of wandering desires and blind impulses" let loose by romanticism and naturalism has to be checked by "restraint or control". In other words, "the energies of the instinctive self" have to be "harnessed by the ethical self", self-expression in art has to be subjected to classical decorum. Humanism is the need of the day since it maintains a deep inner core of fixity that counteracts the flux of human experiences and prevents disintegration by holding tight to the reins of tradition. "Pure humanism" does not use the language of religion, nor does it "accept a formal theology. . ." "for it holds that the value of supernatural intuition must be tested by the intellect". It harmonises science and art but is more akin to religion "in its perception of the ethical will as a power above the ordinary self" (Foerster 1930b: 165-171).

Irving Babbitt (1930) is of the view that a humanist has the "immediate perception" of laws "that are not of today or yesterday", but which transcend the temporal process. "The final appeal of the humanist is not to any historical convention but to intuition" (in Foerster 1930a: 27). T.S. Eliot in his essay "Some Thoughts About Humanism", collected in his book *Selected Essays*, describes humanism as general culture, not concerned with philosophical foundations, but then goes on to say that "it is a mediating and corrective ingredient in a positive civilisation founded on definite belief" (Eliot 1951: 480). Further, he states that humanism "is necessary for the criticism of social life and social theories, political life and political theories" (*ibid.*). While Eliot could not give credence to humanism without religion, T.E. Hulme differentiates between the two: "It is necessary to realise that there is an absolute, and not a relative difference between humanism (which we can take to be the highest expression of the vital), and the religious spirit" (Hulme 1987: 8).

Such a varied response to the idea of humanism accentuates its broad and flexible nature. But it mainly supports a whole or an integrated view of man, perfect in his moral, social and intellectual life, carefully balancing and harmonising his intellectual and emotional faculties.

In the modern context, a reiteration of humanistic values in literature is of prime importance. Various factors have contributed to the dehumanisation of man and fostered the belief that he is the sum of merely his biological drives, subject to economic pressures and to the whims of developing technology.

J.W. Krutch sums up the human condition thus:

> During the two centuries just past more and more human beings have become accustomed to doubt that they are the sons of God and

> that they have immortal souls. Philosophers hint or proclaim that the human being is not essentially different from the other animals and, that all animals are essentially machines whose behaviour is not determined by the choices they are capable of making but by fixed responses to the stimuli to which they were exposed. Since this doctrine began to be widely preached the mechanists have greatly elaborated it without fundamentally changing its implications and they have succeeded in imposing it upon the majority of educated and thoughtful men. — Krutch 1959: 98-99

The culmination of such a view of human life is to be found in *Walden II* by F. Skinner. General conditioning can bring about any expected change in human nature.

In the most esteemed contemporary literature whether American or European, man is projected as an unimpressive and disjointed individual, and his life is described as meaningless and futile. This view of man that negates his essential human quality and reduces him to a machine has ultimately the effect of alienating sensitive intellectuals and thinkers from the main-stream of life. The decadence at the root of modern civilisation is manifested in loss of self, alienation, atomisation and gradual deterioration from the level of the human to the mechanical.

Lewis Mumford analyses the human condition and points to its degeneration:

> Modern civilisation has been arrested in mid-flight: its technical advances in saving labour, perfecting automatism, machanising the daily processes of life, multiplying the arts of destruction, and dehumanising personality have been responsible for this arrest.
> — Mumford 1963: 391

He further comments that the Western man lives in a world given over to "devitalised mechanisms", modern men have become "desocialised organisms", living in "depersonalised societies" (*ibid.*: 395). Similarly, the hero in modern literature is a "faceless and anonymous hero" exposed to "Nothingness" (Barrett 1961: 54), "who is at once everyman and nobody". (*ibid.*)

Modern literature exposes the dark, inhuman powers that engulf man and his failure to come to terms with them. It does not show the man as a hero, in classical style, struggling with universal forces and resigning himself to a beneficial cosmic order, finding in death the meaning and purpose of life, but a fragmented and despairing individual, succumbing to irrational forces in his own consciousness. Alienated from society and his own self, he finds release in violence, madness and suicide. The reason for this dehumanisation is not far to seek. Bullock refers to Jung who in investigating the functions of mythology had concluded that "in every age except our own, men and women have found meaning for their lives in some form of religion or myth", and argues that "many people today are suffering from a sense of futility because although they have discarded traditional beliefs, they need and can no longer find a religion or myth to live by . . ." (Bullock 1985: 148-149).

If religion and myth have been dealt a death blow by the factual realities prescribed by science, there is no other body of belief that can perhaps sustain and ennoble his spiritual life other than humanism. Since the humanist believes that of all the branches of thought and knowledge that have been evolved to educate man's mind and enhance his cultural life, literature holds the pride of place, any literary work, be it poetry, fiction or criticism, should incorporate humanistic ideas. Besides the aesthetic criterion the writer should also follow critical canons that relate literature to life, to understand and value Arnold's proposition that "literature is a criticism of life". The literary critic should not confine himself to purely aesthetic meanings and values. He should bear in mind that "a complete understanding and appraisal of it [literature] necessarily involves its relation to our whole experience" (Muller 1943: 44). The humanistic attitude in literary criticism holds that the critic should be "dispassionate, catholic, flexible, able to perceive the bearings of the diverse activities and admit their validity, able to take his own bearings and enlarge his scope" (*ibid.* : 45).

If modern American criticism has failed to propagate humanistic standards that relate literature to life, it is because there is always a striving in critics to fulfil the demand that they confine themselves to purely aesthetic meanings and values, and take into account the individuality of every writer and the uniqueness of every work. While the New Critical view sought "to restore the concreteness of sensuous materiality in the face of scientific abstraction, to rehumanise the world which science and logic had dehumanised" (Reising 1986: 169), it was not enough to revitalise critical theories. By declaring historical and social considerations "extrinsic and therefore ancillary to literary study", and "often denying or devaluing the referential nature of literary discourse", (*ibid.*: 15) they did a great disservice to cultural theories based on humanistic considerations.

The scientific method based on rational interpretation only of observable facts, resulted in a positivistic stereotype approach to nature and human life, and this is also reflected in literary criticism. The reality that literature, seeks to portray in an age of realism and naturalism, is not the ambiguous, mysterious inner reality, but the social reality: the political system, the economic effects, material conditions and sociological derivations all of which affect and involve human beings. The writers focus attention not upon the uniqueness of man but upon his commonplace attributes and desires. Since the mid-nineteenth century, fiction has become subservient to scientific, sociological and psychological theories, the writer's main anxiety being not to depict man in his humaneness but to illustrate some scientific or sociological thesis he has accepted about him. For instance, Zola's belief that heredity and environmental factors determine character and behaviour, is reflected in his novels. We are forced to conclude from much of modern literature that men are predictable items which circumstances have produced. Sociological problems such as the plight of the worker, the mentality of the bourgeois or psychological trauma of the post-war generation, find a ready place in literature. The result of all this seems to be in the emergence of a literature which in the words of Krutch has come to be "a less and less effective corrective while the sociology upon which it leans so heavily becomes more and more drab as it more and more insolently disregards the intangibles and reduces human nature to the few crude needs, wants and desires which it can recognise and measure" (Krutch 1959: 109).

The reason why culture does not possess the strength to hold the minds of men in modern society is the sense of alienation one develops at the picture of man and society which sociology and psychology offer and which by common consent of scientific minded men has been accepted as the truest picture. Krutch states that there is "an epidemic sense of alienation" caused by the sociological view of man. His mental and emotional life is believed to be adequately described in terms of his "sex satisfaction, his impulse toward conspicuous consumption and his desire for status" (*ibid.*: 113, 114).

The scientific age has seen the surrender of humanism to technology. The creation of the "mass-man", a feature of the democratic age, has added to the deterioration of high ideals. A positivist philosophy has taken hold of the minds of intellectuals who interpret man wholly on the basis of physics, chemistry and animal behaviour. Humanism, with its firm belief in a higher reality to which men may aspire has been attacked by science. The emergent picture is of a "one-dimensional" human being, dangling precariously over a modern wasteland, where there is no hope for the life-giving waters.

Since we have seen the dangers of adhering to what Foerster calls the "naturistic" mode of thought based on science, we may now turn to humanism to see whether it still possesses for us the necessary elements to see us through our modern impasse. If man still has a consciousness unable to interest itself in either mere animal survival or wealth, speed and power alone, he will go on searching for values that distinguish him from the natural order. Science which has taught him disregard for the past and explained man and the universe by "deterministic monism" will cease to interest him further. Nor can he continue to feel along with the scientist that the phenomenal world is the only kind of reality. His own inner world of human impulses and their power over his behaviour interest him more. He needs a philosophy which will make the ethical and moral life a necessary fact in human existence. Among transient, mechanical facts that threaten to engulf his personality, he will always be looking for those perennial objects of his ardent strivings that can help him to survive as an individual in his environment, in his own human right, not as part of a larger social set-up. Instinctively and emotionally conscious that he is an ethical man, he will find worthwhile meaning only in a social order based on moral values the decline of which in the course of history has produced his present dehumanised condition.

In ancient times it was God and religion and myth making that ensured man's happiness on earth. In the Middle Ages his faith in a divine order, of an anthropomorphic God and a rational universe held intact his conception of a moral order in which he could find happiness and certitude. In the Renaissance, when classical influences were increasingly affecting European thought, men were emancipated from the bonds of the medieval religious, moral and social order. They had inherited from the medieval world-view a coherent system of beliefs in the social order. The creation consisted of linked degrees of being from the four elements to the pure intelligence of angels. The divine will governed the course of the universe; nature was an instrument of God and the social hierarchy was an established concept. Subordination and unity were the natural law and man submitted to them in the belief that he could enjoy a civilised form of happiness if he accepted the visitations of divine wrath and human suffering as inevitable. The main task of human reason was to subordinate his body to his soul and prepare for the next life. To accomplish this end it was necessary to develop one's individualism and assert it in the face of medieval authority.

The humanists, therefore, looked to classical antiquity for a moral and intellectual revival. The recovery and imitation of Greek literature in the Renaissance Age exerted a great deal of influence on life and letters, an influence which was to last "till the Romantic Movement of the eighteenth century, as it was to last in the field of education till the latter part of the nineteenth century, when it was gradually superseded by the authority of the modern sciences and modern languages" (Foerster 1930: 10). The Renaissance humanists were poet-scholars. They studied and imitated the classics and also made them the objects of their literary criticism. According to Foerster "We must call the Humanist a scholar-poet-critic" (*ibid.*: 14). Their literary criticism was mainly aimed at searching for values in order to establish norms for the "good life", which means a life of many-sided, harmonious development. The man of learning in the Renaissance age was a man of knowledge, taste, insight and critical sense. The classics divulged not only the literary formats for creative expression such as the epic, tragedy, ode or sonnet, but also quenched his thirst for the sublime and the beautiful. He was fascinated by the heroic character of the classical protagonist and the richness of life represented in these works. More so, the appeal to a universal moral order for the perfection of man's baser impulses, gripped his imagination.

Another important feature of the Renaissance Age was Christian Humanism—a fusion of classical wisdom and Christian faith. According to Douglas Bush, "Humanism in the Renaissance normally means alliance with Christian faith with God-given reason, which is the most human faculty of man" (Bush 1968: 54). It provided a way of life that kept the individual in touch with God and prevented him from succumbing to his lower nature. The focus was upon man as man, aspiring to the higher realm of divinity and staying free from the bestial level by imposing ethical control upon his wild impulses. The essence of humanism was for man to recognise this middle position he occupies in the scheme of nature. He was to follow the golden mean, which is a characteristic attitude appearing in almost every system of Greek philosophy. It preached the motto of measure and harmony as against excess and disproportion and was a way of checking violence and impulsiveness of character. Will Durant says, that Aristotle found "the middle way", "the golden mean", the real "guide to excellence". He also finds that Plato had the same thing in mind "when he called virtue harmonious action",

Socrates too followed the same ideal when he identified virtue with knowledge. "The Seven Wise Men had established the tradition (of the middle path) by engraving, on the temple of Apollo at Delphi, the motto *meden agan*—nothing in excess" (Durant 1967: 75, 77). Through the proper exercise of reason man could keep himself on the middle path.

The veneration for the classics and ancient Greek and Roman philosophers and writers in the Renaissance had only one end in view. It meant faith in high standards. The aim of humanism in England was training in virtue and wisdom along classical principles and Christian values, so that the individual could be prepared to live an active Christian life, especially public life. The humanistic writings of authors like Sir Thomas More, Erasmus, Colet and even Milton provided an educational and moral standard stressing the virtues of commonsense, reason and ethical discipline.

The Renaissance tradition of Christian humanism, was, however, attacked by scepticism and naturalism generated by the new science. Astronomy posed great questions which undermined the ideas and beliefs hitherto accepted as eternal truths. It expanded the universe and dislodged man from his supremacy over natural objects. According to Bush, "What had been a relatively small world created by a fatherly God for the benefit of man . . . became a mechanical system in which human dignity shrank to nothing and God the Father became a logical postulate of motion" (Bush 1968: 90).

Scientific theories shook the absolute authority of the classics and the traditional humanistic discipline. The seventeenth century marks the rise of the physical sciences and the decline of medieval concepts. Throughout the sixteenth century human reason at different times had asserted its independence of authority and challenged scholastic methods of thought as is evident from the writings of Machiavelli, Erasmus and Montaigue. An awakening began with Roger Bacon which reached its fullness in the astronomy of Copernicus and Galileo. The result of all these scientific experiments was that knowledge grew, fear and reverence of the unknown were replaced by ambition to conquer it.

A deterministic attitude in the seventeenth century paved the way for a better moral world through acquiescence and resignation and liberated the mind from the fitful pleasure of passion to the high serenity of contemplation which sees all things as parts of an eternal order and development. The scientific movement produced an era in which men were no longer satisfied by supernatural explanations of natural phenomenon. The rational approach of science deemed the universe as the Great Machine "working by rigidly determined laws of material causation . . ." (Willey 1967: 4). But the belief in the Divine was still a potent force in the society. The Great Machine that was the universe ran by laws that were meticulously thought out by God. Therefore, the new philosophy of the Age of Reason "was anti-supernaturalist, but not anti-religious" (Willey 1967: 4).

Science was also able to provide the rational basis for a belief in a divine universe. This was because the "findings of science, uptodate, could fuse harmoniously with the presuppositions inherited from Christianity" (*ibid.*: 12). Science had revealed that the universe was guided by laws that pointed to the existence of God. Nature was designed and planned out and everywhere there was order and law. The great scientists among whom Newton stands supreme were theists. The laws of nature that they discovered were to them also the laws of reason. There followed therefore "a new vision of life, postulating the unity instead of the former dualism of man and nature" (Foerster 1930b: 34). Right conduct based upon the dictates of right reason proceeding from within the individual was the ideal to be followed. "To the question what must I do to be saved? Natural religion therefore made answer: Follow Reason, the God within . . ." (Willey 1967: 14).

This was indeed a very optimistic way of looking at man who thus learnt to accept the universe—to reconcile the material with the spiritual. Man regarded himself as fallen no doubt, but he could also feel "that he had not yet lost his original brightness" (*ibid.*: 22). He demanded liberty, equality and fraternity.

The Age of Enlightenment is unique in its harmonisation of science, religion and morals. The study of man as the proper objective of all studies paved the way to a secular form of humanism. Science gave a rational basis to religion by stripping away superstitions. It engendered reliance upon observation and experiment and brought forth a realism opposed to the supernaturalism of the earlier ages. The reliance upon free inquiry and liberty from authority strengthened individualism and the perfecting of social institutions aimed at creating maximum prosperity and happiness for man.

In the latter part of the eighteenth century, the romantic movement gained ground over the scientific. Rousseau was the new philosopher of the romantic ideas of individualism, freedom and inherent goodness of man. Romanticism began as a revolt against scientism in seeking to overcome the claims of reason, by celebrating the powers of the imagination. The romantics believe that natural instincts are suppressed, through rationalism, and men are thereby converted into agnostics. Rousseau taught that man was by nature good, and that it was only bad laws and customs that had suppressed him. Man had infinite possibilities which were repressed by social institutions. Once the repression was removed, these possibilities could have a chance of bringing in progress. The classical view according to Hulme saw man as an extra-ordinarily fixed and limited being "whose nature is absolutely constant. It is only by tradition and organisation that anything decent can be got out of him". The root of all romanticism consists in the belief "that man, the individual, is an infinite reservoir of possibilities"; and it is society that hinders their full development (Hulme: 1977: 166). Whereas Hulme upholds the classical view and sees it not as materialism but as the normal religious attitude (*ibid.*: 117) Romantics like Rousseau proclaim the grandeur of liberty which makes it synonymous with heroism. Such an attitude resulted in romanticism in literature and liberalism in political science.

Wylie Sypher's characterises romanticism as "essentially a counter attack of the self on the world outside—on the world invented by Descartes" [which conceives of the universe as the Great Machine] "and Newton and the scientists who followed them" (Sypher: 1961: 20). The Romantic's assertion of the personal will makes for what Sypher calls, "irresponsible freedom" breeding rebellion and anarchy. He further comments that "at its extreme, the romantic ideal of freedom is a form of disrelationship of the self from other selves" (*ibid.*: 20).

Rousseau's concept of man as a "noble savage" was to point out the simplicity and innocence of primitive life, to show that primitive life had values which no civilisation could afford permanently to forfeit. It had its roots in the belief in a natural order. But, as Lewis Mumford says, "there is a difference between idealising the noble savage and believing in a natural order". The two should not be confused. "The latter belief is a salutary corrective to human wilfulness and misunderstanding . . ." (Mumford 1963: 276), while romanticism, in its rebellion against "the tyranny of a mechanical, impersonal world order" (Sypher 1961: 21) results finally in isolation.

The middle class ideals of liberty permeating nineteenth century thought were the outcome of romanticism. From personal liberty of the romantics, the liberals like John Stuart Mill and Jeremy Bentham proceeded to social liberty. They brought in the notion of utilitarianism that aims at the greatest good for the largest number of individuals. Such a notion, while striving for the general good was apt to limit personal freedom. John Stuart Mill's *On Liberty* recognises the danger to individual rights by State interference. Sypher is of the opinion that Mill was "one of the first to recognise" that the "free self" would be in danger of extinction when it "entered into relations with society". Referring to the fifth chapter of Mill's autobiography which is called *A Crisis in My Mental History*, Sypher identifies the crisis as one of "romantic liberal thought, and a point at which an originally romantic idea of the self begins to change over into an existential idea of selfhood"—the self in relation to society (Sypher 1961: 23-24). Deterministic laws based on nature and society reduced man to a "hollow man". He was a man with an impoverished spirit which does not actually possess any freedom, shaped as it is by social and natural laws. There followed a quest for finding some centre within the self to recover from institutionalised determinism. This quest is characterised as the search for identity, integrity and authenticity.

The 'romantic self' which can be referred to as a heroic concept thus became the source of further alienation until "loss of self" became a permanent idea in the modern context. "Romantic flight" was substituted by the journey into the "buried life" within as Matthew Arnold confirms in his poem.

The autonomy given to the self in the modern age by the liberal political policies of democratic governments has in the absence of any central moral control, tended to foster the freedom of the self in its most anarchical forms. Anti-social behaviour amounting to criminal acts have been rationalised as acts underlining individual rights and so tolerable. As such, authenticity does not lie in being true to ourselves, however anti-human, anti-rational or anti-social it may be, but in projecting our "best selves" as Arnold would have us believe. Our "best self" lies buried within and is the repository of traditional, moral values that integrates us to a larger moral order. Therefore, Arnold distinguishes between our ordinary self and our best self. He emphasizes the point that in the democratic world, when more and more men of less and less intellectual, moral and imaginative faculties are liberated politically, then the best self should be allowed to prevail. "Doing as one likes", the policy of the liberals is bound to breed anarchy in the social sphere and mediocrity in art and culture. His book *Culture and Anarchy* was written to warn people in his age against unbridling their ordinary selves and alienating themselves from the ideals of humanism which rests upon "reason" and the "will of God".

How far Arnold was justified in his fear of the masses is reflected in Ortega Y. Gasset's book *The Dehumanisation of Art.* He holds in contempt the mass man and the technician who are separated from the main current of traditional values and wholesome human impulses. The technician is a specialist who has no interest in anything that lies outside his field of activity. He is the prototype of the nineteenth century personality rooted in his smug self-satisfaction and lacking in self-scrutiny and what Arnold calls "curiosity". Science, technism and democratic policies have contributed to the inauthenticity of lives lived by ordinary men and women. The compulsion to be different and the necessity to confirm to mass-based ideologies are in conflict. The hero in nineteenth century literature "resists the ordinary, which is the inauthentic but he fails to gain the authentic" (Sypher: 41). Diderot's *Rameau's Nephew* is an example of the protagonist striving to confirm and ending up with many inauthentic selves.

The reason for this fragmentation of the self is not far to seek. The individual could not find a centripetal force by which to hold in rein his anarchical tendencies. Myths, moral values and revealed religion become obsolete with the rapid development and changes brought in by scientific discoveries. Reason "which had originally an instrumental use, to pose awkward questions and reveal the hollowness of orthodox opinions and conventional wisdom . . . hardened into dogmatic rationalism" in the scientific age (Bullock: 156). Rationalism directed the attention outside into the objective world making the life of the emotions, the myth-loving consciousness, a scientific impossibility. It led to the negation of all that was held dear by the tradition-loving, orthodox individual, who believed in a life devoted to faith in human and religious values. Reason, which was originally meant to elevate and perfect man, is an essential element of humanism. It is the means by which the individual is expected to rise above the natural into the human level by successfully harmonising the subjective world of the senses and the objective world of nature. Reason was to set a standard of values by which the individual could live an ethical life in society. But in the age of Science reason was replaced by scientific rationalism. Scientific development depended on methods based on the rational interpretation of observable facts. The scientific temper resulted in the development of man's intellect at the expense of the imagination. It is this one-sided development based on either complete rationalism or unhindered romanticism that humanism strikes out against.

Bullock gives us the example of Goethe who can be called a true humanist:

> To Goethe, the poet who devoted so much of his time to the study of nature, it was the union of all the human faculties—an equal grasp of the objective and subjective worlds—that brought a man to the highest pitch of development. —Bullock: 156

Reason for Coleridge meant "the combination of Imagination with Method" (Bullock: 156). Such a 'combination' was the basis of the "unified sensibility" that marks a 'whole' man. In contrast to this, is the picture of man as a fragmented being whose intellect and emotion do not work in a smooth co-ordinated manner. David Riesman's theory of the other-directed and inner-directed man points to this division or fragmentation. From the nineteenth century onwards, science saw the degeneration of reason into rationalism. Darwin and Huxley became the new prophets of change and reformation of social and political values. According to Foerster ". . . science worked out the idea of organic evolution and placed man in nature, not spiritually as the romantics had sought to do, but psysically" (Foerster 1930b: 36).

The scientific method revealed a world of positivistic laws that reduced all human instincts and impulses to mechanistic processes. The development of psychology, for example, was based on the supposition that "mechanism prevails even in the inmost recesses of the soul" (Durant: 494).

It was against this "over-organised and over-rationalised civilisation" (Bullock: 134) that Nietzsche struggled; he exalted instinct and emotion and was fascinated by the irrational. He posited the dangers of nihilism that the "death of God" makes evident. When he declared that "God is dead", he meant it in a wider philosophical sense. According to William Barrett, Nietzsche meant that "the whole realm of super-sensible reality—Platonic ideas, the Absolute", everything that philosophy "posited beyond the sensible realm, and in which it has located man's highest values" has been negated by mechanistic science (Barrett 1961: 181). Nihilism lashed out against all moral pressures which weigh upon the inner lives of the individual. It declared war on everything which was not based on pure and positive reason.

The modern man realises himself as being imprisoned by political, social, scientific, ecological and psychological laws and hence has lost sight of his purpose of living. He has ceased to believe in his spirit as a means of transcendence owing to the rampant materialism of a highly civilised state taking his cue also from the socialist realism of Marx and Engels which emphasizes "that economic production moulds the institutions and ideologies at a given time; life is not determined by consciousness, but consciousness by material life" (Ellman and Fiedelson 1965: 229). Marx saw the individual as a social and economic man, "rich in vocations and values, multifaceted in wants and talents, gifted with free time and a sense of wholeness" (Miller 1982: 13).

But this vision of man is not wholly satisfactory. Marx saw man as a social individual and his theory reduced human wants to economic goods and hence negated the existence of the spirit. The later liberal political and economic theories project man as an autonomous, self-reliant, acquisitive and self-interested person, in conflict with the community. The function of the liberal state was to "assume a negative role mediating the interaction of individuals, since without a minimum of public regulation, the utopia of monadic individualism threatened to degenerate into a nightmare of selfish egos competing for scarce resources" (Miller: 14).

Thus, we see that the long effort of man to obey the injunction "Know Thyself" has resulted in nothing except the knowledge that he is low in every way. Myths of his divine origin and of his immortality have been systematically destroyed, and gradually he has come to accept himself as a machine produced by circumstances. He is not a "united I, but only the shifting and dissolving configuration produced at a given moment by the interaction of his instincts, his reflexes, his complexes and his traumas" (Krutch 1929: 100).

Knowledge about the human condition as derived from science and technology has dehumanised man. Society recognises no other kind of knowledge because nothing else except rational scientific knowledge can offer such positive answers, can pretend that all questions pertaining to human nature can be answered so readily.

We can sum up the gradual process of man's alienation and dehumanisation by studying the events of the last three or four centuries. Humanism can be "said to have passed through three well-marked stages . . . of progressive de-Christianization. First we have the God-centred humanism of men like Erasmus, Hooker, Donne, Milton or Locke. Next the man-centred humanism of the eighteenth century of the Encyclopaedists and of the idealistic romantic poets and philosophers" (Willey 1964: 118). This is a period in which morality is dependent not upon supernatural sanction but upon utilitarianism—"that is a matter of consequences of actions in terms of well-being or happiness—or a matter of the Kantian imperative, that is obedience to the law of man's own nature" (*ibid.*). The last stage is "the positivistic stage represented by Comte, Mill, Marx and their followers in which all possibility of contact with metaphysical reality is denied, man becomes God and Humanity a religion" (*ibid.*: 118-119).

A mechanistic deterministic philosophy that denies the existence of a supersensual or transcendental reality, from which the self derives inspiration and motivation has pervaded modern thought. By disregarding the spirit, this philosophy has harmed civilisation and culture. Scientific education is aimed at training individuals to adjust to social mores, by denying him the right to recognise his own spiritual nature.

The moral and spiritual nihilism of the modern world, therefore, is a poison that threatens to destroy civilisation, and must be dealt with. Humanism began with lofty claims for human individuality and dignity, but has failed to realise them. Religious humanists would agree with Basil Willey when he says:

> When man forgets that liberty is the service of God, he becomes a slave to his own passions and appetites and finally to a dictator or state machine which directs those appetites towards the end of power politics. When he forgets that he is a person, that is, a spiritual being, responsible to God, he becomes a thing, subject to natural and political determinism. — Willey 1967: 119

There may not be any such concept as a permanent human nature now because men are conceived of as being born with a "blank slate" (*tabula rasa* of Locke). What follows from the Lockean belief is cultural and moral relativism that denies morals, a permanent human nature and a particular system of ethics. Modern culture is seeking to do away with the past, with values, with the pre-occupation with the spirit. It has sacrificed concepts of the Good or the Beautiful or the Sublime; in other words modern culture has perpetrated forces of dehumanisation and the only way out of the predicament seems to be to submit oneself to social conditioning and to accept comfortably this conditioned existence. Any sensitive, imaginative, thinking man will naturally suffer from the malaise of anxiety and tension at the horror of modern life. But "the mass-man", a product of the industrialised, democratic, mechanised society, "is the creature who has to some extent escaped the malaise by ceasing to be a man at all" (Krutch 1959: 162).

Thus, we have seen how the heroic vision of human nature is lost upon us. The Age of Shakespeare could see the human being in his totality. Bullock contends that "there has never been a more comprehensive representation of the human condition" than in Shakespearean plays which he feels have "a secure and central place in the humanist tradition" (Bullock 1985: 43). Hamlet "the humanist prince" is made to exclaim, "what a piece of work is man! how noble in reason! how infinite in faculties!" Yet, the disillusioned prince exclaims that man is also the "quintessence of dust", who "delights not me". These are the two poles of the human condition from the humanist angle in contrast to the existentialist view of the contingent conditions that converge in angst.

Literature in the modern age has not been able to project an organic view of life, nor has it been able to give a complete image of man. On the other hand, in the attempt to liberate man from the inherited patterns of the past and to elevate the individual over social existence, modern literature has accentuated his idiosyncracies and peculiarities and highlighted his alienation from general culture, which is mostly the outcome of what Eugene Goodheart characterises as "a powerful utilitarian psychology born of a triumphant industrialisation" (Goodheart 1973: 22) and hence "repressive" of humanistic values of individual human dignity and the integrity and freedom of the human spirit. There has followed a search for alternatives to counter the repressive culture, a search that does not go back to the past to discover meaningful ideas, but a search that has resulted in a spate of experimentation in the arts under which reality is obfuscated. The threat to civilisation posed by the commercial culture or the "counter culture" of today requires the beneficial effects of a high holistic culture to dispel its negative influence. In the words of Goodheart: "Though the exponents of the counter culture enjoy the prestige of being radical, they show little interest in the life of the mind in its radical aspect" (Goodheart 1973: 31). They look with suspicion at intellectual and artistic culture, exhibiting a philistinism that is the enemy of humanism and the higher life. Hence, humanists have always pleaded for a literature that keeps the traditional culture alive in us and opens our mind to receive ideas from all cultures and ages to upgrade our present cultural situation and make for a richer social base for culture to flourish in the future. This challenges the phenomenon of "growing up absurd" that characterises the development of human beings in the technological and Benthamite civilisation in the modern world.

All humanists prescribe the study of great literature because it contains a picture of human dignity and human life that can counteract all attempts of positivism and relativism to reduce man to a mechanism. Literary criticism by being truly humanistic should be able to turn the mind of the modern Western man to his great literary past that conceives man as a dignified individual, whose intellect, spirit and body are cultivated proportionately, and who possesses immense capacities for self-development. The past is not to be dismissed as something outgrown and to be discarded (just as imperfect technology is discarded for new ones). An acquaintance with the history of mankind as reflected in great literature is the surest way to moral awareness. It is perhaps the only way that will teach the physicist that the nature of man is more important than the nature of the atom and that his studies should help man to be aware of his own humanness. Scientists ought to realise that "art too is a real way of knowing the real world" (Muller 1943: 258). Hence in the modern age, literary criticism has an important humanistic function.

Humanistic critics interest themselves in social origins and uses and keep turning into social philosophers. They have enriched literary study by emphasizing the human element in literature. In an age of science and technology social critics have tried to create the awareness that literature is not to be taken as an impractical, imaginary and false depiction of reality, but a depiction of life emerging from the combination of the powers of reason and imagination, hence more complete. It is not to be regarded as a "harmless narcotic", but as a "legitimate, mature, important way of knowing and dealing with reality" (Muller 1943: 266). As long as man's powers of intuitive and effective perception are not recognised as legitimate, as long as his emotions are not respected, as long as it does not become imperative to study human nature, literature can evoke only a marginal interest in society.

To redeem society from disintegration, fragmentation and dehumanisation, the study of literature is essential. The works of writers like Shakespeare, Wordsworth, Carlyle and Emerson point to the great cohesive force of literature. They were influenced by the belief that literature has the capacity to heighten each person's power of imaginative participation in the actions and ideas of others and thus literature helps us to know the thoughts and beliefs of others which can enrich our own experience. It helps us to inculcate the necessary mental resilience to incorporate great ideas from different sources to enrich our own life. Literature "provides an exercise of the senses, the imagination and the experiencing powers not available anywhere else in the curriculum. Knowledge of this kind, particularly because it reaches down below the level of abstract ideas into the life of feeling, is an invaluable defense against moral nihilism that seems to company technological thinking" (Marx 1975: 18-19).

Modern humanists of the stature of Irving Babbitt, Paul Elmore More, T.S. Eliot, F.R. Leavis, E.M. Forster and Lionel Trilling in our age have all largely followed Matthew Arnold in protesting against romanticism and naturalism and their effects on life and culture. They are convinced that the problems of modern man cannot be solved by technological, scientific or economic adjustments, for these can benefit him only in the material sense. The real problem faced by man in the modern age, they feel are cultural and intellectual. The New Humanists of America, Babbitt, More and Foerster being the most prominent among them, contributed significantly towards improving critical standards in American literature. They "were the first to wage a substantial attack against the naturalism and relativism that had gained consent with the emergence of Darwinism and pragmatism at the end of the nineteenth century and the beginning of the twentieth" (Hoeveler 1977: 3). They were conservative as they re-affirmed tradition, the relevance of the past and the need for moral and spiritual values. They stood up against the liberal thinkers whose influence on American life and culture was total and almost irrevocable. They maintained that man should learn to subject himself to something higher than his ordinary self and therefore went against the liberal doctrine of complete freedom. They taught that through the power of the inner discipline and conscious exercise of restraint, man must conquer his lower nature through the help of the higher. Hence, it is an absolutely secular form of humanism that found recognition in the modern age. It was a humanism that put perfection within reach of man and saw man in his dual nature of being both good and evil, but possessing the capacity to perfect his nature through the power of inner discipline and conscious exercise of restraint.

To sum up, humanism saw the development of an independent secular scale of values. "From the beginning, the direction of their [humanists] thought had been towards a more secular view of human life focussed on this rather than 'the other' world of the medieval imagination, an historical in place of a metaphysical view" (Bullock 1985: 29). European humanism was based on the great assumption that it is possible to mould the human personality by education. It celebrated an achieved condition of refinement and order in the civic life. It attacked the superficial and artificial aspects of civilisation that made for a cultivation of external properties as against more human needs and impulses. It stressed the need for moral values in social life. Humanism is not at war with the basic assumption of science that the way to determine the existence and value of any and all realities is by means of intelligent inquiry. But humanism lays particular stress on the assessment of their relation to human needs. The belief of humanists is that "humanism will affirm life rather than deny it; seek to elicit the possibilities of life, establish the conditions of a satisfactory life for all not for the few" (Kurtz 1969: 370). The implication of this view is that the human being, the full complex human being, is the standard that the humanist adumbrates. Man is the measure of all things was the assertion of Protagoras. Today when the world has become a global village with information networks altering the modes of our consciousness all over the world, the image of man that the Renaissance humanists had posited or which in a more rational manner Alexander Pope had dilated upon in his "Essay on Man" has a meaning and relevance that was stressed by Arnold when he said that with the advancing doctrine of orthodox religion, poetry would take its place increasingly, poetry may not actually save our soul but it can perhaps make it worth saving. If we replace the word poetry by literature, we can easily gauge its importance and that importance can be brought out and explicated only by the humanist literary critic because he is most powerfully conscious of the play of the life-denying forces of spiritual destitution, cultural deracination and above all of pervasive dehumanisation, thereby making human life nasty, short and brutish. Sweetness and light which underpin humanism in its intrinsic sense cannot survive under such conditions. Like Wordsworth, the humanist too feels a pang in his heart when he scans the modern scenario of anarchy and futility and perceives what man has made of man. The humanist critic subscribing to the central concept of the dignity of man as deciphered by his reason, therefore, has to face a challenging task of rehabilitating humanistic values in the modern world.

WORKS CITED

Babbitt, I., 1930. "Humanism an Eassay at Definition", in *Humanism and America*, ed. N. Foerster, 1930a, New York: Farrar.

Barrett, W.,1961. *Irrational Man*, London, Melbourne, Toronto: Heinemann.

Bullock, A., 1985. *The Humanist Tradition in the West*, London: Thames and Hudson.

Bush, D., 1968. *The Renaissance and English Humanism*, Toronto: University of Toronto Press.

Durant, W., 1967. *The Story of Philosophy*, New York: Washington Square Press.

Eliot, T.S., 1951. *Selected Essays*, London: Faber.

Ellman, R. and Fiedelson, C.J. Jr., 1965, ed. *The Modern Tradition*, New York: Oxford University Press.

Foerster, N., 1930b. *Towards Standards*, New York: Farrar.

Goodheart, E., 1973. *Culture and The Radical Conscience*, Cambridge, Massachusetts: Harvard University Press.

Hoeveler, J.D., 1977. *The New Humanism*, Charlotesville: University Press of Virginia.

Hulme, T.E., 1977. *Speculations*, London and New York: Routledge and Kegan Paul.

Krutch, J.W., 1929. *The Modern Temper*, New York: Random.

————, 1959. *Human Nature and The Human Condition*, New York: Random.

Kurtz, P., 1969, ed. *American Philosophy in the Twentieth Century*, London: Macmillan.

Marx, L., 1975. "Technology and the Study of Man", in *The Sciences, The Humanities and The Technological Threat*, (ed) W.R. Niblett, London: University of London Press.

Miller, J., 1982. *History and Human Existence*, London: University of California Press.

Muller, H.J., 1943. *Science and Criticism: The Humanistic Tradition in Contemporary Thought*, New Haven: Yale University Press.

Mumford, L., 1963. *The Condition of Man*, London: Mercury Books.

Reising, R.J., 1986. *The Unusable Past*, London and New York: Methuen.

Sypher, W., 1961. *Loss of the Self in Modern Literature and Art*, New York: Random.

Willey, B., 1964. *The English Moralists*, London: Chatto and Windus.

————, 1967. *The Eighteenth Century Background*, London: Chatto and Windus.

2

THE HUMANISTIC TRADITION IN THE LITERARY CRITICISM OF LIONEL TRILLING

> The critical faculty is ". . . the faculty of selection and retention, the weighing of cause and effect, the constant and active assumption of the past in the present, by which the events of life are no longer regarded as isolated and fortuitous moments but are merged into a unity of experience".
>
> — Paul Elmer More (*Shelburne Essays*)

This chapter traces the humanistic critical tradition in literary criticism by examining the major premises of Dr. Johnson, Matthew Arnold, T.S. Eliot, F.R. Leavis, Irving Babbitt, and Paul Elmer More. Their critical writings have gone towards the formation of the humanistic critical tradition in literary criticism and Lionel Trilling has contributed effectively towards the strengthening of this tradition.

The modern age has seen a remarkable upsurge of critical theories and experimental writing. This has arisen out of a need to shock readers out of complacency with traditional literature, mainly romantic in sentiment or propagandist in character. While classical literary works could reveal a higher reality, such a vision is denied to readers of modern literature. The modern writer "works with unfamiliar forms; he chooses subjects that disturb the audience and threaten its most cherished sentiments; he provokes traditionalist critics to such epithets as 'unwholesome', 'coterie' and 'decadent'" (Howe 1970: 3).

Modern literary criticism has accomplished little towards restoring the traditional values and aiding the establishment of a healthy literary climate. It has, on the other hand, concentrated on devising a science of literature on the models provided by the social sciences, "using even such tools of quantification as statistics" (Wellek 1982: 33). At the other extreme, criticism has sought to interpret texts along the lines of Freudian or Jungian psychology or through existential philosophy. The attempt of the New Critics to negate the socio-historic bases of literature and their impatience with cultural consideration have resulted ultimately in impersonal technicality and a literature which is of unabiding interest. There is no denying the fact that most modern theories have ceased to interest us. William E. Cain in his book *English in America Reconsidered* speaks against much of modern American criticism "... all that 'theory' has accomplished is to provide new ways of explicating texts, texts that might otherwise have seemed exhausted, 'used up', unable to grant still more readings" (Cain 1980: 88-89). He also attempts to find out reasons why deconstruction theories, for example, are on the verge of collapse, although they had once gripped the imagination of critics and readers. They are "extra-ordinarily dense and difficult, and very resistant to appropriation" (*ibid.*: 90). These critical theories have led to a re-definition of art that can include the ugly, the obscene, the formless, to Dadaism, Surrealism and even the literature of silence. In stretching out for new modes and new enterprises there may be discerned an initial recoil from a dogmatism or canonical approach that is perhaps to be lauded. But criticism subscribing to a doctrine of irrationalism as in the case of structuralism and including deconstruction may be the prime cause of the present malaise. Post-modern criticism uses philosophy such as phenomenonalism and existentialism—hence its density. The effect of all this is the rise of such concepts as "death of literature", "literature of exhaustion", "end of art", "anti-art" and "death of culture". These new theories have legitimatised "complete liberty of interpretation", leading to a "new anarchy" and even of a "self-confused nihilism" (Wellek 1982: 102).

The return to humanistic criticism based on a comprehensive principle of evaluation seems to be an acute need today. The function of literary criticism must be to negate the effects of neutral scientism and indifferent relativism and to secure for the human being freedom from social, political and economic conditioning. Writers and critics who look to art as one of the most important means to a fuller and richer life, cannot for long ignore the beneficent effects of the philosophical stance, in the light of which human life may be understood and judged. Robert Shafer, in his book *Paul Elmer More and American Criticism* (1935) is of the opinion that "... in an age such as ours, which has called everything into question, criticism is forced back to its primary basis in philosophical inquiry: and no better illustration of the necessity of this return to sources could be found than the muddle headed anti-criticism and chaotic art of our day" (Shafer 1935: 148). Similarly E.D. Hirsch (1976: 13) views with alarm the "downfall of humanistic values" and the literary tradition in the "anti-rationalism, faddism and extreme relativism" of Derrida's theory, his "private associations and playful self-indulgent prose" (Phillips 1991: 196).

In such a context of near anarchy the importance of a literary critic as Lionel Trilling can hardly be over-emphasized. His moral fervour and pre-occupation with literature and culture and a strong grasp of the main currents of European and American humanistic tradition make him a voice in advance of his times. At a time when his contemporaries in England and America were committed to verbal analysis and explication of literary texts, termed as "New Criticism", he declared that his interests had led him:

> . . . to see literary situations as cultural situations, and cultural situations as great elaborate fights about moral issues, and moral issues as having something to do with gratuitously chosen images of personal being, and images of personal being as having something to do with literary style. . . . (Trilling 1965: 13)

Richard Chase and Leo Marx also belong with Trilling to the group of cultural theorists who bemoan the lack of tradition in American letters and the harmful effects of modernisation and technology. Although, René Wellek places Trilling in the tradition of the New Critics, "One among the older New Critics" (Wellek 1982: 106), he went beyond New Criticism in bringing into focus the role of literature in society. During the 1930's, when proletarian art was dominant and politically based literary criticism had become the trend, the New Critical movement became a measure to counteract the historical and political narrowness encountered in American criticism confined to phenomena like immigration, urbanisation and industrialisation. Such a tendency was uncongenial to great art and therefore the attempt made by the New Critics to revolutionise critical opinion by adopting the linguistic approach was justified. As such they resisted the prevalent impressionistic criticism by concentrating on form and content. But according to Reising they erred in stating that historical and social considerations were "extrinsic" and therefore ancillary to literary study, and in excluding from contemplation all those books and literary pieces which made explicit references to social questions (Reising 1988: 15). Their methods have led to the progressive alienation of criticism from its social function.

To recall literary criticism to its major humanistic enterprise on the lines prescribed by Lionel Trilling seems to be of great importance in the modern context. It is relevant to discuss here the humanistic ideas that have guided the minds of major English and American critics. They have felt the necessity of establishing a scheme of values gathered from tradition and its dissemination through literature. From a comparative study of their works it is possible to observe their common purpose of making literature and literary study relate to our experience of life. More importantly, it is necessary to argue the point that these writers wrote with an awareness of the classical literary tradition that emphasizes a moral vision in order to establish the fact that the emergence of Lionel Trilling on the Anglo-American scene was a significant literary event. He stands as a major figure in the great English and American critical tradition of humanists, in line with Dr. Johnson, Matthew Arnold, Irving Babbitt, Paul Elmer More, T.S. Eliot and F.R. Leavis. He believes with them that we cannot have great literature without genuine and cogent criticism as also a great critical and literary tradition if we do not have a genuine concern for and pre-occupation with the human condition.

T.S. Eliot, has analysed the "dissociation of sensibility" that took place some time in the seventeenth century with the advent of the Renaissance and the Newtonian science. The history of Western philosophy shows man from this point of time becoming increasingly divided, alienated with the progress of industrialisation, specialisation and secularism. The humanists hold out some hope for the reconstitution of the original wholeness enjoyed by man in the integrated communal societies of the pre-industrial era. There have been writers who from the sixteenth century onwards have been thinking in terms of the total man, possessing a unified sensibility, combining intellect and feeling, that science and scepticism have separated. Such an integration is possible through the rejection of a technological civilisation, through a return to religion or to a re-organisation and re-construction of society on the basis of concepts like an ideational culture, (Sorokin) smaller communities (Mumford) or revival of religious ideals (Maritain).

The twentieth century would do well to look back upon the eighteenth century as a period which saw the humanistic tradition achieve a high degree of maturity. The reason why such a point can be made is that it laid a heavy stress on the social, moral and human implications of civilization and society. Freed from religious dissensions, humanistic impulses declared man a social being. The "insistence that man is a social being was such as to mean in effect that all his activities, inner as well as outer, that literature took cognizance of were to belong to an overtly social context" (Leavis 1976: 186). The writer was aware of a tradition within which he wrote. That tradition was one of decorum, social deportment and moral responsibility. Dr. Samuel Johnson can be taken to be the foremost critic of this period because of his interest in intellectual activities and the importance he gave to the free play of the mind.

Boswell praises Johnson as being "general and unconfined in his studies". He could not "be considered as master of anyone particular science, but he had accumulated a vast and various collection of learning and knowledge, which was so arranged in his mind as to be ever in readiness to be brought forth". He was also excellent in "the art of thinking" in "the art of using the mind", he was a man of "actual wisdom" (Boswell quoted in Leavis 1976: 101).

Dr. Johnson was competent to discuss matters of philosophical, theological or even scientific interest. The "common sense" which Dr. Jhonson's view of humanism deploys is actually the wisdom that is derived by synthesising knowledge from all sources, aimed to guide an intelligent person in what Lewis Mumford calls "the conduct of life", and a critic in evaluating and interpreting literature. Dr. Johnson was a humanist in the sense that he accepted "certain current assumptions, traditions and standards of value which are never called in question . . ." (Leavis 1976: 103). The Augustan spirit of rational controls and critical cautions was thus helpful in developing a civilised age and Dr. Johnson, a critic of stature and common sense, is its strongest representative. This civilization rested upon "sound intelligence, healthy instinct, and a fundamental sense of tradition . . ." (Humphreys 1957: 399). Dr. Johnson addressed himself to a society where there was a general air of assent. The common man could be relied upon for having sound taste and true judgement formed with the help of the humanistic tradition perpetuating moral ideas, a tradition that went back to the classical age in Greece and Rome. The truths that Dr. Johnson expressed as a critic were concerned with the central moral needs of human life and human nature as revealed in the classics and hence were basic to the cultural ethos. The truth he relied upon was not peculiar or individual, "but the truth of a tradition of which Anglicanism was the presiding faith, the humane arts the exemplars, and human nature within that tradition the norm" (*ibid.*, 400). He favoured moral philosophy in place of physical science because the former was concerned with providing examples needful for the proper conduct of life, whereas the latter provided information requisite to the growing materialism.

René Wellek in his *History of Modern Criticism* has criticised Dr. Johnson for having "ceased to understand the nature of art and who in central passages, treats art as life. . .", but concedes that a "new view of art comes out very clearly in Johnson's famous preface to his edition of Shakespeare (1765) as a "vehicle for the communication of moral or psychological truth . . ." (1955: 79).

In his preface he praises Shakespearean drama because it "is the mirror of life", "human sentiments" are expressed in "human language", "gleaned by diligent selection out of common conversation, and common occurrences" (Raleigh 1908: 14). He endorsed the view that literature is "a just representation of things really existing and actually performed" and that "the legitimate end of fiction is the conveyance of truth" (Hill 1905.3: 255, 1: 271). This truth as he states in *Rambler* Number 4 is "human manners" (Murphy 1823.2: 21). He elaborates his meaning of reality by saying that one must imitate nature, "but it is necessary to distinguish those parts of nature, which are most proper for imitation". Literature should be a means whereby we "get the power of counteracting fraud, without the temptation to practise it". If vice is to be portrayed consonant with the theory of realism, it "should always disgust" (*Rambler* No. 4).

For Johnson, moralism and realism should combine in order to teach and elevate the moral standards of the society. His preoccupation with both these critical criteria makes him favour and adopt generalised and universal truths. He can stoop to the level of the actual and the practical to derive universal moral truths that are of significance to men of all times and all places. Of Shakespeare's characters he says: "they are the progeny of common humanity. . .", they "act and speak by the influence of those general passions and principles by which all minds are agitated . . ." (Raleigh 1908: 11-12). Further, he makes the point that "great thoughts are always general and consist in positions not limited by exceptions" (Hill 1905.1: 21).

The historical sense also informs much of Johnson's criticism. In his respect for tradition and prescription of classical norms, he relies upon the past. Defending Pope's translation of Homer he speaks with sufficient historical insight. "Time and place will always enforce regard. In estimating this translation consideration must be had of the nature of our language, the form of our metre and above all the change which two thousand years have made in the modes of life and the habits of thought", since Pope "wrote for his own age and his own nation" (Hill 1905.3: 238-40). He viewed English literature as one continuous effort towards the establishment of a tradition based upon the writings of Pope and Dryden.

We can take Dr. Johnson to be the first great English literary critic who related literature to life. His demand of literature that it should minister directly to experience is linked to the firm religious and moral structure of his thinking. He is important to the study of humanistic thought because he did not see himself as a "pure" critic. He valued wisdom which meant for him moral discipline of the mind which in turn would promote the increase of virtue rather than learning. At a time when most of his contemporaries were attracted by the new scientific discoveries he had the wisdom to visualise their negative aspects. Scientific knowledge he felt, was "less suitable to the state of man" than "consideration of the moral discipline of the mind" (*Rambler* No. 24). In a passage of the same number he praises Socrates for having drawn Greek philosophers "from the vain pursuit of natural philosophy to moral inquiries". He turned their thought, from scientific discoveries to the contemplation of the nature of human life.

Paul Kent Alkon in his book *Samuel Johnson and Moral Discipline* (1967) contends that Johnson associated himself whole-heartedly with the long tradition of Socratic humanism rather than with the concerns of liberal arts or the newer branches of mechanical science.

Johnson has strengthened the tradition of that kind of critical inquiry which has concerned itself with the problems of civilisation and the perfection of the individual. *The Rambler* and *Lives of the Poets* popularised "for a general reading public a literary criticism previously associated with pedantry and personal abuse", and made it evident that "literary criticism inhabits no autonomous aesthetic sphere but belongs with 'general ideology' " (Eagleton 1984: 33). Hence we see that to become an effective tool for social amelioration, literature should be supported by a critical tradition that is humanistic. J.W. Krutch enlists qualities essential to the humanistic design: "penetration of mind, tact of address, subtlety of response, concern to refer to a mature standard; deliberation in judgement and responsibility in decision" (Krutch 1929: 97). Such literary criticism will succeed in creating a humane consciousness amidst the material pressures and dehumanising forces of modern world, and in bringing to bear upon literature and life a mature sense of values.

The literary persons who have followed the humanistic ideal have surrendered their individualism to larger concerns. They have realised that art is fundamental to man because its end lies in the revelation and inculcation of the ideal of perfection. Perfection means the development of the human personality, its material and spiritual aspects. As Lesley suggests culture which is the result of "conscious, strenuous and prolonged effort" (1979: 2) to attain the ideal of perfection is the prime concern of humanism.

The strongest representative of this tradition of humanism in literary criticism after Dr. Johnson is Matthew Arnold who emerged as a great literary force in the nineteenth century. Like Dr. Johnson, he was against all ideological apparatus. Like him, he was a poet-critic and hence his observations on literature came from his personal experiences as a poet. Unlike Johnson, however, Arnold had to write against the trend of his time, which was one of complete disillusionment with human values. The eighteenth century tradition was a modified classicism: writers were asked to beware of breaking the rules, but critics were advised that they should not judge mechanically by them. Arnold had to contend with romantic subjectivism, and ended by rejecting it in favour of classicism. To achieve this end Arnold retrieved the ancient classical norms and helped their onward transmission. His oft-quoted dictum that literature is a criticism of life, has found a permanent place in literary criticism. His most famous essays, "The Function of Criticism at the Present Time", "The Study of Poetry" and his book *Culture and Anarchy* are of seminal importance. In these works, he makes bold statements in keeping with the classical tradition. He proves that the critical activity is not inferior to the creative by refuting Wordsworth's remarks that it is better to be an indifferent poet than a critic. To a generation burdened by utilitarian doctrine, and given to the pursuit of science and materialism, he advocated the study of poetry as a substitute for the religion it had lost. His analysis of the Victorian society and the anarchical conditions prevailing in all spheres of life as a sequel to industrialisation made him conclude that men were straining under the effects of a grave spiritual crisis which would in future worsen the human condition.

In order to understand fully the importance of Arnold to social criticism we must bear in mind that romanticism had encouraged a primitivism that taught man to return to a natural state and assert the complete independence of the self. It meant the rejection of traditional values, the rejection of history and egocentrism. All inherited norms were flouted on the grounds of a human being's claims to total freedom—

to do as one likes. To his generation of men who were 'Light-half-believers' of 'casual creeds'; to the world of 'sick hurry' and 'divided aims' ("The Scholar-Gypsy") and to the world 'swept with confused alarms of struggle and flight', ("Dover Beach") Arnold prescribed the obvious answer: culture. Such an assumption that culture could overcome forces of disruption and anarchy in a society rested on the view that it is a disciplining process. It follows the classical ideas of humanism which stress the need for human perfection by inducing man to strive towards an ideal beyond and higher than the individual man.

The call which Arnold gave to the establishment of a high cultural climate was justified. The democratisation of society and relaxation of standards were conducive to the growth of a mass-based literary output. The kind of society which this mediocrity would produce was a question that continually disturbed his mind. Being a liberal in political matters and an upholder of equality, he was, nonetheless, fearful of the masses whose presence was becoming increasingly menacing to the process of culturisation. His liberal leanings did not in fact blind him to the dangers inherent in a free society consisting of dehumanised individuals. He feared their narrow provinciality, lack of value-based social ideals, and an absence of intelligent understanding of the purpose and meaning of human life. He believed that culture, the basis of which was "the best that has been thought and said "(*Culture and Anarchy*) could teach an entire generation how to live a full life in a fast-changing democratic and industrial society.

For Arnold, culture did not mean only art or great literature but a disposition to work by the light of reason and traditional human values that great literature of all ages undoubtedly contains. It is an internalising process of value gleaned externally, and the control of individual impulses by the critical, rational faculty. A remarkable feature of Arnold's humanism was his belief in the 'best self' resident in man and trained by culture, to subdue his lower, impulses that border on the bestial. His conception of a state authority comprising the 'best selves' and empowered to resist anarchical forces surprised many liberals. Although he was a liberal, "he was nevertheless mistrustful of the libertarian notions that formed a large part of the moral atmosphere of nineteenth century England. Arnold was understandably repelled by the unholy alliance between freedom and philistinism in the nineteenth century which he satirises to a considerable effect in *Culture and Anarchy* in the chapter, 'Doing as One Likes" (Goodheart 1973: 22).

At a time when science was threatening the very basis of religion, Arnold adopted a distinctly secularised view by advocating culture in its stead. Culture, like the religion of the past was a means to teach man to be committed to something beyond himself. In religion it was God; for Arnold it was perfection. It is a continuous process, "not a having and a resting" but "a growing and a becoming" (*Culture and Anarchy*).

Arnold's essays reveal that he had the foresight to work for the reconciliation of the humanities with science. He aims at the synthesis of two cultures: the humanist based on emotion and imagination, and the scientific, based on reason and good sense. He advocated the inculcation of knowledge from varied sources, as knowledge fostered a state of mind which made synthesis and integration desirable and possible.

The central tenets that emerge from Arnold's writings that have shaped modern humanism are: opposition to narrow provinciality, faith in the 'best-self' in man as a redeeming force and the formation of a body of beliefs based on the best that has ever been said and written to act as a standard of values by which the individual should judge and act.

There were several writers who have thought on similar lines and have helped to strengthen the humanistic tradition, both in England and America. "Throughout the latter part of the nineteenth century, a whole generation of intellectuals who were coming of age in the eighties and nineties, seized upon the doctrines of Arnold as gospel . . ."; his critical writings inspired in many literary men, "a devotion that practically assumed the form of a cult" (Raleigh 1957: 47).

After Arnold's visit to America, his influence on American intellectuals grew. The English Club was founded at Sewanee with Arnold as a nucleus. It started systematic studies of the age: its religion, ethics, politics and literary criticism, on the strength of Arnold's view that criticism was an equally prestigious literary pursuit as creative writing. John Macy, in "The Critical Game", an essay presented with many others in James Bownan's *Contemporary American Criticism* says "Every man who plays with literature at all must be ambitious to succeed in some form of art that may be called 'creative', as distinct from critical—a distinction which, since Arnold taught us our lesson, we know does not exist" (Bownan 1926: 261). The need for good criticism arose because it "tends to make an intellectual situation of which the creative power can profitably avail itself" (Arnold: "The Function of Criticism at the Present Time"). Norman Foerster in his *American Critical Essays*, (1930: VII, IX) finds that ". . . the critical movement is attracting more and more writers and readers to the effort to achieve 'an intellectual situation' capable of sustaining a new creative movement".

Among American writers who were inspired by humanism and who turned to Arnold for guidance was Irving Babbitt and Paul Elmer More. They founded a new critical movement that was termed New Humanism. When contemporary society became degenerate, incapable of bringing moral and intellectual redemption, and criticism did not have the required strength to curb its indecencies, there was felt a need to follow new models. Dominating the criticism of this period were the liberal critics such as Howells, Garland, Van Wyck Brooks and Mencken. Liberal criticism gained importance after the first World War responsible for the mushrooming of decadent American literature. The liberal critics, armed by the debunking spirit, more often than not, corrupted the best traditions of criticism. By bringing in a shallow understanding of society, they misrepresented reality. Their works consisted of studies in political determinism and victimisation of individuals by the state. They rarely delved below the surface of social and political reality to expose the harm inflicted on the psyche by social institutions and political ideologies. They were unable to deal with the deeper relations between art and society, literature and belief. As Kazin remarks aptly, "It was a conception of criticism which had begun by the need to characterise society and to define the artist's place in it, but soon exhausted itself by bewailing the fate of the artist in a hostile world, a criticism, self-consciously aristocratic and unwittingly sentimental", (Kazin 1942: 272). In its attempts to incorporate the scientific spirit, liberal criticism failed to be "scientific in intention" and adopted "a method of analysis" which "was even arrogantly anti-rationalist, but soaked up the fashionable jargon of science" (*ibid.*: 267). They chose to criticise authors who expressed dissatisfaction with the society and saw failure everywhere. They never felt the necessity to question the adequacy of the writer's personal resources and imagination. Kazin makes this clear: "That there were creative spirits abroad who though conscious of the sickness of their age, were able to meet it with their gifts, their capacity for life, their need to convert the largest possible quantity of experience into conscious thought, did not concern them" (*ibid.*: 272). It was against these liberal tendencies that the New Humanism was directed. Babbitt and More were the early exponents of this movement.

Babbitt was a scholar who assiduously studied the classics of the East and the West, and was able to diagnose the root cause of the sickness of his age. It was "the wrong type of individualism", he says "where the individual has repudiated outer control without achieving inner control" (Babbitt 1919: XXIII). The New Humanism professed by Babbitt and More was an attack on naturalism in literature and impressionism in criticism. They shared an abiding taste for classicism and love for the usable past and therefore felt uneasy with the laxness of standards characterising the American socio-political scene. They at first aroused much ire for their 'conservative' attitude and were regarded as enemies of all progressive, liberal and democratic forces. But they later came to have many followers who saw the relevance of their statements.

The major premises of the New Humanism were contained first in Babbitt's *Literature and the American College* (1908) which attacks the craving of the age for material prosperity and neglect of spiritual development and subservience to science and romanticism. It criticises the educational policy that encouraged the pursuit of science to the detriment of the humanities and which replaced the older common curriculum with one which encouraged specialisation. In other words, he derided, and so did the other humanists, the encouragement given by the universities to the propagation of a materialistic culture. These ideas were further elaborated in *The New Laokoon* (1910). In this book he studies the influence of romanticism on aesthetics. The *New Laokoon* was named after Lessing's *Laokoon* which made a distinction "between painting as an art of space and verbal narrative as an art of time" (Wimsatt and Brooks 1957: 373). Later Herder asserted that there could be no such distinction made because the ultimate end of all art medias was to produce an immediacy of experience of what the shaping spirit of the artist or writer had itself felt. His theory was based on a trend that sought to assimilate "all medias to spirit itself" (*ibid.*). Babbitt's work, therefore, studied this trend that sought to bring all the arts closer together on the basis of aesthetic theories of romanticism and assented the primacy of reason and the virtue of restraint in literature. The importance of *The New Laokoon* can best be understood if we consider what Allen Tate has said in connection with Babbitt's book: Babbitt fought against the vogue to merge the arts. The result of such merging would be that painting would try to be like music, poetry like painting and ultimately all the arts would strive towards the condition of music, "till at last seeing the mathematical structure of music", the arts would become "geometrical and abstract and destroy themselves" (quoted in Wimsatt and Brooks 1957: 276). He wrote the *Masters of Modern French Criticism*, a survey of the important French Critics and aestheticians of the nineteenth century and the influence of science and romanticism on them. The most important treatise for the New Humanists was however *Rousseau and Romanticism* (1919) in which he exposed the sources of the contemporary malaise and stressed the importance of self-discipline, traditional moral values and the recovery of sane human law as an effective measure against romantic individualism. His critical survey of the intellectual past and relating it to the modern context shows his strong historical sense. That Babbitt was drawn to the literary criticism of Matthew Arnold and was influenced by it is evident in his essay on Matthew Arnold contained in *Spanish Character and Other Essays*.

Babbitt praises Arnold as a positive and critical humanist. He cites Arnold's awareness of the "best self" which stands out against the commonness of his "ordinary self" as a centre of control. The best self has elements of permanence that can withstand relativism inherent in a fast changing political and social set-up, whereas the ordinary self is apt to be swayed by changing tastes and passing fashions. In Arnold he found all the requisites of a humanist programme and was moved by the completeness of Arnold's critical positivism: his perception of the importance of man's inner self as opposed to the philistine belief that material advancement can serve as a remedy for moral anarchy.

Babbitt also wrote on the political problems of his day. In *Democracy and Leadership* he examines democracy as the political expression of naturalism, and maintains that there should be leaders observing high standards of leadership. Where there are no true leaders and a code of conduct based on the highest principles of leadership, there can be no true democracy. He detects a disintegration of American culture and society wrought by a weakening of the inner life, sham spirituality, quantitative habits of mind and intemperate commercialism. But perhaps the strongest point in Babbitt's favour was in his regarding literature as an inter-locking system of ideas, and his insistence on an ethical comprehension of life without which literary criticism is incomplete.

Critics have found Babbitt rigid but it must not be forgotten that he was primarily responsible for the development of humanism in America. If he appears to be a main force on the American literary scene, it was because of his wide scholarly activities. That Babbitt was not rigid or uncritically conservative may be deduced from his comments on science and humanism: "The man of science is like the humanist at his best, at once highly imaginative and highly critical. By this co-operation of imagination and intellect, they are both enabled to concentrate effectively on the facts, though on facts of a different order" (Babbitt 1919: 362). His refusal to connect humanism to religion and his denial of the need for a transcendental value system is Arnoldian, and well-suited to a society that could never hope to regain its original religious faith. Babbitt was, however, not against religion. He felt the necessity for the setting up of some pattern or model for imitation in society and humanism could provide it in the absence of established religion. He pointed out the difference between the two. "Humanism however, differs from religion in putting at the basis of the pattern it sets up, not man's divinity, but the something in his nature that sets him apart simply as man from other animals . . . a sense of order and decorum and measure in deeds and words" (Babbitt 1930: 28). Alfred Kazin makes an interesting remark: ". . . Babbitt liked to think himself as another Dr. Johnson, an archpriest of Toryism furiously lashing out against the weakness and sentimentality of mankind. But he never knew anything of Johnson's profound religious sensibility" (Kazin 1942: 296).

Paul Elmer More had a profound literary sensibility. He suffered from grave religious doubts and this made him an ethical critic of literature. He rejected the disbelief in modernism and unlike Babbitt, he tried to dwell on human perfection. His view of perfection was akin to Christian humanism. It was a craving for higher truths that a relationship of man with God naturally brings about.

His criticism of literature and society is suffused with moral intensity and religious purpose. He felt that it was not enough to be morally earnest, humanist critics should realise the necessity of a positive principle capable of uniting in an effective manner, the spiritual, moral and aesthetic sense. "More's own devotion to religion was the thing his admirers were least interested in" but "he pleaded earnestly with them to see that their doctrine was futile without religious faith" (Kazin 1942: 310). He made a stern appeal to order and authority, to character, discipline and moral responsibility. Like Babbitt, he brought to his task of literary evaluation, an extensive learning.

More helped to define the New Humanism in his *Shelburne Essays* (1904-1921). They were published in eleven volumes and contain criticism on religion, literature and philosophy. These essays show his affinity with Arnold and Babbitt. The central idea that runs through the essays and provides the critical standard by which More judged the wide range of topics and persons he examined is "the dual nature of the human soul" which was for him "the indispensable fact of human nature . . ." (Hoeveler 1977: 13). He identified the cause of man's spiritual decline in the inability of his higher self to oppose the propensity of his lower self for evil and spiritual inertia. In professing such a view he has tried to tackle the most difficult and most important of all the problems that may set a humanist—that of man's nature and destiny.

Since he considered that literature was a reflection of life and a corrective force, he soon recognised the need of standards in criticism. In "The Demon of the Absolute" he states that every man has a standard by which he consciously asserts his choice: "The real question is not whether there are standards, but whether they shall be based on tradition or shall be struck out brand new by each successive generation or by each individual critic" (Glicksberg 1951: 265). His belief in a constant element in life which withstands the absolute sway of change and forms the criterion by which to judge new ideas is a transformation of the idea of the best-self of Arnold. Tradition and continuity are really derived from this conception.

A society the taste of which is shaped by such a literary tradition can boast of a culture that is formed by the best that has been said and thought; in other words, by holding the past as a living force in the present.

More has also dealt with romanticism in his *Shelburne Essays*. He recognised the soundness of the romantic theories of the autonomy of the self. He was convinced too, of the high intention of the romantic movement. Therefore, he proceeded to make plain the reason for their failure to stand against scientific naturalism: it was the glorification of the self detached permanently from history and tradition. What he admired in the romantic writers was their effort to preserve a living sense of man's spiritual nature and a sense of mystery surrounding existence that science was doing its best to destroy. Therefore Robert Shafer admires More's criticism as having been written "in the very spirit of disinterested critical activity . . . avoiding unqualified or sweeping judgements" (Shafer 1935: 179).

More propounds the theory of dualism in his essays. Humanism entails a true understanding of human nature and dualism helped More to explain it. In "Definitions" which is to be found at the end of the Eighth Series of *Shelburne Essays*, he gives us an exposure of the human condition, and the ultimately irreducible fact of human life. Man, he says is subjected to two disparate influences: inner desires and outer impressions, and an inner check exercised as a force contrary to theirs. As we look deeply into ourselves, consciousness, he states "tells us that we are ceaselessly changing, yet tells us that we are ever the same. This dualism of consciousness, it seems, is the last irrational fact . . . the reality which only stands out the more clearly the more it is questioned . . ." (quoted in Shafer 1935: 165).

Reason is the source of the inner check: it is an act of volition, an exercise of choice, whether to surrender to impulses or to act in the light of an inherited traditional value-system, modified by the needs of the contemporary situation. To heed the inner check is essential to become truly cultured. It also provides us with knowledge of the self and integrates our personality, making us distinctly human. To acknowledge honestly the mystery at the centre of human nature for More, is the true sign of a humanist. To More man appeared as an "incomprehensible union of opposed forces neither of which can be denied or ignored without complete disaster, both somehow working together to produce intelligence, character, and a free responsible personality" (*ibid.*: 169).

This view of man which takes into account man's struggle with himself and informs the philosophy behind More's writings, opposes the relativism of naturalism and romanticism in a good deal of twentieth century criticism. A focus upon an inner reality as an important element in the response of an individual to outer reality retrieves for man the dignity he has lost in being considered as a determined organism. It also broadens the perspective from which a man is to be judged and from which literature, which is the record of his experiences, may be properly assessed. It also anticipates Freud whose analysis of the mind and the role of the unconscious, Trilling feels, has complicated the view of the human condition and added a tragic dimension of his situation in the modern world.

More resented the dehumanisation of art by liberating it from the moral obligations of life. In his essay 'The Humility of Commonsense' which is really a part of 'The Demon of the Absolute', he criticises Croce for having declared that the artist can have no social or moral obligation and that art has nothing to do with morals or philosophy. He even cautions us against considering the value of a work of art as an expression of the artist's self, against judging its worth in relation to the sincerity with which it is expressed. According to More, a critic has also to take into account the nature of the subject and decide whether the character of the human experience put into it is worthy of discussion. In other words, he is pleading for a just selection of human experiences, a selection characterised by moral righteousness. He deals critically with modern realism. In his comments on Joyce's stream of consciousness technique, Dadaism, Surrealism and the Naturalism of Zola. They present a picture of man which is either wholly mechanistic or beastly in character. We may take note of a statement made by Babbitt in "Humanism: An Essay at Definition": "Humanism appears . . . in the act of selection, in the final imposition on mere multiplicity of a scale of values" (in Foerster 1930: 30). Modern literature has repudiated its faith in such a scale of values and in the name of individualism, has given priority to the eccentric and the abnormal in human experience.

As Arnold has pointed out in "The Function of Criticism at the Present Time", there is an inherent relationship between criticism and literature and literature and society. Good criticism creates the background of taste; a good literary tradition ensures high cultural aspirations in human beings. With this we come to important questions regarding the basis of culture, its relation to civilisation, its effect on education and its relation with religion. T.S. Eliot belongs to the tradition of humanism although he openly insists on its alliance with religion, a thesis that Babbitt could never endorse. Eliot agreed with the New Humanists in America that classicism summed up an outlook which was valid for literature. From the mid 1920's Eliot recognised the futility and the dangers of isolating literature and its criticism from other human interests, since literature itself necessarily involves such non-literary truths. In the *Criterion* which he ran for several years, he advocated classicism in literature and emphasized the relationship of literature with life. He felt that one can "never draw a line between aesthetic criticism and moral and social criticism" . . . "between criticism and metaphysics", ". . . however rigorous an aesthete you may be, you are over the frontier into some thing else sooner or later" (Eliot 1951: 55).

This critical background enabled him to sympathise with the New Humanistic movement. In 1929, Eliot contributed an essay "Religion without Humanism" to Norman Foerster's volume of essays *Humanism In America*, making his humanistic stand clear. Eliot published two essays, "The Humanism of Irving Babbitt" (1928) and "Second Thoughts On Humanism" (1929) which were reprinted in *Selected Essays*. In the former essay he argued that Babbitt's secular humanism which placed control on human impulses by a counter force inherent in the individual himself, was inadequate. He considered it to be "a romantic, individualist and in tendency anarchic social theory" and affirmed that "the inner control of the individual should have "the external sanction afforded by Catholic religion" (Eliot 1951: 477, 473). His conception of the "whole man" was a combination of intellectual and spiritual qualities.

Eliot met the demand of literary aesthetes that the critic should confine himself to purely aesthetic meanings and values, with the rejoinder that literary standards are not sufficient for the judgement of literature. Eliot assumed that criticism should concern itself with the greatness of literature and this does not necessarily involve the sacrifice of literary standards, on the contrary, extra-literary standards—theological, social, political and philosophical, provide a true understanding of literature.

About objectivity in art he was very much insistent, but differed from the purely aesthetic criteria by maintaining that the artist's personality encroaches upon a work of art, but it has to be "fused" with the impersonal and the general, not completely extinguished. True objectivity is attained when the artist's personality is formed by a literary tradition and is enriched by the best ideas current at the time a concept brought out in "Tradition and the Individual Talent". In his strong reliance on the past he is akin to Babbitt and More and Arnold. He believes that there is an integral relation of the present to an alive past ". . . the vitality of the past enriches the life of the present". Eliot recognised the role of the psychological unconscious in the creative process. The past exists as "the collective historical, psychological unconscious which is important to the writing of poetry . . ." (Skaff 1986: 139).

This is not very different from Babbitt's teaching at Harvard that standards should be derived from the classical tradition in art and that it is necessary to withstand an egocentric subjectivist romanticism. Hence, Eliot's ideas of "tradition" and the "historic sense" are a synthesis of Arnold's "the best that has ever been thought and said, and Babbitt's classicism. But he has explicitly stated how the literary past is to be apprehended and made use of if the critic is to avoid any deliberate and mechanical application of classical rules to literature. He will respond spontaneously revealing in his statements the effect of a collective historical unconscious of which he is a spokesman. The mind within tradition is "a mind which changes", but "this change is a development which abandons nothing en-route: which does not superannuate either Shakespeare, or Homer, or the rock-drawing of the Magdalenian draughtsman" (Eliot 1951: 16).

The most striking element in Eliot's theory of tradition is the affirmation of a continuity, that links the great ideas of the past to the present. It challenges the ideas of flux, of relativism in literary theories, and makes disintegration of values nearly impossible. It also acts as the "inner check" which Babbitt talks of, and prevents corruption of art. In all these ways, it goes beyond liberal criticism.

Eliot was greatly interested in the steady application of thought to social questions. The lectures which were published as *After Strange Gods: A Primer of Modern Heresy* indicate hope for a politics suffused with Christian doctrines. He frankly admits that he hopes to see Christian standards of orthodoxy coming into prominence. He makes a variation of terms by substituting the classicism of New Humanism for orthodoxy and heresy for its romanticism. Other features of his argument are the criticism of modern writers and insistence on the need for intelligence to govern social life. He finds liberalism inadequate to sustain tradition and culture as it encourages rampant individualism through tolerance. The need of the times, as he states in *After Strange Gods* is the conservation of traditional wisdom, and an establishment of a connection between the individual writer and his tradition. He was against the mass-values that a liberal democracy promoted and found the most conscious level of culture amongst the elite.

In this way, he was different from Arnold. Arnold hoped for a classless society by the propagation of culture, but Eliot who wrote in a far difficult time saw the futility of such a hope. Eliot's concept of culture was broadly similar to Arnold's, but where Arnold was secular, Eliot was religious. For Arnold culture meant a secular code of values. Eliot felt that secularism would not be sufficient. It might lead to the worship of strange gods as in D.H. Lawrence. Culture was to be rooted in religion; for Arnold it was to be rooted in the best ideas—as found in classicism. It is the difference between secular humanism and spiritual humanism. Eliot was less liberal than Arnold in his views on education. He preferred a high educational standard confined to smaller groups, to mass-based low educational standard. "What I plead for is what Matthew Arnold spoke of as 'the knowledge of the best that has been thought and said in the world . . .' that this knowledge of history . . . should be the common possession of those who have passed through the higher grades of non-specialised studies . . . that it might well form for most of them the foundation for many of the more modern studies which now tend to be substituted for it" (Eliot 1965: 120). Finally, Eliot commits himself to the humanist function saying: ". . . it was our business not so much to make any particular ideas prevail as to maintain intellectual activity on the highest level" (Eliot 1967: 118).

F.R. Leavis has also been influenced by Matthew Arnold's dictum that literature is a criticism of life and advocated it in his own literary criticism. He too can be placed in the tradition that has been traced from Dr. Johnson, a tradition that holds that there is no distinction between literary values and moral and spiritual values. He is a humanist in the sense that he gave priority to considerations that related literature to the individual consciousness, and made moralism the main criterion of literary judgement. Like the other humanist critics discussed before, he believed with Matthew Arnold that literature represents the best that has been known and thought in the world; that great literature has established a tradition of thought based on human truth and human wisdom, and that such a tradition, if followed and maintained can enrich culture and civilisation. Further, Leavis explained the relationship between traditional culture and literary culture which was one of inter-dependency. Of literary judgement he says, ". . . a real literary interest is an interest in man, society and civilisation. . . ." A critic needs ". . . a living critical inwardness with literature, and a mind trained in dealing analytically with it. . . " (Leavis: 1976: 200). In commenting upon Eliot's *After Strange Gods*, he asserts that "moral or religious criticism cannot be a substitute for literary criticism. . . . It is only by demonstrating convincingly that his [Eliot's] application of moral principles leads to a more adequate criticism that he can effect the kind of persuasion that is his aim" (*ibid.*: 241).

We find that Leavis adopts a more intellectual approach to criticism than Arnold. Although he displays very little intellectual interest in examining religious issues, and is more concerned with society and culture, he was unlike Arnold in many ways. Culture was not for him the pursuit of harmonious perfection, not a process, but the attainment of a sense of discrimination, through the power of art and literature. Arnold was more idealistic when he expressed the hope that a literary education would develop the sensibilities of the masses in mass-democracy. Leavis is only too acutely aware of the levelling of standards in a democracy and therefore adumbrates an elitist bias of culture. He confined the cultural group to a very small minority.

In "Mass Civilisation and Minority Culture" (1930) he attacks the evils of mass society which are technical advancements and utilitarian policies. He found America lacking in tradition and culture, a characteristic common to most modern industrial societies. It was a matter of grave concern for him that the machine age with its mass production of consumer items, should also see the advent of mass culture, pop art and degenerate morals, that it should also view art as a consumer item, whose utility lies in pleasing the greatest number of individuals. Advertisement and the media he felt, have added to the depersonalisation of art and the dehumanisation of man.

In defending a minority culture he states: "In any period it is upon a very small minority that the discerning appreciation of art and literature depends . . . upon this minority depends our power of profiting by the finest human experience of the past; they keep alive the subtlest and most perishable parts of tradition" (Leavis 1961: 143). The minority for Leavis is the literary intellectual who has not submitted to the pressures of specialisation prescribed in the professional courses in universities. This conscious minority is the most suited to transmit culture.

Leavis's sympathy with the few, the elite, reveals an anti-Marxist strain. He strongly opposed Marxist ideas which gained ascendency during the 1930's in Europe and America. Being a traditionalist, he viewed with disdain the revolutionary base of Marxism and its tendency to crush the human spirit. He was also opposed to Marxist approaches to literature as also to popular culture: ". . . the sole possessor of culture is essentially a literary minority" (Leavis 1932: 31). His faith rested upon a "school for English" in a University ". . . to make provision for keeping alive . . . and developing that full human consciousness of ends and values and human nature that comes to us . . . out of the long creative continuity of our culture" (Leavis 1969: 2).

Leavis's book *The Great Tradition* affirms the value of common morality. It discusses five novelists who constitute for him the great condition of the novel in England—George Eliot, Henry James, Joseph Conrad, Jane Austen and D.H. Lawrence. He chooses to put them into one tradition because they are "significant in terms of the human awareness they promote; awareness of the possibilities of life" (Leavis 1977: 10).

Lionel Trilling sums him up thus: "Dr. Leavis is not a critic who works by elaborated theory. As between Coleridge, on the one hand, and Dr. Johnson and Matthew Arnold, on the other, he has declared his strong preference for the two latter—for the critic, that is, who requires no formulated first principles for his judgement but only the sensibility that is the whole response of his whole being" (Trilling 1957: 102). In his attitude to science, he is in agreement with the humanists. In his reply to Lord C.P. Snow's address called "The Two Cultures", Leavis challenged his main assumptions. He maintained that literary persons were not impoverished by leaving out scientific study. "It is in the study of literature . . . that one comes to the 'third realm'—the realm of that which is neither merely private and personal nor public in the sense that it can be brought into the laboratory or pointed to. But it is something in which minds can meet. . . . It [English literature] gives us the nature in general of what I have called the 'third realm' to which all that makes us human belong" (Leavis 1962: 28). Therefore, it is in relation to his beliefs in tradition, in his indictment of modern culture and of a literature that suffers from a discontinuity of consciousness with the past and his moralism that he belongs as W. Walsh contends, to the "grand line of English tradition" (in French 1980: 51).

Keeping in view the assumptions and ideas of the foregoing critics it may be said that although humanist criticism does not fit into any ideologies or dogmas, it requires the critic to be intelligent, observant, unprejudiced, with a highly developed moral and historical sense. The criteria applicable are the maintenance of standards, commitment to culture, and a tragic sense of life.

America, during the early part of the twentieth century, shared the same atmosphere as the bourgeois culture of Victorian England. It was marked by "disintegration through the dynamics of bourgeois division, proletarian development, progressive specialisation and artistic alienation" (Fekete 1988: 17). The cultural sphere was isolated from the socio-economic sphere, and the latter gained ascendency over concerns relating to human nature and values. Since the new theories in American literary criticism derived from the belief in art for art's sake, and were designed to resist the dilemmas of the Victorian ethics they were welcomed. But soon they proved themselves inadequate to give an integrating and wholesome picture of life, which cultural theories could provide. "The new theory accepts the place of the artist in the division of labour and in that context what had been rebellion (against scientific naturalism in art) moves towards hedonism: the heightening of the intensity of the aesthetic experience" (Fekete 1988: 12). It was also felt that a community of good taste and reason essential to the humanistic literary enterprise was fast disappearing.

It is against this background of disintegration in literary standards and loss of human values that Lionel Trilling came into prominence as a critic in America. With the publication of *Matthew Arnold* in 1939 his stand on humanism became clear. It was from him that he derived ideas regarding literary and cultural criticism. The ideas and attitudes that influenced him were that literature is a criticism of life, that a really sensitive individual has to acquaint himself with the best that has been known and said in the world, and in this way to establish a link with the past; that humanisation of man in society is essential to a civilisation. These views were no longer current in the America of the 1930's. The dominant intellectual climate was specifically radical. Trilling, being a liberal at heart, could neither commit himself to political liberalism nor to Stalinism nor to Trotskyism. He was not primarily interested in politics but in literature, nevertheless politics interested him in just so much as it intruded upon and affected literature and culture. He was for such attitudes often denounced as a conservative. In 1939, Trilling made his position clear: "My own literary interest . . . is in the tradition of humanistic thought and in the intellectual middle class which believes that it continues this tradition" (*Matthew Arnold*). Arnold had similar hopes on the middle class, as perpetuators of culture. Trilling sought to revive interest in cultural theories at a time when they were becoming stale and when humanism was being attacked by naturalism and scientism. Ihab Hassan says: "In this restoration of literature to a larger view, Lionel Trilling plays a special part . . . he provides an alternative to formalist doctrines, and at the same time, a corrective to liberal and radical ideologies, the very same ideologies against which formalism itself stands" (Hassan 1973: 15). But perhaps the most striking feature of his criticism is the intellectual balance he maintains "between the great ideas of the Enlightenment and the great passions of Romanticism" (*ibid.*: 16).

In attacking liberal notions that have attained the status of ideologies, he displays a truly Arnoldian spirit of allowing a fresh current of thought to play upon stock notions. In *The Liberal Imagination* (1950) he begins by correcting various misconceptions of progressive liberal criticism. In his essay "Reality in America" he redefines the meaning of reality by adopting a counter progressive attitude. This was accomplished by transferring "the grounds of reality from economic and political systems to human psyches" (Reising 1986: 95). He saw the need for literature to reflect "natural, direct human feeling", manners and customs and a realism which he calls moral—realism, a "product of the free play of the moral imagination" (Trilling 1950: 219-22). Trilling can be judged as one of the few American writers "who perceived the human complexity and the ambiguities beneath the affirmative surface of American life" (Reising 1986: 95). He could not give himself up to any one particular mode or critical theory, for they would be inadequate to interpret life whose variety and complexity are apt to evade any doctrinaire approach. He strove for a means to depict the violation of human life by technological systematization and the harm inflicted upon the psyche by a dehumanised, impersonal, mechanistic culture, and the means by which he could achieve his aims was by the fusion of Arnoldian aims and Freudian ideas.

The essence of Trilling's humanist philosophy seems to be contained in his book *Matthew Arnold*. According to Trilling Arnold had to struggle with the spiritual disease that arose from a social organisation "in which the wisdom of society can no longer be accepted" and hence which is not fit enough to lead it. Therefore, "the burden of ethical judgement "rested entirely upon the individual self" (Trilling 1982: 130). Eliot had talked of a centre of control: the Anglo Catholic elite or the intellectual elite professing a minority culture; an imposition of discipline from without. Leavis is equally concerned with the training of the sensibility by a literary critical method. Such trained individuals constitute the minority. Trilling, in fixing the responsibility of moral development on the individual self echoes Babbitt's views on the "inner check" and More's "dualism of consciousness" that shape the development of the spirit. The self-proceeds on a quest for a properly balanced relationship between the individual and society. Defining Arnold's disinterestedness and objectivity, Trilling says that a really objective criticism must as Arnold states "praise elements that for the fullness of spiritual perfection are wanted, even though they belong to a power which in the practical sphere may be maleficent. It must be apt to discover the spiritual shortcomings or illusions of powers that in the practical sphere may be beneficent" (quoted in Trilling 1982: 205).

His reliance on Freud to depict the human condition points to the secular character of his humanism. The Freudian element in his criticism replaces Eliot's religious approach. Freudian psychology was an aspect of science that Trilling accepted and fused it with his humanist creed. It helped him to understand the distinctive qualities and values of subjective life. Through this he was able to explain how social sanctions are repudiated in the individual's search for self-affirmation. In Freud's *Civilisation and Its Discontents* he found the grounds whereby he could defend his views on moral realism and define the tragic condition of modern man. He reveres Freud because the latter's views have not narrowed and simplified the world for the artist as the liberals were trying to do, "but on the contrary" they have "opened and complicated it" (Trilling 1950: 57).

Trilling's views on culture evolve out of his democratic liberalism. He believes that there is a close relation between culture and the artist and each one modifies the other. He speaks of culture as "not a flow nor even a confluence, the form of its existence is struggle or at least debate—it is nothing if not dialectic" (*ibid.*: 9). Culture is an attitude of mind which enables the self to weigh and judge when it encounters difficulties and complexities, and either to take an adversary position to its environment or to become resigned to it.

In the manner of Arnold in *Culture and Anarchy*, Trilling opposes liberalism as practised by politicians. He appreciates liberalism as an idea, but observes that when liberalism becomes "active and positive" its limitations are exposed. Although it contains the "vision of a general enlargement and freedom and rational direction of human life—it drifts towards a denial of the emotions and the imagination" (Trilling 1950: XII). Liberalism has tended to divorce mind and imagination as legitimate objects of consideration. Therefore, "the job of criticism is to recall liberalism to its first essential imagination of variousness and complexity and difficulty" (*ibid.*: XIV). Being a liberal humanist Trilling firmly believed that the "recalcitrant" material of life could not be compartmentalised to a few simple problems and judged by material standards. Like Leavis the shaping and strengthening element in his criticism is moral feeling.

In *The Opposing Self* (1955) and *A Gathering of Fugitives* (1956) Trilling is confident that the individual self and the surrounding culture can achieve harmony. Many of the essays presented in these volumes are searches for 'heroes' who have harmonised themselves to the surrounding culture. "The arguments implicit in both these collections is that such adjustment was easier in earlier times" (Chace 1989: 101). The reasons why he thinks Keats to be a hero is that he "believed that life was given for him to find the right use for it, that it was a kind of magical confrontation requiring to be met with the right answers. He believed that this answer was to be derived from intuition, courage and the accumulation of experience" (Trilling 1955: 4, 5).

These being the humanistic virtues championed by Trilling, it is not surprising to see why, when the general trend advocated the opposition of the individual self to culture, Trilling was trying to salvage from the past, examples of writers and characters who possessed the tragic view of life in the classical sense and who utilised it to confront contemporary reality, to come to terms with it and to achieve harmony with it. Trilling was positive that a balance between the individual and the society was possible. His belief in this idea of cultural stability was however shaken when he became conscious of the nihilistic encroachments of modernity in novels of writers like Kafka, Conrad and Dostoievsky. In *Beyond Culture* (1966) he focusses his attention on modern literature and its tendency to break away from traditional norms and from society itself. While admiring avant-garde literature he also expresses his disenchantment with it, because of its destructive nature. He comes to the conclusion that "the tragic mode is not available even to the gravest and noblest of our writers". The ethical mode has submerged itself in the non-ethical, and the anti-hero "who is indifferent to, or who hates ethical nobility" has replaced the hero. Trilling complains that we achieve "the acculturisation of the anti-cultural, or the legitimization of the subversive" when the avant-garde becomes the norm (Trilling 1966: 26).

In *Sincerity and Authenticity* (1972) he makes a more serious attempt to understand the nature of the self. With great historical insight, he gives an account of western culture through four hundred years. He differentiates between the relationship of the self to culture, as seen in traditional literature and modern literature. The former he discusses as sincerity—"the avoidance of being false to any man through being true to one's own self", and the latter as authenticity—the compulsion to revolt against a given cultural situation, on the strength of the autonomy of the self. Cultural situations are responsible for the loss of sincerity, which is the power to transcend the self by believing in universal and permanent human values. Authenticity is what is left to us, the assertion of the self, the releasing of the artist's primal, non-ethical energies, an escape from the "hell of dehumanisation that inauthenticity is" (Trilling 1972: 102).

In his later writings Trilling travels away from literary criticism to philosophy. But this tendency of philosophising was with him even in his literary criticism. He was a true humanist with a moral vision, preoccupied by the problems confronting the individual in the modern society. His few short stories and a full length novel *The Middle of the Journey* show him as a creative writer, sympathetic to the human cause. They help us to understand him not only as a critic of great power and intelligence, but as a creative talent imaginative, perceptive and sensitive.

The Middle of the Journey is in one sense a political novel about "the moral and intellectual implications of the powerful attraction to communism felt by a considerable part of the American intellectual class during the thirties and the forties" (Trilling: Introduction to the Novel 1975). But it is also a story of a real human being, struggling with the complexities of human feelings and thoughts and moving in a journey which has meaning and purpose only as long as it remains human. It is a journey akin to Dante's in the *Divine Comedy* where the most difficult juncture is the middle state between the lower and the higher, where the self begins to feel the pressure of fate and destiny.

Laskell the protagonist finds himself awakened to the belief that his moderate liberal faith may be inadequate to grapple with questions of suffering, anxiety and death that assail the self.

Trilling's ultimate conviction was that the life of the mind is the life most worth living. In the all encompassing technological dispensation our mental life is apt to suffer from dimunition. In such a dispensation there are two alternative courses the mind naturally follows: submission to mechanical effects which annihilates self-hood; or assertion of selfhood and escape from conditioning through recourse to madness, violence and intoxication, aspects of modern life that have attracted the attention of post-modern writers like J. Lacan and M. Foucault.

Viewing with alarm the increasingly adversarial stance towards society adopted by modern literature he expressed doubts about its ability to educate people in moral realism. Reason and morality pursued by a mind given to objectivity and dis-interestedness could perform the task of civilising and humanising society. He meant literature to tell "the best kind of truth" that will promote will and mind. True liberty as Babbitt remarks in his essay "Genius and Taste" consists in resisting impulse, and not by yielding to it", perfection is reached "not by the throwing off but by taking on limitations" (Scott 1962: 39). Trilling's essays strongly reflect this view of the intelligent mind.

Although Trilling was non-ideological in his approach to literary criticism he steadfastly held on to the moral view-point, he belongs definitely to one of the major traditions of English criticism as revealed in the writings of Johnson, Arnold, Leavis and Eliot. In America this tradition was followed by Babbitt and More. Trilling, belongs to this tradition in literary criticism which is both British and American.

At a time when positivism was intimately tied to the birth and development of modern literary criticism and was engaged in the process of applying the method of science to studying texts, Trilling provided the humanistic method as a counterpoint. Literary criticism can be a socially active force and this is primarily the message that humanist critics like Trilling have succeeded in giving the modern age. The method of literary study is not the application of theories of quantification, structuralism, semiotics and post-structuralism originated by positivism. It is to examine the socio-historical matrix of literature and to redefine its function as a value-shaping force in the modern world of alienation, atomisation and pervasive dehumanisation. Trilling being able to convince us of the responsibility that writers owe to their society, deserves to be considered as a major figure in the humanistic tradition.

WORKS CITED

Alkon, P.K., 1967. *Samuel Johnson and Moral Discipline*, Evanston III: North Western UP.

Babbitt, I., 1919. *Rousseau and Romanticism*, Boston, New York: Houghton.

————, 1930. "Humanism: An Essay at Definition" in *Humanism and America*, ed., N. Foerster, New York: Farrar.

Bownan, J., 1926, ed. *Contemporary American Criticism*, New York: Henry Holt.

Cain, W.E., 1980. *English in America Reconsidered*, Baltimore: Johns Hopkins, University Press.

Chace, W.M., 1980. *Lionel Trilling: Criticism and Politics*, California, Stanford, University Press.

Eagleton, T., 1984. *The Function of Criticism*, Norfolk: Thetford.

Eliot, T.S., 1951. *Selected Essays*, London: Faber.

————, 1965. *To Criticise the Critic*, London: Faber.

————, 1967. *Notes Towards a Definition of Culture*, London: Faber.

Fekete, J., 1978. *The Critical Twilight*, Henley and Boston: Routledge and Kegan Paul.

Foerster, N., 1930, ed. *American Critical Essays*, London: Oxford University Press.

French, P., 1980, ed. *Three Honest Men: A Critical Mosaic*, Manchester: Carcanet.

Goodheart, E., 1973. *Culture and The Radical Conscience*, Cambridge, Masachusetts: Harvard University Press.

Glicksberg, C.I., 1951, ed. *American Literary Criticism*, New York: Hendricks.

Hassan, I., 1973. *Contemporary American Literature*, Princeton: Princeton, University Press.

Hill, G.B., 1905, ed. *Lives of the Poets*, Vol. 3 (Pope), Vol. 1 (Waller), Oxford.

Hirsch, E.D., 1976. *The Aims of Interpretation*, Chicago and London: University of Chicago Press.

Hoeveler, J.D., 1977. *The New Humanism*, Charlottesville: Universitv Press of Virginia.

Howe, I., 1970. *Decline of The New*, New York: Horizon.

Humphreys, A.R., 1957. "Johnson" in *The Pelican Guide to English Literature*, Vol. 4, ed., Boris Ford, rep. 1970, Penguin.

Kazin, A., 1942. *On Native Grounds*, New York: Harcourt.

Krutch, J.W., 1954, *The Measure of Man*, New York: Bobbs Merrill.

Leavis, F.R., 1932. "The Literary Mind", *Scrutiny*, 1: 20-32.

————, 1961. *Education and the University*, London: Chatto and Windus.

————, 1962. *"Two Cultures?"* London: Chatto and Windus.

————, 1969. *English Literature in our Time and the University*, London: Chatto and Windus.

————, 1976. *The Common Pursuit*, Penguin Books.

————, 1977. *The Great Tradition*, London: Pelican.

Lesley, J., 1979. *The Cultural Critics*, London, Boston: Routledge and Kegan Paul.

Murphy, A., 1823, ed. *Works*, 12 Vols. London.

Phillips, W., 1991. "The Crisis in Our Culture" Conference on "The Changing Culture of the University", *Partisan Review*, 58.2: 192-226.

Raleigh, J.H., 1957. *Matthew Arnold and American Culture*, Berkeley, Los Angeles, University of California Press.

Raleigh, W., 1908, ed. *Johnson on Shakespeare* (Selections), London.

Reising, 1988. *The Unusable Past*, New York and London: Methuen.

Shafer, R., 1935. *Paul Elmer More and American Criticism*, New Haven: Yale University Press.

Skaff, 1986. *The Philosophy of T.S. Eliot*, Philadelphia.

Scott, W., 1962, ed. *Five Approaches to Literary Criticism*, New York: Collier, Macmillan.
Trilling, L., 1950. *The Liberal Imagination*, London: Secker and Warburg.
———, 1955. *The Opposing Self*, New York: Viking.
———, 1957. *A Gathering of Fugitives*, London: Secker and Warburg.
———, 1966. *Beyond Culture*, New York: Viking.
———, 1972. *Sincerity and Authenticity*, London, Oxford University Press.
———, 1982. *Matthew Arnold*, Oxford University Press.
Wellek, R., 1955. *A History of Modern Criticism, 1750-1950*, New Haven: Yale University Press.
———, 1982. *The Attack on Literature and Other Essays*, Chapel Hill: University of California Press.

3

LIONEL TRILLING: CRITIC OF THE INTELLECT AND SPIRIT

> The noblest Greek art was a union of the two ideals, the restless masculine power of Dionysus and the quiet feminine beauty of Apollo.
>
> — Will Durant (*The Story of Philosophy*)

The objective of this chapter is to give a general estimate of Lionel Trilling as a critic and to point to the dialectical nature of his discourses on literature. It focusses mainly on the ambivalence of attitude that governs his critical stance and agrees that this ambivalence is the right course for the critical spirit to maintain in order to stem the tide of mechanistic and positivistic philosophies that engulfs literary thought of the modern age. His ambivalence is the result of the harmonization of the powers of the intellect and the spirit, making him critical of too much intellection on the one hand, and complete freedom of spirit supported by an imaginative faculty that has lost touch with the world of objective reality, on the other.

Trilling enjoys an undisputed eminence in American literature and culture. He emerged as a major presence in American literary life in the mid 1940's, with the publication of his remarkable essays in the *Partisan Review* and the *Kenyon Review.* Since then his essays have been anthologized by him and "now constitute one of the great and beautiful achievements of the American literary intelligence in our time" (Scott 1973: 153).

His death which occurred in November 1975 was a major loss to the world of humane letters. The obituary in *Times* of London bore the headline: "A Literary Critic of Major Stature". But he was not only a literary critic, he was a true humanist whose interest in the human condition led him to talk about literature. He saw the modern condition of man as a division between his rational mind and his free romantic spirit, an oscillation between Apollonian control and Dionysian impulses. Trilling, in his essays, examines critically the nature and function of the intellect and the spirit and arrives at a liberal philosophy of life, negating neither, but holding both in a healthy dialectical tension.

The popularity that Trilling enjoyed as a critic was due to the objectivity which he brings to bear upon the divergent topics he discusses. Steven Marcus's tribute to Trilling is incisive. He declared that Trilling's writings "are now a permanent part of our culture's heritage". Douglas Bush wrote that Trilling's place would henceforth be "akin to that of the Victorian sages and prophets". Roger Sale who had never evinced much interest in his writings was fascinated by his popularity and felt that he was perhaps the only literary essayist read by important non-literary intellectuals (quoted in Chace 1978/79: 49).

He was accorded praise by social scientists and historians alike who admired the suppleness of his mind, his broad learning and disinterested pre-occupation with man and culture. His literary essays made it clear that literature was not just the product of an ephemeral imagination, but a chronicle of abiding human experiences, the pulse of an entire culture, its breath and finer spirit. It can be studied for its political, social, cultural and humane values, as also for its fictional and aesthetic nature.

"One reason for Trilling's sway [over intellectuals] is that he gave general consideration to history, politics and morality and thereby extended himself beyond the traditional confines of an English department . . . he welcomed to his thinking disciplines other than his own" (*ibid.*: 51). That is why a poll in 1970 among the intellectuals in the U.S. placed him as one of the top ten most prestigious contemporary American intellectuals (French 1980: 101). William Barrett says that in his view Trilling was the most intelligent man in his generation—"or at least the most intelligent man I knew" (Barrett 1982: 177).

Trilling's writings had a wide appeal. They were both morally satisfying and intellectually provocative. "It was the prose of the great nineteenth century critics and essayists, yet it was a clearly modern idiom and it proposed to bring to the discussion of literature a seriousness and cogency that such discussion merits but rarely finds".(Marcus 1977: 268). Trilling viewed the study of literature as a study of human life and so he brought into his criticism of literary texts a concern with moral, psychological and cultural issues. He did not merely proceed along the lines of the prevalent critical approaches: explication and analysis of texts and judgment of their aesthetic merits. He enlarged the frontiers of criticism on the assumption that the literary text was the product of the race, milieu and moment and hence inseparable from moral and social intentions. As Steven Marcus remarks, "In American academic literary life it is extremely uncommon to find someone who actually believed that literature has some determinate and important relation to the world, to the society and culture out of which it arises and which it helps in turn to form" (Marcus 1977: 270).

During his life-time there were excessive attacks on Trilling. Joseph Frank described him as a conservative in a derogatory sense. Many critics charged that Trilling aimed at defending and defining the post-war *status quo* (Reising 1986: 218). David Hirsch remarked that Trilling in criticizing Parrington's concept of reality that it is always reliable, always the same, easily to be known ended with making the same assumptions (Hirsch 1971: 35). How far he was right in his charges is debatable. Richard Sennet accused Trilling with "you have no position, you are always in between". Trilling replied, "Between is the only honest place to be" (quoted in Shoben 1981: 191).

His "betweenness" shows the aversion he had to ideological or dogmatic approaches to literary criticism and mostly revealed a historical and relativist bias, yet he is deemed positivist in his "expectations as to how the social is to be represented in the aesthetic" (Reising 1986: 219).

What gives Trilling his distinctive cultural stance is the spirit of the times. We have a picture of the period in his own words. "The 30's marks the radical movement creating the American intellectual class which was leftist". From their radicalism came the "moral urgency, the sense of crisis and the concern with personal salvation that mark the existence of American intellectuals". The doctrine followed by politics affirmed freedom: "The doctrine was directed towards the richness and fullness that would eventually be given to human life" and hence pointed to "a solicitude for mankind in general. . . " (Trilling 1966: 43, 49).

Trilling did not confine himself to such humanistic beliefs, although a liberal. He did acknowledge the "historic role of the working class and the validity of Marxism", but his own literary interest was "in the tradition of humanistic thought and in the intellectual middle class which believes that it continues this tradition" (Trilling 1939: 111).

He addresses himself to the intellectual class in whom he finds a "dramatic contradiction". "Its living with the greatest possibility (call it illusion) of conscious choice, its believing itself the inheritor of the great humanist and rationalist tradition and the badness and stupidity of its action" (Trilling 1939: 112).

Trilling has shifted his priorities during his literary career, and revised some of his key conceptions. But he remained a cultural critic throughout. He was the contemporary of the New Critics, Allen Tate, Cleanth Brooks, Robert Penn Warren, but was not a pure formalist. He belonged to the first generation of New Critics who were interested in the relevance of general ideas of society and culture to literature. Like Trilling, Philip Rahv, Alfred Kazin and Irving Howe argued against pure formalism as did Robert Penn Warren. There were two main groups of critics who made their presence felt at this time. "The Southern New Critics and the New York intellectuals were opposed in their ideologies and in their conceptions of literature and culture, but sociologically they resembled each other . . . theirs was an amalgam of traditionalism with modernism" (Krupnick 1986: 10).

Irving Howe remarks that during the 1950's when the New Critics enjoyed great prestige it was "only Lionel Trilling among the critics living in New York" who "did not suffer a loss of standing" (Howe 1982: 174). Even though Trilling criticised the ahistorical and apolitical thrust of New Criticism ("The Sense of the Past" in *The Liberal Imagination*), John Crowe Ransom, a prominent New Critic and editor of the *Kenyon Review*, associated him with the magazine for several years. That he also served subsequently, as advisory editor for the quite different *Partisan Review*, indicates his intellectual flexibility and imaginative appeal. Through the writings of men like Trilling, Rahv, Stuart Chase and F.W. Dupee "a useful tension was [also] set up between the New York Critics, whose instinctive response to literature was through a social moral contextualism and the New Critics, whose formalism may have been too rigid yet proved of great value to those who opposed it" (Howe 1970: 238).

Trilling followed the ideal of centrality which meant the incorporation of selective modern elements into the tradition of the past. This has become rather unfashionable in modern critical theory which searches for novelty of expressions and themes. Trilling's ideal makes for sanity and authenticity, as it has a long history. His critical method is enshrined in the criticism of Johnson, Arnold, Eliot and Leavis. Tradition, which is a key element in cultural criticism is associated with conservatism and hence it is considered old fashioned, detrimental to socialistic principles in political thought and Marxist ideologies in literary criticism, which were fashionable in his time. Now, after the demise of Communism in East Europe and the U.S.S.R. it is the right time to ponder on the correctness of Trilling's approach to life and literature which saw the discrepancies between the ideas and ideals of Marxism and the character of societies which are guided by these ideals. Paul Hollander (1991: 107) has commented on the long and tenacious Western misconceptions of the Communist system and which Trilling had himself battled against.

Even though we find political, social, historical and philosophical elements in Trilling's literary criticism, his primary preoccupation was with the complete human being and the self in relation to culture. He deplored the gradual disintegration of the self in its struggle against culture. His consciousness of the self in man was the cause of his early radicalism, his anti-Stalinism, his anti-liberalism and an aversion to utilitarian, progressive and mechanised culture. He regarded the American cultural scene as being dominated by liberal political ideas, that somehow permeated literature and the minds of intellectuals. Being a true critic, it was but natural for him to take an adversary position to contemporary ideas in politics, literature and the social sciences that were harmful to universal values and general human nature.

Unlike the prevailing opinion, Trilling did not think of culture in any institutionalized way. Political propaganda dispenres ideas of vested interests, which influence the intellectual milieu, giving rise to a culture alienated from the personhood of man. Trilling realized the danger to selfhood in a restrictive culture. This idea, which constitutes the core of his essay, "Mind in the Modern World" is also found in the *Loss of Self in Modern Literature and Art* by Sypher and *The Self in Literature* by Glicksberg. Man is not only a political creature or a social creature or purely a creature of passions and emotions—but an amalgam of all these, a complex entity full of possibilities. No political regime, however progressive and secure, can contain the effusiveness of his spirit. Trilling, like many intellectuals, recognised the importance and indomitable quality of the self in man and its adversary posture to the culture that shapes it. But where he differed from them was that he gave primacy neither to the self, as was to be seen in cultures based on the philosophy of Romanticism, nor to coercive culture, as was evident in the Stalinist regime. The first accounted for disorder, alienation and solecism; the other for neurosis, spiritual crisis and nihilism. Both these conditions bring about cultural decline leading to dehumanization, fragmentation and disharmony in society.

The self and culture were inter-dependent. There should be a culture based on tradition, shaping the self and there should be a self incorporating the best elements of the past and present, shaping culture by criticizing it and urging upon it new options. The attitude that he prescribes for the self is a constant vigil and refusal to be dominated by ideas propagated by culture, other than those that promote "innocence", "simplicity" and "integrity of life" (Trilling 1957: 62). Trilling also enjoins upon the self, the necessity of resignation to repressions that are aimed towards cultural upgradation, and acceptance of suffering as the chastisement of the spirit to refine and renew it. He believes in the discipline of the inner life, in the development of a true inwardness.

Trilling questioned nearly all the basic assumptions of his generation. In criticising liberalism, he does not undervalue its doctrines; he denounces the attitude of the liberals and accuses them of a lack of liberal imagination. He knew that liberalism is bound to fall short of its aims in the hands of men who serve vested interests. It can be saved by remaining aware of its deeper meanings. Hence, he revalues the liberal tradition in the light of objectivity and open-mindedness. His impatience with definitions and preference for subtlety, comprehensiveness, mental flexibility and imaginativeness make his essays complex and difficult. He repeatedly made use of his adaptation of Keats's conception of negative capability: the capacity to remain in doubts and uncertainties and to avoid easy or dogmatic conclusions. As Tom Sanet says, "He knew that difficult questions are rarely answered in any ultimate satisfying way; he thought it sufficient to hold the terms of debate in a state of mutually sustaining position" (Sanet 1979: 169-70).

Critics have argued that Trilling's evaluation of the liberal imagination is not systematic. This is because Trilling had developed an ambivalence that was the result of an inherent suspicion of easy and final solutions to complex cultural questions. It was not a sign of weakness, therefore, that he maintained an ambivalent attitude to the urgent problems of his day. On the contrary, his literary essays show his sincerity in trying to figure out in a morally responsible manner the nature of society, the place of culture, the predicament of the self, the function of literature and the aims of criticism. More importantly, Trilling was careful that he should not become a prey to ideas even if they were his own. He was aware that life overflowed ideologies and coercive systems, and therefore he brought to his sharp intellection, the tempering effects of intuition and perception. In this way he asserted the freedom of the mind.

Barzun's comments on Trilling point to the way he countered relativistic and posivistic ideas ". . . his affirmations were opposed not solely to cover schemes of social and political repression charged with philanthropic intent, they opposed equally all other fixities professing to be sufficient or complete whether derived from natural science, psychology or peremptory moralising" (Barzun 1976: 82). In this way, he taught a whole generation of men and women to think for themselves.

His ambivalence is also marked in the way he tries to find out the proper relationship of self and society. Selfhood cannot be attained in isolation from society, for it is the cultural environment that gives it shape; nor is it possible for the self to achieve fullness by submitting itself wholeheartedly to the conditioning of social forces without intelligent discrimination. At different times, therefore, he either advocates or opposes the conditioning forces of culture. Robert Boyers is of the opinion that "the pleasure we take in his enduring work is a pleasure in confronting a unified sensibility whose general absence our cultural has bemoaned. . . " (Boyers 1977: 1). Even in the treatment he gives to a single idea, we find the minute workings of a subtle intelligent mind, for he believed implicitly that an idea is founded upon contradiction. Even in his creative works, he proceeds as a critic. His novel, *Middle of the Journey* for instance, is based on ideas, and depicts the very process of thought itself as the narrative unfolds. Such sensibility is important in the modern context as it saves the mind from "acculturisation" by anti-cultural ideas.

The ability of Trilling to change his opinions and postures shows the development and growth of his ideas. In his books *The Opposing Self* and *A Gathering of Fugitives,* he dwells upon the possibilities of realising the self through culture. In *Beyond Culture* he develops a new adversary position *vis-a-vis* both environments, the literary and the cultural. This refusal to adhere to any particular mode or idea is the right approach of a critic. It makes it possible for him "to discover fresh ideas for the use of the poet who could then invigorate the mind and the feelings, providing alternatives to those received truths awakening in effect an unthinking and self-satisfied cultural life" (Kubal 1978-79: 283).

In resisting liberalism he was more of a liberal than his self-satisfied counterparts. He saw in the American society the loss of imagination which only can effectively comprehend moral realism. The liberal imagination that is evident in his writings was aimed at defending culture and society against the attacks of political barbarism and cultural philistinism. The moral realism achieved in his criticism is the result of the exercise of the liberal intelligence, a repudiation of reason which is mechanical and a prescription of sanity and sobriety.

Averse to the uses of both intellect and imagination as reflected in the liberal thinking of the right and the radical attitude of the Stalinists, he nevertheless combined some elements of both and followed a middle path. He took the main elements of conservatism and applied them to the liberal attitude by declaring that "progressivism has no true awareness of the deep instinctual roots of man . . . what awareness it does have is likely to be a hostile one . . . and in this respect it is in full accord with the acquisitive, competitive society it wishes to revise" (Trilling 1948: 246).

It must not be deduced from such assertions, that he was an orthodox conservative. Trilling admitted his misgivings about the conservative position in his remarks on Eliot's "deficiencies", his "cold ignorance", his "fierce puritanism", and his "confusion of morality with snobbery or conformity" (Trilling 1940: 372).

Trilling made use of his knowledge of Freudian psychoanalysis to add complexity and variety to his ideas on liberalism. Prospects for moral perfection and social reform were so complicated that the narrow liberal policies could not deal adequately with them. For, what was human and belonged to the spirit was out of bounds for progressive liberals. They lacked the vision to understand the human predicament as a whole. Trilling looked for support on some principle that would adequately define the human condition in the modern world and he found it not in the social sciences but in Freud's theories of the unconscious.

Such a study of the human mind in depth was an urgent necessity for him as modern literature was helping to introduce and make explicit what was dark, primitive, violent and non-ethical in man. Modern literature that belonged to high culture perpetuated ideas that were subversive of general culture, and as they were taken to be the expressions of the alienated self of the highly intelligent writer, they set the trend of the intellectual process. Modernist writers thereafter based their adversarial attitude on false assumptions and incorrect appraisals of Freud, made popular by his followers. The works of the most important modern writers Dostoievsky, Gide, Conrad, Joyce while being admirable testaments of the personal being, asserted the autonomy of protagonists who did not possess heroic qualities worthy of emulation. The notion of escaping from society into a state of unconditioned existence as illustrated in the novels of these writers was disturbing to him. The bitter line of hostility to civilization evident in modern literature arises out of a dissatisfaction with the cultural order itself. Students of modern literature were apt to respond in a positive way to the subversion indicated and to be influenced by the idea of power depicted therein.

Trilling concluded that culture was not the only source of repressive autonomy that the self struggled against. Society was essential for the self and to stand beyond society did not give freedom to the self. The study of the unconscious revealed that the mind possesses surrogates of societal pressures in the form of the superego. Man was subjected to biological drives which were repressed by the superego, the repository of historical, cultural and social values. The self alienated from society had also to contend with the conditioning of the superego. The only way, then to achieve selfhood was to escape from the mind itself to irrationality, which in one sense was a total negation of the human.

Trilling, in trying to reinterpret Freud to his generation enabled it to see that social contract required the de-authenticization of the self. But it was equally true that the unconscious appropriated a part of the aggressiveness of society and tyrannized over the self resulting in neurosis. The inherited past and the summation of all social, historical and cultural pressures stored in the unconscious continually intruded upon the conscious causing misery and suffering when it encountered the tyrannical inauthenticity of the social world.

Alienation must be overcome, Trilling felt. It must not be allowed to become a romantic and sentimental convention. Michel Foucault, R.D. Laing, Norman O'Brown are some of the authors responsible for popularising the view that inauthenticity can be overcome by no means other than madness. Trilling has shown that there is nothing very grand or noble in madness; it is not a way to authenticity, nor to divinity. Man by asserting his self, by becoming more himself was not living the life of pure spirit. On the other hand he was travelling back to the underground to confront his own hell.

The ultimate release lay in acquiescence in a universal order that noble characters in great literature achieve. Adversity and suffering have to be accepted as natural to man and there could be no escape from them. As Scott aptly remarks, "it is just this stern vision of the ultimate mystery and intractability of our basic woe which in the world of contemporary radical thought is felt to be an intolerable affront" (Scott 1973: 208). Trilling's writings make it evident that modern criticism has romanticised nihilism by recognising only "the world's false image of strife" without "the true emotion of reconciliation", and by denying the virtues of human existence (Trilling 1975: 187).

This was the moral realism Trilling arrived at after his study of Freud. He was able to face the irrational component in human nature that liberalism with its imaginative bankruptcy could not do. It cannot also be denied that in re-discovering the truth of self affirmation through self-denial he had come close to some sort of a religious process.

Trilling's diagnosis of the modern self as a "disintegrated consciousness" (*Sincerity and Authenticity*) is seen as an alienation from traditional humanism. Hegel's view that it is the nature of spirit . . . to seek existence on its own account", when taken to extremes has undermined the life of the mind, which seeks order, continuity and harmony. He proposed another alternative to the modernity of the autonomous self—that challenges of life have to be met with the stoicism of heroic composure.

Trilling advocated heroism that could affirm qualities and virtues lost to his generation. But he also contends that alienation or separation from one's culture is not only painful but inevitable. "It is the very process by which the self resolves its own contradictions and pushes towards fulfilment. This 'strange, bitter, dramatic' process is at the very centre of personal existence made social. It is what becoming 'cultured' in a serious and not merely fashionable sense happens to be" (Chace 1980: 5). This vision was enshrined in what Trilling calls the "other culture", a culture that saw the production of such masterpieces as *Oedipus, Hamlet, The Brothers Karamazov.* Trilling felt that directing the attention of literary critics to what was large and magnaminous would help them regain that moral vision. But in the ultimate analysis Trilling's writings were aimed at "the clear purpose of detaching the reader from the habits of thought and feeling that the larger culture imposes, of giving him a ground and vantage point from which to judge and condemn, and perhaps revise, the culture that produced him" (*Beyond Culture*: IV). To stand beyond culture really means to inculcate an original approach to culture and criticism, to think in a new way, to transcend ideas and perceptions that generally mar our autonomy of judgment—in short to have as many options as possible to bear upon our habitual mode of thought. In this context we may refer to R.P. Blackmur's assessment that Trilling was "an administrator of the offices of the mind" (1950: 34).

The public stance taken by Trilling in his writings is one which is ever watchful that the autonomy of mind is not hampered by ideas which are merely fashionable or current at any time. He adopted a posture which was simultaneously an acceptance of and a detachment from life in civilization. Trilling himself achieved the autonomy of perception he prescribed for others through his critical essays. At the risk of being criticised as conservative, hence inimical to progressive democratic ideas, he advocated spiritual affirmation and archaic heroism. At a time when modernism held sway over the imagination, he depended on writers like Jane Austen and Henry James who displayed the imagination of felicity that "presents the idea and descriptions of an innocent and happy humanity" (Trilling 1965: 51). Wordsworth he admired because he represented the idea of innocence and exposed the native dignity of man. To formulate the conception of modernity he brought in Arnold's, but felt that "To anyone conditioned by our modern literature, Arnold's ideas of order, convenience, decorum and rationality might well seem to reduce itself to the small advantages and excessive limitations of the middle class life of a few prosperous nations of the nineteenth century" (*ibid.*: 16). The attainment of spiritual poise he knew was not through negation of culture but through the assertion of traditional humanistic ideals of order, peace, honour and beauty.

Of seminal importance is his essay "Mind in the Modern World" contained in *The Last Decade*. He deplores the separation of the intellect from feeling, imagination and will. The fragmentation of the individual mind is consonant with the fragmentation of the collective conscious. The alienated artist speaks in a personalised idiom incomprehensible to men who lack social empathy. Wordsworth, he writes, conceived of an imagination that was universal. His poet was a man speaking to men in the idiom of common men. He had the privilege of possessing what was normative and human, rather than special and peculiar. He could even conceive of a harmony of poetry and science, for it was a science readily comprehended by literary intellectuals. In the modern world such a harmony is inconceivable because scientific ideas are expressed in technical language and are highly specialised.

It has now become impossible to think of a "whole man" and the universities are responsible for producing individuals trained only for specialities or super-specialities. They are not induced to make an effort to train a strong general intelligence. By discrediting "certain humanising and liberalising disciplines, among which literature is pre-eminent" (Trilling 1965: 214), they have forsaken a highly moralised intention. For Trilling, literature was that disciplining agent that could civilise society and help to disseminate a moral and intellectual education, thus making an individual fit to face any situation in life.

From the discussion of Trilling's method of following a dialectical course in dealing with complex social, moral and literary ideas, it follows that he possessed a truly contemplative mind. His efforts in literary criticism were not directed to arrive at specific answers and formulations of theory. As he himself states "To summarise any good, developed idea is to betray it, we must have not only its conclusions but its dialectical growth" (Trilling 1943: 41). He realised quite early that, literature was a humanistic discipline and to theorise about man and life was practically impossible. In this connection we may review the modern theories that have done little to bridge the gap between literature and reality. On the other hand, they have helped to widen it by stressing the fact that literature is the expression of the writer's autonomous self, a product of the creative imagination, exalted and estranged from base social existence. Structural linguistics served to disintegrate reality further and hence failed to give a coherent view of life based upon real human experience. Criticism became an intellectual activity, an offspring of the analytical reason, not an objective appraisal of life. Trilling's essays in criticism enable us to reconsider our basic assumptions on life and literature, and help us to imbibe wisdom and equilibrium in an age that has progressed far on the Kantian imperative to follow one's own nature and to express without any restraint the urgings of the autonomous spirit. To Arnold this was anarchy.

WORKS CITED

Barrett, W., 1982. *The Truants: Adventures Among The Intellectuals*, New York: Anchor, Double Day: Garden City.

Barzun, J., 1976. "Remembering Lionel Trilling", *Encounter*, 47.3: 82-88.

Blackmur, R.P., 1950. "The Politics of Human Power" in *The Lion and the Honeycomb*, New York: Harcourt.

Boyers, R., 1977. *Negative Capability and the Wisdom of Avoidance*, Columbia: University of Missouri Press.

Chace, W.H., 1978-79. "Lionel Trilling: The Contrariness of Culture", *American Scholar*, 48: 49-59.

————, 1980. *Lionel Trilling: Criticism and Politics*,Stanford: Stanford University Press.

French, P., 1980, ed. *Three Honest Men: A Critical Mosaic*, Manchester: Carcanet.

Hirsch, D., 1971. *Reality and Idea in the Early American Novel*, The Hague: Mouton.

Hollander, P., 1991. "The End of Communism?" *Partisan Review*, 58.1.: 107-15.

Howe, I., 1970. *Decline of the New*, New York: Horizon.

————, 1982. *A Margin of Hope*, San Diego: Harcourt.

Krupnick, M., 1986. *Lionel Trilling and the Fate of Cultural Criticism*, Evanston: North Western University Press.

Kubal, D., 1978-79. "Lionel Trilling: The Mind and Its Discontents", *Hudson Review*, 31: 279-395.

Marcus, S., 1977. "Lionel Trilling" in *Art Politics and Will*, ed. Quentin Anderson, New York: Basic.

Reising, R.J., 1986. *The Unusable Past*, New York and London: Methuen.

Sanet, T., 1979. "Lionel Trilling and The Social Imagination", *Centennial Review*, 23: 159-84.

Scott, N.A., 1973. *Three American Moralists*, Notredam: University of Notingham Press.

Shoben, E.J., 1981. *Lionel Trilling*, New York: Ungar.

Trilling, L.. 1939. in "The Situation in American Writing: A Symposium", *Partisan Review*, 6.5.

Trilling, L., 1940. "Elements that are Wanted", *Partisan Review*, 7.5: 370-75.

———,1943. *E.M. Forster*, Connecticut, New Direction.

———, 1948. "Treason in the Modern World", *Nation*, 166.

———, 1950. *The Liberal Imagination*, London: Secker and Warburg.

———, 1957. *A Gathering of Fugitives*, London: Secker and Warburg.

———, 1965. *Beyond Culture*, New York: Viking.

———, 1966. "Young in the Thirties", *Commentary*, 41.5: 43-51.

———, 1975. *The Middle of the Journey*, London: Secker and Warburg.

4

TRILLING'S THEORY OF CRITICISM AS A MOULDER OF CULTURE

> One must escape the solipsistic self in order to move outwards towards a true sense of community. From there one is able to situate a particular community or culture in relation to significant developments in the Western tradition and in the mind of Europe, that is, the achievements of European culture. . . .
> — Robert Con Davis and Ronald Schleifer (*Criticism and Culture*)

The focus of this chapter is on Trilling's theory of criticism as a moulder of culture. It traces his attitude to literature, his ideas on the place of the critic in society, the function of criticism and the social consequences of bad art or anti-art that subverts tradition and culture.

Trilling as critic can be placed in the Arnoldian tradition of disinterested moral and intellectual inquiry, tempered by Forsterian awareness of the ironies, pitfalls and paradoxes confronting the liberal humanist intellectual. Though, like most American critics of his generation he was affected by the theory and practice of New Criticism, the ideas of the autonomy of the work of art was never congenial to him. On the contrary he was inclined by temperament and conviction, to emphasize the ways in which works of literature both effect and reflect the cultural contexts in which they are produced and consumed. As a literary critic, Trilling did not follow any rigidly established method or ideology. He aimed at fostering a social and cultural appreciation of literature, for which he deplored the "tangential" relationship between American literature and American reality and in his literary criticism, he tried to bring literature closer to life as modified and conditioned by social and cultural forces. For fulfilling his purpose of humanising and liberalising literary study, Trilling relied on the ideas of a tradition that went back to Renaissance humanism, Samuel Johnson and Matthew

Arnold as has been suggested earlier. We do not find traces of prevalent American literary canons like the Adamic, the romance, the pastoral, the symbolic, the world elsewhere, guiding his approach to literary texts. Rather, his interpretations and analyses result from the synthesis of the emotive, cognitive, ethical, political, historical and aesthetic view points. Trilling's criticism, seen in the light of new critical canons such as the structuralist, deconstructive and self-reflexive theories in recent American criticism in the formalistic, feminist and racial approaches, exposes their limitations and deficiencies. Trilling's broad humanistic concern makes him look at literature as a "criticism of life" and at criticism as an instrument of social change and cultural amelioration. Although his concern is really with ideas rather than aesthetics, his insistence upon the necessity of culture as an undeniable fact in literary production and his stress upon literature as the arbiter of culture, have helped him develop a theory that amply demonstrates that a truly aesthetic experience can only be derived from literature, if it reflects the fullness, freedom and potency of life. His stress on culture as a summation of the human efforts through the ages to make life refined, humane, subtle and harmonious is, to an extent, similar to Eliot's idea of culture as a harmonising inner agency.

Trilling is of the view that "the literary life . . . is quite indispensable to culture" (Trilling 1950: 50). By this he means that literature reflects the consciousness of society as well as it forms and refines it. It exposes the writer's whole milieu which also derives moral sustenance from him. As such, literature is a social institution, the essence and summary of all history. As Morris Dickstein confirms, ". . . a great writer is not simply an individual but a crystallization of his time and place" (1992: 437). Hence literature occurs only in a social context, as part of a culture. It brings us closer to the "sources of life" and develops our imagination to include a concern for "moralised taste" and a habit of discrimination. The development of discriminatory powers which a literary sensibility inculcates, makes the judgement and evaluation of culture valid. It helps us to value such aspects of culture as are indispensable to the refinement of the human faculties. Trilling recognised the power of literature to influence attitude and behaviour, and its role in the formation of a truly liberal imagination. Therefore he enjoins upon criticism the task of sharpening the general intelligence and refining the general moral tone of society, by proceeding on the sound principles of the humanist critical tradition.

Surveying the literary-intellectual climate of his time, Trilling found that "the culture of humanism was at a point of crisis" and that "the society that had sustained this culture was in due straits" (Trilling 1982a: 235). What was lost was the link with forces that unite, harmonise and shape the human faculties, will, imagination, reason and spirit, and make human ties possible and essential. For Trilling culture was an inclination of the mind to receive truth. It was a moral reorientation involving the intellect, the imagination, the emotions and the will that culture should strive to bring about, Trilling's stand on culture is similar to Arnold's. Arnold states that culture is that totality of the "imaginative reason" which must be applied to our social and political life if anarchy is not to prevail (Trilling 1982b: 429). At a time when the modern spirit is questioning the validity of religion as a shaping force for the spirit, critics of the stature of Arnold and Trilling have pointed out the possibility of literature and literary studies taking its place. Arnold had declared that in us there is a central moral tendency that links us to the universal order. Trilling supports this claim (*ibid.*: 341) and puts his faith in criticism as a civilizing agent, instrumental in negating the effects of cultural philistinism. F.R. Leavis also holds a similar view regarding the value of literary critical study in our age.

Trilling avoids the approach generally adopted by modernist critics: an exaggerated concern with formal criteria and preoccupation with style and literary technique. He states that the "judgement of literature is overtly and explicitly a moral and intellectual judgement. The cogency, the appositeness, the logicality; the truth of ideas must always be passed upon by literary criticism" (Trilling 1957: 135).

What Arnold calls the imaginative reason. Trilling interprets it as the synthesis of the intellect and the imagination. Noting with an increasing sense of alarm, the trend of modernism which puts excessive faith in the reasoning powers, Trilling enjoins upon critics to bear in mind that their reason should not be the "cold and formal reason that makes the mind a machine". On the other hand, he should develop "faith", "but not the escape from earth-binding facts" (Trilling 1982b: 194).

How criticism can mould culture is a pertinent question. Criticism, to follow Arnold's arguments closely, is the propagation of ideas—the best that have ever been known and thought. Critics must study and propagate ideas from different disciplines that are conducive to the fullness of moral and spiritual life. According to Trilling the spirit of criticism is that which measures the actual social reality and aspects of the practical sphere by the ideal. This ideal is to be deduced from cultures of other nations, of other ages and from the critic's own "sense of life" (in the sense of Henry James) and made to bear upon his own cultural environment. Although he adopted a sympathetic attitude to the formalist's exhortation to "return to the text", he was also particular that the textual analysis must be supplemented by extrinsic evidences. Extra-literary ideas from social, psychological, political, historical, and the moral sphere, must be allowed to influence the critic if literature is to be taken seriously as a criticism of life.

Trilling's own criticism shows that literature is a study of human life in the widest sense. He brings to the consideration of literary texts a concern with moral, psychological and cultural questions. As a culture-critic he gives priority to the political sphere as it is politics which arranges and organizes the life of men in society, gives them their values by institutionalising the very organs of culture. He views politics as an essential part of culture as it presents "choices to all elements of the individual, including his imagination and his sense of the quality of his own being", politics was for him "an activity in which the individual stakes all the cherished elements of his being on the chance of securing their safety" (Trilling 1946: 658). He was himself engaged in the criticism of liberal politics and in redefining the meaning of the liberal imagination. As Mark Krupnick remarks, "Trilling's cultural redefinition of politics . . . was itself a political act, an attempt to displace the cultural attitudes that accounted for Stalinism's hold on liberal intellectuals" (Krupnick 1986: 16). Trilling's early criticism is an attempt to invigorate liberal thought, by questioning the assumption and attitudes it encompasses. The liberal tendency, as he states in the introduction to *The Liberal Imagination* is inadequate and therefore he wants criticism to "recall liberalism to its essential imagination of variousness and possibility, which implies the awareness of complexity of difficulty". These being also the qualities of great literature the liberal spirit in criticism should be properly organized to come to terms with the "variousness, possibility, complexity and difficulty" of any literary, political or social idea. From Forster, Trilling took the ideas of "moral realism" and "dialectical intelligence" to to confront the unimaginative and oversimplifying ideas and attitudes of his liberal contemporaries. Such an attitude has been responsible for an overt ideological stance in literary judgments. He believes that ideology is reductive in essence, and makes man lead an "unexamined life", and that it oversimplifies the complexity of human experience. The "moral imagination" should be another attribute of a critic; it is the capacity for adopting an open attitude in order to recognise the ambiguities and antimonies that culture contains.

Induced by the liberal spirit of his day, many American critics followed an uncritical and, unregulated course in discussing modern literature, and endorsing the validity of the individual self's complete detachment from culture. Their social criticism was without imagination. According to Kazin, they were liberals "by acquiescence" and lacked the full understanding of social forces. It was either "curiously decadent" or "frankly conservative" (1942: 270). But their most important contention was that the artist was limited by hostile forces in culture and as a result had to stand beyond culture to assert his own superior individuality.

Trilling's literary criticism was directed against these critics. He could not conceive of a person standing beyond his culture. In fact the whole being of an individual depends upon his culture. It is culture that has given him:

> his categories and habits of thought, his range of feelings, his idiom and tones of speech. . . . No personal superiority can place one beyond these influences. . . . Even when a person rejects his culture and rebels against it, he does so in a culturally determined way.
>
> — Trilling 1965: 12

Although he did not give credence to the liberal critic's position regarding the culture and the place of the writer in it, he was deeply concerned about "the opposing self's predicament. He sees the individual striving for self-realisation in a cultural environment that both nurtures his self-hood and ruthlessly bends his will to its dictates. The task of criticism in such circumstances would be to tone down the irrational urge for freedom inherent in the spirit of the individual, while encouraging him to retain his self-hood as a sensible, honest and intelligent being. He was aware of the implications of the modern self struggling against the repressive forces of culture and with fate. But he concludes that human nature could be relied upon to achieve harmony and quiescence if he allows his "imaginative reason" to function in a way which would connect him with his culture, so that the best aspects in it would develop and refine his "moral intellect".

In his essay "Art, Will and Necessity", Trilling views with concern the tendency of the modern self to repudiate its culture in favour of a kind of untrammelled autonomy. The idea that cultural limitations exert a beneficial influence upon men in a civilization is being discredited in the modern world. Today will is no longer seen as the power through which the individual controls his impulses and refines his sensibilities in the light of the best ideas that are propagated by high-culture. Rather, that vision of the will has been replaced by a blind, irrational will, "the will of the undeveloped ego, unresponsive to necessity" (Trilling 1982a: 146-47). Trilling finds that modern man no longer values the will power through which impulses are organised to follow principles relating to a universal moral order. There are a number of causes that have alienated the individual from the main currents of true culture, the foremost among them being the spread of democracy and the lure of total freedom. Trilling does not undervalue the freedom of the individual but he feels that criticism can play a great part in providing values by which the individual could be guided to act and think in an independent way, and refine his manners and responses at the same time.

Such refinement consists in an intellectual and emotional acquiescence to the limitations and conditions that life in society entails. He believed that the will when detached from cultural necessities exhibits "weightlessness" and depletes life of all meaning and purpose. A social imagination fosters a sense of commitment to culture and a desire to work for its perfection. This commitment has been described by Trilling as the outcome of "the notion of the interdependence of men" and the need for "human responsibility" and the awareness of "the delicacy and intricacy of social life" (Trilling 1980: 139), a notion that reminds us of E.M. Forster to a great extent.

Trilling's understanding of the will offers an immediate contrast to the modern view of Lacan. He deplores the use of the will-power for winning "felicity" and for "survival" in a universe subjected to the "inevitable rule of harsh necessity". Trilling feels that the human race might find its real purpose if it made the right use of its mental powers. It is clear from Trilling's works that his theory of criticism has much to do with developing the life of the mind and enriching the temperament, because culture rests more upon man's inner qualities than upon his material progress. The mind, freed from the limitations of understanding becomes subtle enough to grasp complications, and thinks up new ideas when it faces difficulties and contradictions that arise in its encounter with culture as a form of reality itself. Such a fresh spate of ideas is always welcome as it is of "particular value for the establishment of man in society and the universe" (Trilling 1950: 286). In this context, it is of importance to note Trilling's anxiety that ideology should find no place in the critical temper for, "Ideology is not the product of thought" (*ibid.*). It is mechanical adherence to a habit of thought . Hence any critical theory which prides itself for being "at the service of the emotions and life itself should turn a very strict and jealous gaze upon an intimate relationship between literature and ideas, for in our culture ideas tend to deteriorate into ideology" (*ibid.*).

In Trilling's view literature and ideas are inseparable. By a "literary idea" he means "only such ideas as can arouse and traditionally have aroused the feelings—the ideas, for example, of men's relation to one another and to the world" (*ibid.*: 287). This is a definite humanistic stand taken by Trilling reminding us of John Donne's famous phrase that no man is an island and is a reaction against naturalism, realism and objectivity in art, all of which were post-Renaissance or post-Enlightenment developments in Europe. Further, by stressing that ideas can also generate and underpin emotions, as they do in regard to the intellect, he projects a unified, synthetic approach to literary criticism that makes the experience of literature a wholesome and lively one.

The position of the critic, therefore, should be one of alertness. He should judge the social and political conditions around him and try to determine their causes. As a literary intellectual he should also study contemporary writings to see how far they have been instrumental in spreading ideas that are either adding to the intellectual and moral anarchy of the society, or democratizing art and helping mediocrity prevail. This last function is of special importance in the modern world of standardization and mass man where we see everywhere, the lowering of standards and a cynical attitude to high art and culture. The idea that art and culture have a large part to play in producing intelligence, character and a free and responsible personality should be allowed to permeate the modern consciousness.

The critical temperament for Trilling as it was for Arnold, is the disinterested effort to see the object as it really is, without regard to personal prejudices or prevalent notions. To him as to Carlyle, the man of letters "is a priest, a hero and a seer" and thus coequal to the political leader and the rival of the scientist.

Trilling viewed with alarm the dominant trend of modern literature which has conventionalised alienation to the extent of glorifying it. It has broken all connection with the past and discredited human values and questioned the validity of all established norms:

> It asks every question that is forbidden in polite society. It asks us if

> we are content with our marriages, with our family lives, with our professional lives, with our friends.
>
> — Trilling 1965: 8

In the process of its disenchantment with the past it has perpetrated grave dissatisfaction with a conditioned existence and favoured an attitude of self-autonomy, which gave precedence to the will and reason, rather than to the emotions and the imagination. Of greater concern was the devaluation of traditional social and ethical values that modern literature demonstrated. Hence his faith in literature as a social stabiliser began to wane and he began to investigate the causes that led to the devalued condition of human nature as reflected in modern literature. When other critics were turning their attention to formalistic theories, Trilling continued to delve into the social origins of the new literature, because for him society was of ultimate concern. In Delmore Schwartz's words he had "the most serious misgivings about the extremism, the bias and the methods of all modernist authors" (Schwartz 1953: 60). He termed the effect of the new literature as the "adversary culture" since it was characterised by a radical attitude to established norms of culture and social behaviour. Trilling laid a great deal of importance on manners which he describes as being "generally the product of the very basis of character" (Trilling 1957: 159). He found contemporary literature doing very little in the way of refining them. It did not possess that which was "good and beautiful" (Trilling 1965: 27), or that which endorsed conventional morality. Instead of maintaining his early position about the beneficial effect of literature, which he believed stimulated and extended the individual's moral imagination and connected him with his fellow citizens, he was obliged to see the harmful effect it had in denying the validity of the social connection and in divorcing morality from imagination.

Daniel Bell makes the same point. He states that "genius" has become democratised and institutionalised, ". . . the search for release has become legitimated in a liberal culture and exploited . . . by commercial entrepreneurs . . ." (1976: 145). Further he goes on to say that the avant-garde has displaced the conventional and the traditional art forms and occupied such a firm place in the minds of men that there cannot be discerned any real tension between the new art that is meant to shock and the society that is to be shocked.

Beyond Culture portrays modernist trends in literature as a seductive force that annihilates moral and ethical values. Trilling suggests in his preface that "art does not always tell the truth or the best kind of truth and does not always point out the right way, that it can even generate falsehood and habituate us to it" (xvii). The truth he expects literature to deal with "is the truth of the self, and also the truth about the self, about the conditions of its existence, its survival, its development" (Trilling 1965: 102-103).

Trilling takes a courageous stand as a literary critic by suggesting that creative imagination and art are not the best means of judging authentic human existence; reason and morality can serve the purpose better. The development and refinement of reason and the inculcation of moral values is the true end of critical endeavour. In his later works Trilling gives more attention to the nature of the self in culture than to individual works of art or to individual authors as such. His approach which is cultural and non-literary, draws upon the works of outstanding philosophers and critics and social scientists such as Hegel, Rousseau, Carlyle, Nietzsche, Schiller and Freud, whose writings represented for him the history of European culture. A survey of the past was essential for him to understand the present malaise which was, as he says, the "socialization of the anti-social, or the acculturation of the anti-culture, or the legitimization of the subversive" (Trilling 1965: 26).

Taking his cue from modern literature which develops the idea of the opposing self to an extremity by devaluing man's life in society and over emphasizing the life of the spirit in all its isolation from culture, he was led to the study of the nature of the modern mind. The mind for him was the repository of cultural values that could help the individual in placing himself beyond his own inadequate culture, and at the same time provide him with a source of authority other than the culture he repudiates. He found Freud's ideas enlightening since they helped him to understand the ideal relationship of the self and culture, and the role of the mind in helping the individual attain a state of composure and poise in the face of cultural vicissitudes.

The chief ground of his theories of criticism, morality and social action seems to be that "man can be truly himself and fully human only if he is in accord with his cultural environment, and also, only if the cultural environment is in accord with the best tendencies in himself" (Trilling 1965: 108-109). But this is a condition scarcely reached in modern culture—either the culture is too repressive or the individual self too rebellious. Trilling's criticism, unlike the general trend of political thought does not give absolute authority to culture; nor does it put absolute faith in the adversarial position of the self. Following Freud's arguments closely he deduces that individuals in a culture could extend some kind of autonomy through their biological selves, which can judge and reject culture. This function of the individual biological self is seen by Trilling as the most beneficial aspect of culture: "This intense conviction of the existence of the self apart from culture, is as culture knows, its noblest and most generous achievement" (*ibid.*: 118). Nevertheless, the fact that despite culture's repressive or seductive forces, there is yet a residual human element (the biological self), that can transcend culture and express itself, makes Trilling's arguments acceptable to us. In the final analysis, it means that man is not purely a social being as the Neo-Freudians, Harry Stack Sullivan, Erich Fromm or Karen Horney would have us believe. By de-emphasizing biology and the "instinctual roots of man", they averred that man was a social being, not a biological being. Trilling's support of biology as a "given" in human fate "far from being a reactionary idea", is actually "a liberating idea. . . . It suggests that there is a residue of human quality, beyond the reach of cultural control, and that this residue of human quality elemental as it may be, serves to bring culture itself under criticism and keeps it from being absolute" (*ibid.*: 113).

Therefore, Trilling's cultural criticism is a means to reassess the position of the self in culture. In modern literature, he finds a particular concern with the "self in its standing quarrel with culture" (*ibid.*), and that all notions that bear semblance to religious ideas or stress the importance of values in shaping lives, have ceased to be of interest. His most important treatise on human nature and its possibilities of attaining an integrated and authentic existence is *Sincerity and Authenticity* (1972). The essays contained in the book show the historical, moral, social, cultural, philosophical and literary leanings of Trilling. The range of knowledge depicted in the book is extensive and gives evidence of the richness of the mind of the author who combines intellectual subtlety, moral insight and aesthetic control and evinces a deep and sympathetic interest in the human condition.

Trilling defines those values and conditions that give actuality and meaning to human life in an affluent and technologically advanced society. He recalls Keats' statement in one of his letters: "Call the world if you please The Vale of Soul-making! Then you will see the use of the world. . . . Do you not see how necessary a World of pains and troubles is to school an Intelligence and make it a Soul?" (quoted in Trilling 1955: 44-45). In the last decade of his career we have a Trilling who is non-political in his approach to culture, and who evinces a nearly religious strain in his argument on the human condition. In his assertion of positive belief as a necessary condition of self-fulfilment, Trilling goes counter to the modern tendency of institutionalised negativism dominant in the American adversary culture. In this way he acts as the adversary self to the adversary culture of his times, which had its roots in the desire to break with the past and to repudiate all inherited values, in life as in art. Trilling's criticism is based upon a belief that can be found in a Judeo-Christian tradition that supports an integrated authentic existence based on "the sentiment of being" in contradistinction to the existential mode of intensities of being, and giving credence to irrationalism and a fragmented, disjointed existence. All said and done, Trilling, in *Sincerity and Authenticity* shows his personal preference for the type of personality formed in adversity. Trilling's theory of criticism invalidates the existential craze for "more life", as in Dostoievsky's *Notes from Underground* and reiterates the need for a perdurable unified self. It denounces the progress of spirit through self-estrangement and madness in favour of a composed and harmonious relation to culture. With prophetic insight he had diagnosed the source of the modern malady:

> The extremity of our condition makes us value extremity in ourselves, for men adopt as their own the nature of whatever overawes and oppresses them.
>
> — Trilling 1949: 10

Being ever conscious of the ethical effects that cultural forms have upon individuals in society, he deplored the radical negativity of some of the most characteristic modernist art and thought like Beckett's writings, although he fully appreciated the undeniable power of that negativity.

If modern society lacked the authority of a body of beliefs and ideals taken from religion and morals to aid it in living a meaningful life, then the next alternative was the imitation of literary figures, both characters or authors. In this respect he would most certainly have us follow the humanism of Forster rather than the radicalism of the raw hero, the Underground Man. Hence it was the task of American higher education to train the modern mind to judge and choose its own ideal of personhood from literary sources. The task of criticism in this endeavour was no less important.

Trilling's ideas on literature countervail the French theoreticians like Lacan, Derrida and Foucault. Their ideas which form the new avant-garde in literature make for heterogeneity, disunity and disintegration. In contrast, "the sentiment of being" that Trilling recommends is a sentiment of wholeness and can act as a corrective to the modern inclination to disunity and discontinuity. The disinterested play of critical intelligence that Trilling's essays exhibit, brings out the glory of committing oneself to an artistic culture and refraining from a philistinic devotion to alienation from the traditional ethos. Trilling has a cogent case to make out against postmodern counter culture that finds place in the curriculum of universities in America. He found that the advanced critical theories and ideological analyses of literature were completely out of touch with the larger realities of American society. How far such theories could advance the cause of general culture and art was a question which continually intruded upon his thoughts.

In "The Authentic Unconscious", the final chapter of *Sincerity and Authenticity,* Trilling discusses "the specific developments in our contemporary arts by which the preoccupation with authenticity expresses itself" (1972: 134). He is led to remark that the concern for authenticity has drastically reduced the narrative content in literature and broadcasted the Lacanian belief that "madness is health, that madness is liberation" (*ibid.*: 171). For Trilling, this distrust of the narrative mode in the art of the novel, is symptomatic of the impatience of modern writers with the conventions of a past literary tradition, and a controverting of mimetic theories of art. More so, it represents in the words of Lukács (1957), the "attenuation of reality and dissolution of personality" (in Lodge 1972: 480). Trilling deplores the modern literary aesthetic of anti-realism, which while negating man's relationship with his environment, takes no pleasure in the simple unfolding of a plot with a traditional hero and a moral lesson to be imparted. It may be argued that modern criticism, following blindly the methods of the formalists, may be adequate to deal with texts which are aesthetic in intent, but can lead to a myopic view of a work of art which has an underlying philosophical or moral purpose and a consistent world view. We may refer here to Trilling's *The Middle of the Journey* which has a sketchy yet coherent narrative content but where the philosophy is steadily built up by a ruminative dialectical process.

Perhaps Trilling's comments on Henry James' criticism will help us understand him better:

> . . . part of our experience of his work, which we see [is] not as a collection of particular aesthetic objects but as an intention, the enterprise of a life-time, which has its own coherence and form and is thus in itself an aesthetic object of a kind.
>
> — Trilling 1982: 74

In other words, a writer should be sincere and wholehearted in his response to a particular situation. A critic's sincerity is to be judged by the effectiveness with which he blends moral and literary qualities. His intention should not be overtly moral; the moral experience should be a part of his experience of life as expressed in a literary work. The formalists would do well to remember that it is the urgency of the moral intent which finds release in a suitable art-form, and that in all great literature form and content are inseparable.

It is a definitely humane intention that Trilling sees in the novelists of the nineteenth century England. Their aim was to give detailed representation of the social context in which man is to revitalise his life. To this end, the form, intention, the language and the content should be modified. The aim of all art should be to depict that initiation into society is possible, not the modernist view that poetic virtue consists in the conventionalised form of alienation. In Trilling's words, the duty of the critic is to "project what men should become" (1980: 164) and not to serve the immediate ends of providing pleasure or knowledge which is linked to philosophy, science, religion, or history. If literature is to serve the purposes of a higher life, the knowledge it should in fact provide, is the knowledge of the self and the truth about human nature as Trilling himself has accomplished in his own novel. We may find affinities between the critical attitudes of Trilling and Richards (1924) who holds the view that literature helps us organise and evaluate experience so that we get the knowledge of what is the best life. Such knowledge has a moral tenor. Further, he states that "the two pillars" upon which a theory of criticism must rest are "an account of value" and "an account of communication" (in Lodge 1972: 106). The writer should be able to communicate with his readers on the common ground of emotions, ideas and language, and effect them in a way which corresponds to his own sense of rightness and knowledge of life. This concept of communication which has become prominent in the post-modern era is seen in the writings of Jürgen Habermas and implies a community of readers who share common values. Such sharing becomes feasible in an organic community, which unfortunately declined with the advent of the Industrial Revolution or what Alvin Toffler designates as the "Second Wave". Under such conditions man becomes atomised and communication becomes problematic and we are exposed to "readerly" texts Habermas therefore proposes a model of communicative action based on a field of intersubjective action along with interest in critical self-reflection which resembles to an extent Trilling's conception of communication.

Trilling's theory of criticism, therefore, has the ultimate objective of vivifying the Aristotelian definition of the human being as a gregarious social animal. His individual existence, his self cannot be really distinguished from his social and historical environment. His human significance or his specific individuality cannot be separated from the context in which he lives and has his being. Contrary to the modernist stance he views the artist as integral to the culture: "the artist must accept his culture and be accepted by it, . . . he must be its critic, correcting, even rejecting it according to his personal insight, his strength seems to come from the tension of this ambivalent situation and we must learn to welcome this ambivalence. . . ." All these precautions must be taken particularly because "we can no longer not expect a political effect from a work of art . . ." (1980: 134).

Regarding the New Criticism, Trilling comments that although it has won its way into academic circles, it has failed to deal effectively with the crisis that engulfs modern culture. "It has mistaken method for ideology and pretends that all it offers is method". It may have begun as an endeavour to achieve complete objectivity in criticism, but its technicality while professionalising the study of literature failed to perceive its rootedness in life. He argues that the New Critical approach militated against "the breadth and catholicity of reading which once was assumed to be the goal of the study of English Literature" (1980: 354-55).

Perhaps the most obvious fault of the New Critics that Trilling points out is "in their reaction from the historical method they forget that the literary work is ineluctably a historical fact, that its historicity is a fact in our aesthetic experience" (1950: 184). This brings us close to Trilling's insistence on "the sense of the past", which is a knowledge of the "morals and manners", "philosophy and art" as developed in course of time. The historical sense, as Trilling puts it is the "critical sense", "the sense which life uses to test itself" (*ibid.*: 196). It is the sense that can immediately divine the moral value of literary and historical experiences and judge their relevance. Hence, it is best to remember Trilling's assertion that "the historical-literary mind" is "the best kind of critical mind" (1957: 73). A lack of the sense of history has been responsible for the radicalism of post-modernism that drives the individual into the beyond. Daniel Bell in his essay "Beyond Modernism, Beyond Self" refers to the "moral imagination" of Trilling which is a development of his "historical sense". It seeks to examine the assumptions and attitudes, beliefs and ideas which are the facts of history and of culture.

This leads us on to consider the "authentic unconscious" of a critic like Trilling, an unconscious which is formed out of the deeply inlaid cultural assumptions of the past, from which it is impossible to be completely freed and which conditions the development of his career. Without a clear conception of the past a critic cannot hope to imagine a standard to measure the present, "and so must become content with a sense of universal diminishment, occasionally punctuated by apocalyptic spectacles of one sort or another" (O'Hara 1987: 284).

In "Mind in the Modern World", Trilling makes the point that the exercise of only the mental faculties has been responsible for the modern malaise. In this essay he refers to the destruction wrought by war and the new weapons "that mind had brought into being". In face of such destruction it is impossible for him as a humanist to go along with progressives and scientific-minded men, in being optimistic that the mind would play a beneficial part in human existence. His "diminished confidence in mind", is the outcome of the mind's break with the past:

> From earliest youth into his old age the intense imagination of the past gave impetus to all the shaping minds of the eighteenth and nineteenth centuries, Voltaire, Diderot, Rousseau, Goethe, Hegel, Darwin, Marx, Freud—all were rooted in the past, from which they derived the force with which they addressed themselves to the present. . . . And if now we may be aware of a diminished confidence in mind . . . this is a concomitance of our diminished awareness of the past, of our disaffection from history.
>
> — Trilling 1982a: 105

The importance of criticism with regard to the contemporary critical and literary situation lies in resisting the emphasis on "a self without the old confinements" of historical and cultural necessities, and to formulate ideals "related to the humanistic tradition of the past". In other words it should "offer an ideal of a shaped self, a formed self", a self moulded by the best aspects of culture (1982a: 175-176).

Trilling's chief contribution to critical thought appears in *Sincerity and Authenticity*. One of the first points he makes is that the modern concept of sincerity, is inadequate as a literary ideal. For example, it does not adequately testify to the importance of the impersonality theory. In order to appear sincere to himself, the great modern writer does not project a universal truth (which he does not believe in), dramatised by effective fictive details, but gives shape to a personalised philosophy in a setting which is abstracted to a point as to be utterly cut off from recognised social reality. In Trilling's words, he deals "with the self and the difficulties of being true to it" (Trilling 1972: 7). On the other hand, when Leavis says in his essay "Johnson and Augustanism" in *The Common Pursuit* that "works of art act their moral judgement", he is giving us a more cogent view of the impersonality theory, where objective reality and subjective concerns are fused in such a creative way that the artistic creation becomes as it were an "objective correlative" of a deep ethical preoccupation. In Trilling's opinion, therefore, the criterion of sincerity should be bound up with the idea of impersonality so that the writer achieves transcendence over his work. This can be done by the effective use of irony and other devices by which he distances himself from his subject. R.C. Davis and R. Schleifer point to the kind of objectivity that can be reached by a humanist writer ". . . humanism assumes the transcendental objectivity of 'humanity' itself which can and should serve" as the vantage point "from which to pursue the study of literature" (1991: 56).

Thus how the neglect of the impersonality theory in modern literature affects the readers is Trilling's main concern. He is of the view that: "For all their intention of impersonality, they [the modern writers] figure in our minds exactly as persons, as personalities, of a larger exemplary kind, asking each one of them, what his own self is and whether or not he is being true to it, drawing us to the emulation of their self-scrutiny" (*ibid.*: 7-8). Moreover as Trilling argues, an art which at the behest of the later concept of authenticity becomes radical in nature, and employs a highly personalised idiom, catches immediately the attention of readers who are attracted by the "disorder, violence, unreason" depicted therein.

Trilling next criticises the *Phenemenology* of Hegel that "holds moral judgement to be nothing but retrograde, standing in the way of a true conception of the human spirit" (*ibid.*: 33). He does not agree with Hegel's view that the ideal condition of the human spirit is to seek "existence on its own account" and to free itself from the limiting conditions of state power and wealth power. Nor does he give credence to Hegel's proposition that, "Alienation of self is really self-preservation" (*ibid.*: 38). However, alienation is a condition that has some meaning for Trilling, because it shows the self's capacity to oppose society in order to become something else. It is not the self, static in uncritical agreement with culture, but a self capable of resisting, analysing, rejecting or accepting culture, and in the process becoming itself civilised and refined. Hence alienation for Trilling is a means to an end; it cannot be an end itself.

Trilling's ideas of the self in relation to culture are Arnoldian. Arnold's conception of culture is the development of the self to perfection through its active experience of "the best that is thought and said in the world". but whereas Arnold could speak of "perfection", Trilling could not. Both culture and the self are seen to evolve indefinitely. They act upon each other endlessly, and result in the attainment of self-knowledge.

In the third chapter of the book Trilling studies how modern man establishes "a self of his own devising made up of elements derived from various personages who had figured, to popular acclaim, on the stage of History" (*ibid.*: 70). Therefore, he attempts to give a cultural conception of the self which he says is formed by following of the ideas and attitudes of others in society. David Reisman had called such a person "other-directed" and seen him "as becoming ever more salient in our society" (*ibid.*: 66). He has lost his self, hence also the need to be sincere to his own self. In opposition to this kind of personality is the "inner-directed" individual who has internalised the best elements and influences from history and culture and established a self so strong that it can withstand the changes in intellectual fashion. In the modern age, the critical mind which is inner-directed is the best mind. It can act as a buffer against changes in literary tastes and styles and modes of existence. This interpretation of Trilling resembles that of K. Jaspers who detects the predicament of modern man in the deficiency of inwardness and the Indian conception of "*Sthitadhiti*" (internally stable).

In "The Heroic, the Beautiful, the Authentic" Trilling brings to our notice the full importance of these terms by contrasting the literary cultures of two different periods. The heroic constitutes for him a Wordsworthian stance, of the poet as the repository of values like order, moral beauty and the desire to achieve common good for all. The modernist view of the heroic is "an arrogant disdain of reason, prudence and morality" (*ibid.*: 83) which Trilling disapproves of. He admires what he feels to be Wordsworth's conscious certitude of his own personal selfhood, which is ever in direct contact with the selfhood of others. Trilling quotes from Wordsworth. "Points have we all of us within our souls/Where all stand single". This was said by him in 1805 and for Trilling time has not "diminished the powerful charm of these points of singleness" (*ibid.*: 103). Opposed to this principle of oneness the modernist writer is in conflict with forces of life, of pleasure and culture, and has the vision of a dehumanised and fragmented reality.

In the opinion of a critic (O'Hara 1987: 261) Trilling looks "over the past century and a half or so" and notes that "the power to confer the sentiment of being, of being strongly oneself, has been transferred from every external source of authority—God, nature, society—except one: that of avant-garde art and the culture it authorizes. In our time, the modern artist must provide his audience with the only form of the sentiment of being they can receive, and it is defined wholly in terms of the ideal of personal authenticity".

The rest of *Sincerity and Authenticity* marks the dissatisfaction of Trilling with post-modern literature and critical standards. Regarding the violence of modernist literature he makes the point that such an extreme exercise of personal will was needed to overcome the sentiment of non-being that threatened to engulf men who were convinced of the total inauthenticity of modern society. But post-modernism is a blind acceptance of radicalism. In one way it is even more inauthentic than modernism, because the modernist writers wrote with the purpose of overcoming mechanical thinking in a technological society. They strove for seriousness by accepting literature as a medium for expressing human consciousness which projects a subjectivised picture of the outside reality. Graff remarks: "By contrast, a post-modern fiction tends to carry the logic of such modernist theories to their limit, so that we have a consciousness so estranged from objective reality that it does not even recognise its estrangement as such" (Graff 1979: 208). In other words post-modernism is a result of the extreme authenticization of the self which frees itself form all social conditioning. For example, Michel Foucault, R.D. Laing and Norman O'Brown justify alienation and interpret it as a condition that is consequent of the pressures exerted on the individual by a restrictive society. They declare that in madness there is to be found an appropriate way of dealing with the tyrannous inauthenticity of the social world, a view that is also advanced by W. Barrett in *Irrational Man* in which he deals with the irrational as discovered by psychology and its significance.

Following their trail, post-modernists have treated literature as a reality by itself and the view of life proposed by them has no link with the reality outside. They negate external reality by declaring that the world outside is unreal and hence limit themselves to grammar and linguistic structure. As a matter of course we have Ortega Y. Gasset speaking about the "progressive disrealisation of the world" (1956: 119) in modern fiction and Graff (1979: 13) commenting upon the number of "theoretical strategies for eliminating literature's referential functions" that post-modernism has brought about. All this results in the concept of the irreal which makes literature a kind of will-o-the-wisp and criticism a quest for its seizure all of which are a far cry from the humanistic conception of literature as a repository of humanising and centralizing values. A.J. Cascardi in a similar vein denounces the separation of life from literature which the culture of modernism has striven to keep intact. As long as this continues the "ghettoization of fiction" "by an army of professional readers" will do little towards removing the "incoherent and abstract" nature of our relationship to values (Cascardi 1992: 622, 627).

Trilling rightly opposes the theses of the Post-Freudians that alienation can be combated by the completion of alienation and that "madness is health" (Trilling 1972: 171) by interpreting the human condition in the manner of Freud's *Civilisation and its Discontents*. The book presents Freud's maturest understanding of the relation between mind and society and emphasizes a tragic view of life. It is the superego guided by the Death Principle or Thanatos which controls the id which is guided by the Pleasure Principle or Eros. The combination of the superego and the id relates the mind to the external reality and makes it judge, analyse, accept or reject societal pressures, or modify behaviour. This Trilling interprets as necessity and imputes to it a developmental function.

Trilling's views are aimed at focussing our attention on the superego. The place of the superego in the functioning of the human consciousness is of prime importance to culture. Its repressive nature is not to be understood in a pejorative manner in regard to the human cause, but as an aspect which is to be taken as an advance in the development of the mind (*ibid*.: 153). To become a moral and social being, sharing the life of a community, the strengthening of the superego is essential. It can act as a moral check to the spirit in search of liberation from artificial social bondages and become the centre of values which it derives from culture.

Trilling's essays are as much literary criticisms as they are pure literature. They deal with varied themes: art, literature, society, philosophy, history, politics, ethics and culture like Bertrand Russell, for example. But the central theme that finds place in his writings is the human person or being in all its ramifications. His essays evoke our interest in such a way as to jolt us out of our passive acceptance of the literary culture of our present day. Langbaum (1978: 60) suggests that in an age of over specialisation such essays are "clarifying and synthesizing because they bring together so many disparate subjects . . . in small compass". More specifically, however, they are guided by the aim of restoring literature's social, moral and cultural centrality. In his social writings Trilling laments the fragmentation of modern society, the disruption of tradition, the negation of culture and the isolation of the self. By stressing the inter-relatedness of the individual and his culture and by making the human being the centre of all thought Trilling has laid the foundation of a theory combining society, history and man, by which literary activity can be performed and pursued in the future to attain excellence.

Trilling as a critic adopts an ethical posture in a post-modern age of counter-cultural passions. By endorsing the psychic necessity of suffering, he has helped us to visualise progress as the development of the total personality of man, his intellect, his spirit, his environment and his moral being. All these factors should be directed towards the refinement of self and culture. His totality of vision, his anxiety about the psychic health of the individual and his preoccupation with culture make him a seer, whose leanings are as much literary as they are ethical and moral. Literature is likely to awake to its pristine function to stimulate and refine human sensibilities, if it is again allowed to incorporate the moral vision and humanistic enterprise that he adumbrates.

WORKS CITED

Bell, D., 1976. *The Cultural Contradictions of Capitalism*, New York: Basic.

———, 1977. "Beyond Modernism, Beyond Self" in *Art, Politics and Will*, ed., Q. Anderson, New York: Basic.

Davis, R.C. and Schleifer, R., 1991. *Criticism and Culture: The Role of Critique in Modern Literary Theory*, Singapore: Longman.

Dickstein, M., 1992. "Farewell to the Gilded Age", *Partisan Review*, 59.3, 435-43.

Graff, G., 1979. *Literature Against Itself*, Chicago and London: University of Chicago Press.

Kazin, A., 1942. *On Native Grounds*, New York: Harcourt.

Krupnick, M., 1986. *Lionel Trilling and the Fate of Cultural Criticism*, Evanston: North Western University Press.

Langbaum, 1978. "The Importance of the Liberal Imagination", *Salmagundi*, 41: 55-65.

Lukacs, G., 1957. "The Ideology of Modernism" in *20th Century Literary Criticism: A Reader*, ed. David Lodge, London and New York: Longman, Ist Published 1972.

O'Hara, D.T., 1988. *Lionel Trilling: The Work of Liberation*, University of Wisconsin Press.

Ortega Y. Gasset, J., 1956. *The Dehumanisation of Art*, trans. H. Weyl, New York: Anchor.

Richards, I.A., 1924. "Communication and the Artist" in *20th Century Literary Criticism*.
Schwartz, D., 1953. "The Duchess' Red Shoes", *Partisan Review*, 20.1: 55-73.
Trilling, L., 1946. "The Life of the Novel", *Kenyon Review*, 8.
_____, 1949. ed. *The Essential Matthew Arnold*, London: Chatto and Windus.
_____, 1950. *The Liberal Imagination*, London: Secker and Warburg.
_____, 1955. *The Opposing Self*, New York: Viking.
_____, 1957. *A Gathering of Fugitives*, London: Secker and Warburg.
_____, 1965. *Beyond Culture*, New York: Viking.
_____, 1972. *Sincerity and Authenticity*, London: Oxford University Press.
_____, 1980. *Speaking of Literature and Society*, ed. D. Trilling, New York and London: Harcourt.
_____, 1982a. *The Last Decade*, ed. D. Trilling, Oxford University Press.
_____, 1982b. *Matthew Arnold*, Oxford and Melbourne: Oxford University Press.

5

LIONEL TRILLING'S LITERARY CRITICISM: POETRY

> To see the glory of human experience, the human bard must know the anguish of Tiresias as well as his wisdom, the wounds of the Lapith spears as well as the Centaur's joy, the travail of the Heroes as well as their triumph.
>
> — Lionel Trilling (*Matthew Arnold*)

This chapter argues the point that Trilling's criticism of poetry makes us perceive the limitations of naturalism. It is directed towards restoring the classical vision of grace and nobility in poetry, and at achieving a unified sensibility that envisions a proper understanding of man and nature. Trilling like Blake protests against any single vision of reality and persuades us to find a solution to the problem of reality in a holistic vision of life that undercuts the Cartesian world-view.

To understand how Trilling stood in relation to poetry, it is essential to go through some of his ideas on literary criticism. Trilling was a culture-critic and saw literature as having its roots in culture. Culture being a conscious effort to attain the ideal, to elevate human life, and to bring it close to perfection, it becomes the focal point of his literary criticism. Cultural criticism generally invokes the classical ideal of humanism which repulses romantic primitivism that prescribes a return to a natural state for man. Humanism is anti-naturalistic because it sees man as distinct from naturalistic creatures, pursuing an ideal end for himself. Trilling is of the opinion that:

> To many men, from the nineteenth century on, this primitive relation of human beings to the processes of nature has come to seem increasingly desirable, in itself a source of life. They feel that the rational processes of the intellect which have grown in authority in recent centuries, have resulted in a dryness and deadness of feeling, in a loss of vital power of the primitive imagination.
>
> — Trilling 1967: 128

Trilling follows the humanistic ideal implicitly in his works. He sees literature as autonomous yet inseparable from life. His literary judgments are ethical because they move out from the work to the outer realm of society and life. Moral considerations play a large part in them, linking literature to life. In this he follows the line of Leavis who holds that a genuine interest in literary criticism is an interest in society and civilization.

It is interesting to know why Trilling focussed his attention upon the cultural aspect in his literary criticism. According to him:

> Culture may be defined as the locus of the meeting of literature with social actions and attitudes. English literary life is marked by certain social features to which we in this country (America) have no precise counterpart.
>
> — Trilling 1957: 105

Therefore, we see Trilling turning again and again to the English literary tradition to derive examples that would help him define his special needs and to provide correctives to modern American literatures, that lacked tradition and cohesiveness. The criticism of poetry as a humanistic pursuit has to be concerned with such parameters.

For this reason, in Trilling's literary criticism we do not often find close technical discussion. His focus is upon the nature of reality as revealed in literary works. He did not share the idea of the aesthetic critics that the poetic experience is characterised and heightened by remoteness from practical considerations and that morality and truth are essentially irrelevant to literary criticism. The kind of response he is seeking from literature is related to the cultural reality which the writer is involved in that is, the moral, political, social and cultural issues. He argues with Arnold that moral and intellectual ideas are so much rooted in tradition, in the past that his literary criticism may appear on the surface to be traditional rather than modernist in any sense. But a deeper study reveals his modernism, his refusal to take criticism as an impressionistic response to a literary work, a mode that was used by critics like Pater, Saintsbury, Elton and Quiller-Couch.

His most popular strategy was to bring to bear conceptions of self and society from English literature of the nineteenth century upon his criticism of modern literature and culture. He used critical analysis like the New Critics but did not stop with finding tension or ambiguity. He rightly realised that a work was the product of the race, milieu and moment and that a literary artist was the most conscious point of his age.

As such any work of art was bound to reveal the forces that constituted the spirit of the age or the ethos. And so for him, as a critic remarks, literary analysis "was also an exercise of self analysis and of analysis of the culture through which the self can explore" (Leary 1976: 303). Therefore, we find an inevitable link between literature and the self or the society and the writer's cultural milieu, language itself being a manifestation of culture, Trilling establishes its referential status and thereby exposes the inadequacy of formalist theories which have served to eliminate literature's referential functions.

Trilling aimed at arriving at the best possible answers that would determine what kind of culture could foster the best in the self, or what kind of literature could bring about a developed cultural ethos where the self can function, or better still, how literature could engender the "best self" that accommodates with culture by developing the strategy of an opposing self. This opposition by a dialectical process would reveal the author's attitude to life and his value preferences.

Trilling's concern with moral values has affinities with Mallarme's argument that in proportion as the poet's work is exact, i.e., true to human consciousness and to the nature of man, as it is exact in formulation of desire, so it is durable and so it is useful. Good poetry, we find, maintains precision and clarity of thought and a great poet invests his work with the sanity of thought that appeals to those who are inside literary circles and also to non-literary people as well. It affects individual and communal life and promotes the general good. The moral pre-occupation of a poet, therefore, is to help nurture and develop a sensibility that shall discriminate between good and evil. Baudelaire has also dealt with this problem—the aesthetic sensibility has to distinguish between the ugly and the evil (*Flowers of Evil*). This sensibility touches on the moral order in the sense of mores. Hence literary criticism as it deals with a work of art is finally involved in the moral order. Trilling's concern with the moral order in criticism is akin to Eliot's whose essay on Baudelaire reveals a pre-occupation with the problem of good and evil and its relation to art and life. The moral order affects human life—whether it is beautiful or ugly—and that life is influenced by the social order or civilization. The creation of an ugly decadent civilization, affects human life and then the aesthetic order. Here we may refer to the conception of transcendental pleasure that Indian aesthetics posits as the final effect of a work of art. Where the dichotomy of evil and good is resolved the residual effect is that of *ananda* or bliss and that is realised when moral, evil and good are subsumed under a transcendental vision.

Wordsworth referring to the impulse of the vernal wood reached that kind of an awareness through transcendental nature.

Trilling's moral concern in poetry may be better understood if we recall Arnold's statements regarding the energetic and profound treatment of moral ideas. He says that we must:

> Let our minds rest upon that great and inexhaustible word *life*, until we learn to enter into its meaning. A poetry of revolt against moral ideas is a poetry of revolt against life; a poetry of indifference towards moral ideas is a poetry of indifference towards life.
>
> — Arnold 1960: 86

So Trilling assumed that criticism should be essentially moral in nature and this led him to a pre-occupation with culture and manners, which are the social manifestations of moral attitudes and values. As Tanner says: "He viewed culture as consisting less in great and good ideas and utterances than in social values and behaviour" (Tanner 1988: 78). Through his literary criticism he wanted to go deep down below the surface of civilized assumptions and ideas, to reveal the undercurrents of thoughts and desires that condition the minds of men. In *Sincerity and Authenticity* he defines culture as "a unitary complex of interacting assumptions, modes of thought, habits and styles, which are connected in secret as well as overt ways with the practical arrangements of a society, and which because they are not brought to consciousness, are unopposed in their influence over men's minds" (Trilling 1972: 116). Since literature owes its existence to culture, he felt that "sooner or later, any critic of large mind will touch upon social matters" (Trilling 1957: 112). His cultural stance has caused critics like Denis Donoghue to complain that Trilling was remarkably unliterary in his judgment and appreciations (Donoghue 1955: 379). This is not true. Trilling was surely aware of literary methods but used them sparsely, for his aim was to make literature a criticism of life in the widest humanistic sense, hence he loved to roam about in the realm of ideas that would elevate and purify the poetic experience. He believed along with Matthew Arnold that literature should "study and praise elements that for fullness of the spiritual perfection are wanted" (Trilling 1982: 205). Although Trilling did not refute formalism as a valid critical approach, he felt that an inordinate attention to form as an end in itself as had been practised by the major New Critics, was rather limiting, and the pursuit of purity in literary criticism was a fetish which would soon peter out.

Rene Wellek in his essay published in *The New England Review* of 1979, shows that Trilling was not averse to the aesthetic standards used by the New Critics. He was sympathetic to their exhortations to return to the text, but maintained that social, political, historical, psychological and moral dimensions of criticism could not be ignored if one wished to take literature seriously. The meticulous analysis of language is useful he feels, "but there are moments in literature which do not yield the secret of their power to any study of language, because the power does not depend on language but on the moral imagination" (Trilling 1955: 72). He further remarks that ". . . extrinsic information whether we wish it or not, and whether the critics in their strictness like it or not, often does impinge upon our awareness of a particular poem and becomes an element in our relation to it which we cannot ignore" (Trilling 1967: 105).

Trilling rightly feels that literature is conditioned by many social and historical factors and that literary study, "must in some ways always be a historical study, for literature is an historical art" (Trilling 1950: 184). Literature contains the continuity of the spirit of man and so history is an element of its aesthetic experience. This socio-historical approach precludes any set ideologies and endows literary criticism with refinement and richness. Eugene Goodheart is of the opinion, therefore, that "the very best American discussion of literature was generated" by "critics like Wilson, Trilling, Burke, Kazin, Howe" who "had to ask themselves where ideology ended and art began" (Goodheart 1973: 77).

Cultural radicalism in America was expressed in the modern age as a resentment against culture in its intellectual and artistic aspects. There was a widening counter-culture which owed its existence to the advancement of science and technology, and debasement of moral values. Trilling observed with alarm the subversive attitude of modern literature to culture and an unintelligent assertion of the self in all its genres. This subversiveness resulted in the formation of anti-culture which became the norm by a process which Trilling calls "acculturation of anti-culture" and the "legitimisation of the subversive". Trilling rightly diagnoses the modern American predicament as a "disenchantment of culture with culture" which becomes the basis of a new category—the "adversary culture" (Preface to *Beyond Culture*), which manifested itself in the Hippie movement and the rejection of the American tradition. Writers like Jack Kerouac or Allen Ginsberg came into prominence as a reaction to the modern culture. Haight Ashbury became the Mecca of this counter culture.

Trilling found modernism following blindly the idea that the old forms of pleasure derived from traditional modes of expression in literature were superficial. He saw literature aiming at higher reaches of artistic achievement by striving to depict what was "primal" and "non-ethical" in the human psyche. Hence he remarks:

> The tendency of literary criticism and education has changed. In our time the poet's personal fantasy is given large license and authority. Less and less do we think it possible to ask that a poem conform to some preconception of what a poem should be. . . . We may even incline to the belief that the more alien from our own state of feeling a poem is, the more authentically it represents the poet's feelings and the more authority it has.
>
> — Trilling 1967: 62

Trilling helps us realise that artistic excellence is inseparable from the moral imagination, and that the pleasure derived from the "sentiment of being", is of greater moral significance than the satisfaction derived from the depiction of evil and destruction of human values prominent in modern literary thought. Trilling's criticism of modern literature helps us to review our given assumptions and to question the modern attitude that takes moral or cultural conventions as a mechanical affirmation of inauthentic social values.

Having examined Trilling's ideas on literature, modernism, culture and literary criticism we may now turn to his literary criticism to see how he has diversified and enriched modern critical methods. Trilling has written almost exclusively on fiction. The poets who have influenced him are Arnold, Keats and Wordsworth. His turning to the English poets of the Romantic and Victorian ages shows his dissatisfaction with American poets of the twentieth century. Chace is of the opinion that Trilling's strategy "is to lament the available and to find attractions in the seemingly unattainable" (Chace 1980: 102). But this only shows Trilling's awareness of the past and belief in a tradition. He found in many nineteenth century writers, the existence of a point of view that could adequately contend with modern nihilism, and offer perspectives to modern literary culture.

Trilling's faith in English writers was based upon their sense of reality which he feels modern American writers lack. Trilling's essay, "A Ramble on Graves" is one that we should take particular note of. He takes Robert Graves, a writer of the early 20's as a second rate prose writer, but as a poet of the first rank. Although Graves "cannot have, and does not try to have the large dramatic appeal of Eliot or Yeats", yet he is great, because he is sincere in his style and representation of reality. He does not possess the dark, pessimistic tone of his contemporaries despite the familiarity he shows with the modern situation. The lightness and clarity in his verses may be mistaken for frivolity by modern critics. Trilling remarks in support of his poetic style that it is full of grace, elegance, and even as apparent frivolity of theme which may "preclude the judgment of the highest value" (Trilling 1957: 22). The diction, voice and style employed by Graves in his poems on common life are integral to his themes. He admires Graves because he wrote within the English tradition, and used the English language in a subtle way, giving his poems a hue and flavour, not to be found in modern poetry, with its gross, raw and affected style, and a language which is distorted. Trilling invites our attention to "the quality of the poet's tone, the quality of his voice, which may or may not be beautiful, but which must be truthful" (*ibid.*: 23). Trilling admires Graves's depiction of the English landscape, but what attracts him more is his "passion for integrity of the self—and a passion for civilization" (*ibid.*: 29), and the almost total negligence of the modern passion for asserting "the fierce modern intellectual will". He contrasts Graves with Cummings and brings out the differences of feeling each had for civilization: "Graves is a less abstract writer, less lyrical, his pages are more peopled, more filled with actualities. Cummings celebrates a way of feeling; Graves pre-supposes a way of life. . . ", in Graves there is a "vein of moralizing, very light and ironic, but persistent" (*ibid.*: 29).

According to Trilling, the use that Graves makes of language to depict the commonplace feelings, objects and customs of modern civilization, make him a great poet. That Graves has been able to free himself from prevalent poetical mores, is a point in his favour. The contemporaries of Graves are the war poets Wilfred Owen and Siegfried Sassoon whom he followed in his early phase; he became a prose writer of some renown. But Graves as a poet, consistent "in his dislike of modern culture" (*ibid.*: 21), evokes Trilling's admiration more.

The essay is a key to our understanding of Trilling as a critic. He upholds grace and subtlety and denounces qualities of will and energy in poetry. He is not concerned with only intellectual ideas in poetry, but shows his appreciation of human sentiments of everyday simple living. He quotes from the poem "Warning to Children" which he says is a complex and difficult poem. But our pleasure in the poem is immediate. "It is in part the pleasure of truth and belief: each word is valued, but not overvalued; the rhetoric is right, being the rhetoric of literate colloquial speech, and our sense of the rhetoric, of the easy management of the sentence becomes conscious at the end of the fourth line where the enforced pause on 'Say' gives the word a heavy emphasis and a double meaning (i.e., you say but you don't really mean)" (*bid.*: 24). Here is an example of how Trilling pays close attention to the use of language, and praises it because the meaning of the poem, the words employed, the attitude of the poet to his theme, form a composite whole. We have an instance how moral realism and aesthetic value can cohere. The method here is that of the New Critics: close reading and analysis, but the attitude is different. It is an interest in the poet's sincerity and integrity and not merely in his formal experiments. It is here that Trilling's connection with Wordsworth's theory of poetry in the Preface to *The Lyrical Ballads* becomes visible. Poetry to Wordsworth is a spontaneous overflow of powerful feelings in the language of the common man. But this overflow gets organised by the inner dynamics of the poet's emotion which is the evidence of his moral imagination. Form gets organised by the control of the moral imagination. Here one perceives Trilling's similarity with Arnold and Leavis.

His other poems "Any Honest House Wife" engages Trilling's admiration because it pays attention to common details that present a true picture of a life style. "The Climate of Thought" is described by Trilling as a very witty, but serious poem. Graves gives evidence of his humanistic attitude, "he weights himself with common sense and with an ironic love of the emotions" (*ibid.*: 29).

Trilling points out that without becoming sentimental Graves can accurately portray emotional situations, without seeming intellectually strenuous, he can depict ideas, and even his frivolous themes have an under-current of moralising intent. In short, Graves responds to any cultural situation in an integrated wholesome manner. Graves's poems are then, quite different from modern poetry which employs an obscure, tortured idiom to depict the nothingness that exists at the centre of existence and the alienation of the artist's self from culture. Modern poetry suffers from "weightlessness", a term used by Nietszche to define an aspect of modern sensibility. The word suggests a diminished sense of reality of the world, of other persons and most fundamentally, of oneself.

As is evident from Trilling's essay on Robert Graves, the characteristic method followed by him in literary criticism is to study the cultural conditions that determine the poet's attitude to his theme.

The influence of Arnold on Trilling's literary criticism can be seen very clearly. His interest in Arnold, as a poet and critic stemmed from his tragic view of the human condition, made all the more strong by the study of Freudian psychoanalysis. Trilling is concerned initially with Arnold as a poet whose melancholy spoke to me in an especially personal way" (Trilling 1982: 15).

Trilling's study of Arnold made him conclude that he was "the first literary intellectual in the English speaking world". It made him particularly sensitive to the struggle of the self to maintain its integrity, both apart from cultural conditioning, and as a part of the general culture. His analysis of Arnold's poem "Dover Beach" shows how well he understood Arnold's sense of loneliness and his inability to transcend cultural barriers in order to arrive at a durable, meaningful and satisfying relationship with someone he loves. In that poem Arnold speaks of the world, that is the culture surrounding him, as illusive. Despite the fact that the world appears to lie before him "like a land of dreams/So various, so beautiful, so new", it has "neither joy, nor light,/Nor certitude, nor peace, nor help for pain". Arnold makes a distinction between the world of appearance and the world of reality. A change has occurred in the way a person looks at reality, because the "Sea of Faith", which had encompassed the world, had retreated, leaving behind a bleak and barren landscape, symbolic of moral decrepitude and loss of human impulses. Trilling feels that Arnold is right in his criticism of life, by emphasizing the sad and joyless uncertainty that characterises it.

To recompense the loneliness, the poet pleads for fidelity, abandoning any hope for love or intimacy, or even understanding. As Trilling notes, ". . . perhaps never before in literature has a lover given a reason for love, and a reason, which while asserting its necessity, denies its delight. It is believed by all lovers that love has the power not only of making the world various and beautiful and new, but also of maintaining it in variety, beauty and novelty. But the lover of 'Dover Beach' denies love's efficacy . . ." (Trilling 1967: 89).

About Arnold's comments that "Sophocles long ago" also heard the ocean's "grating roar" which brought into his mind the inevitable fact of human misery, Trilling makes some very insightful comments. He feels that Arnold interprets the condition of the modern mind as being incapable of experiencing vitality and joy due to the loss of self-confidence and due to the diminishing of religious faith in life. Trilling feels that diminution produces another kind of attitude towards life which is reliance on a chain of sensations. This is according to him "animal faith" which can be related to the Freudian pleasure principle, hence it is gross in nature. He asserts that "the energies of men are continuous with and supported by the energies of the world, which are in some way divine" (*ibid.*: 129). In Arnold's poem Trilling marks the loss of spontaneity and gaiety that a human being enjoys at being alive and in believing that his life has a purpose. He further states that Arnold's reference to Sophocles shows his acquaintance with the third chorus of *Antigone* which is a contrast to the joyous note of the second chorus which opens with: "Wonders are many, and none is more wonderful than man". In contrast to this joyous exclamation and optimistic elan, the third chorus depicts the dreadful and inevitable disaster that befalls the members of a certain family under a curse. Arnold has generalized this as human misery in general. The tragic note introduced into the poem depends upon the depiction of intransigent forces dogging human fate, forces that can upset his primitive faith in love as a power to revitalize distressed souls. Hence, it is our awareness of uncertainties and dangers that rob us of all pleasures even in moments of joy.

Trilling feels that the Marguerite poems offer an even more tragic picture of reality for the object under criticism here is not culture but human personality, the alienation shown is not of the self from culture but of the self from other selves or what Yeats described as masks. Arnold takes the ending of a relationship of love as symbol of human separateness. The sorrow suffered tells Arnold that "in the sea of life enisled/. . . . We mortal millions live alone". Between one person and another there arises an "unplumb'd, salt, estranging sea", that forces upon Arnold the realisation that "Thou hast been, shalt be, art, alone". In this world of loneliness, one is not only cut off from the knowledge that resides in other people's hearts, but ironically enough, when one turns within, he finds he is a stranger to himself—"Ah! Who knows his own?" Trilling sympathises with Arnold's predicament, that he can neither expect joy in human relationship, nor live in alienation from the self, in desireless nothingness of being. A natural object like the stars and the sea show complete indifference to man's misery, and a powerlessness to be responsive to their laughter and beauty.

From the poems of Arnold discussed by Trilling, what evokes his admiration is Arnold's contention that since there is no other way out of the conditions enforced by the prevalent culture, one must exist strictly as a human being—by keeping alive the emotions and feelings. The threat to the human passions perpetrated by an industrialized society is a recurring theme in English literature. Trilling points to the withering of human emotions wrought by excessive rationalism; and in the fierce emphasis on the self in modern literature, he detects the supreme motivation of the artist to indulge in the necessity to feel. In Arnold, Trilling finds the belief that there are elements in modern culture that dehumanize men, but men can make the attempt to reorganize themselves in the old way by giving primacy to simple feelings, so that the self can live in some harmony with the individuals in a community. For Arnold, it is not sorrow, or suffering or old age that threatens to break up links between one man and another, and narrow down the imaginative capacities of individuals, but the increasingly scientific industrial and economic life that does it.

From Arnold's poems on Marguerite, it is evident that the more richly we develop and diversify our private, inner lives, the more different we become from those from whom we expect love, and sympathy, and the greater the difference becomes, the more difficult and the more subject to misunderstanding our chance encounters with them becomes. Arnold views the modern man as possessing "A heart of ice, a soul of fire". He is deficient in human emotions but energetic in fulfilling the self's quest for autonomy.

Trilling admires Arnold for his understanding of the psychological phenomenon of the self in relation to culture. The self is alienated from the world and in order to realign itself with life, it meets cultural necessities by assuming a role. Role-playing helps in coping with social demands upon our selfhood, but makes us realise that "What we say and do/Is well, but 'tis not true", and thus, social alienation leads ultimately to alienation from self—to inauthenticity.

For Trilling, Arnold as a poet was very important, for it was he who regarded literature as criticism of life, by dwelling upon the various aspects of the self in its relation to culture and itself. Through literature, he aimed at showing how men could tame their freedom of spirit while being engaged in activities that culture and civilization necessitate. In *Sincerity and Authenticity* Trilling proves how cogent and inescapable the sense of selfhood is. He quotes Matthew Arnold who believed that below the thin surface of civilized life and assumptions, of hypocrisies and self-delusions, there flows "The central stream of what we feel indeed", and that to reach it, to be true to it "involves a lot of difficulty" (Trilling 1972: 5).

This problem of the modern poets like Yeats, was anticipated by Arnold. In the "Dialogue of the Self and the Soul" Yeats confronted this central problem and showed how such an inauthenticity leads to the use of masks in interpersonal relationship. This problem is dramatically rendered by Eliot in *The Wasteland* where communication fails between the speaker and listener who are supposed to be lovers: "Why do you never speak? Speak, What are you thinking of ? What thinking ? What?"

The training of the inner energies of man can bring about the reality of "mankind's best self" that can judge its culture, and resist and revise it. In Trilling's words it is "the residue of human quality" or the "biological reason", which Arnold detected as opposing cultural necessities and determining, in a very limited way, its own destiny.

Arnold found it necessary for the moral life to check the impulses that arise out of the energies let loose by the self. Hence, he concluded that moral life involves a lot of strain and labour and suffering for the self. Arnold's insight into the self corresponds to Freud's perceptions and held great significance for Trilling.

Trilling's essay on Keats in *The Opposing Self* likewise pursues the relationship of the self with culture, and the means whereby the self can come to terms with its conditioned existence. This essay is "at once a tribute to the poet's magnitude and humanity and censure of the smallness to which the present age has been brought" (Chace 1980: 102). The essay deals with his letters, because they show us Keats as a man and is helpful to our understanding of his poems. The essay also comments upon the poetic process, the function of poetry and the poetic mind.

Trilling makes a study of Keats's mind and remarks that ". . . we have the wisdom of maturity arising from the pre-occupations of youth". Wisdom he defines as the acceptance of the tragic life in all its aspects, and at the same time being able to partake of the joy in nature and in the self. In the "Fate of Pleasure" essay, Trilling sees in modern literature "a mutation in culture by which an old established proportion between the pleasure-seeking instincts and the ego instincts is being altered in favour of the latter" (Trilling 1965: 86). In Keats this proportion is maintained from which he derives the heroism to face life's tragic necessities.

Trilling praises Keats's "quick understanding of human feelings" and his "most profound tolerance" (Trilling 1955: 11). He becomes for Trilling an example of the 'whole man', sense and intellect are held in balanced proportions. Trilling confirms that Keats was not anti-intellectual. He found "every department of knowledge . . . excellent and calculated towards a great whole" (*ibid.*: 30). At the same time he knew that sense could not be left behind. Keats's poems and letters do not deny the full autonomy of sense, because, it "generates idea and remains continuous with it" (*ibid.*).

Trilling describes Keats's "negative capability" as the quality of the poet's mind that prevents him from "making doctrinal utterances about the nature of life's goodness or badness or perfectibility, which, if he rests on them, will prevent his going to his full poetic vision" (*ibid.*: 37). Keats's heroism consists in a Shakespearean acceptance of evil. Both these writers gloried in an equilibrium in the face of evil, which is not found in modern literature. Pointing out to the differences in their attitudes to life in a Shakespeare and a Kafka, Trilling observes that in the latter man's suffering and cosmic alienation appears to be more intense and complete because it is not complicated and contradicted by the "sense of personal identity" (*ibid.*: 38) that is, his characters lack substantiality.

In Keats, Trilling finds, the knowledge of evil, suitably contradicted by the knowledge of the good together with the vital and the positive health of the self, and therefore this is a fitter picture of reality than the one shown by Kafka. The "negative capability" enabled him to balance the "reality of the self and the reality of circumstance" (*ibid.*: 41). Realizing that the very elements and laws of nature are hostile to man, he yet confirms that the world is "the vale of soul-making".

At the centre of Keats's heroism Trilling discovers, his resistance to evil and its pressures. Such a stance, he feels, has become impossible. Modern culture has allowed the negative forces to overwhelm and destroy the self. Although Keats lived perpetually in physical agony and horror of death, he was able to transcend their evil effects and maintain composure. Trilling avers, "It is in terms of the self confronting hostile or painful circumstance that Keats makes his magnificent effort at the solution of the problem of evil, his heroic attempt to show how it is that life may be called blessed when its circumstances are cursed" (*ibid.*: 42) Although Trilling affirms that Keats's "heroic vision of the tragic life and the tragic salvation" through the soul accepting the fate that defines it "will not serve us now" and that the "unified sensibility" that was Keats's peculiar strength as a poet, is a modern impossibility, nevertheless he maintains that it is right to struggle towards achieving such a vision. The modern sensibility is incapable of accepting limitations. It always stretches towards a beyond. It aims at reaching beyond culture, even beyond the self. But Keats possessed the capability to remain within human limitations even though he was aware of the adverse circumstances surrounding the human condition. This is evident in "Ode to a Nightingale" where he shows more concern for the tragic human condition of death, illness and pain than in "Ode on a Grecian Urn". In the latter poem he speaks of aesthetic transcendence to escape the burdensome human reality, while in the former, his sense of reality enforces upon his imagination an admission of the actuality of the pain of human life and so he returns to his "sole self" after identifying himself with the nightingale which is also a symbol of transcendence, like the urn. Trilling points out that the tranquillity Keats evinces in the face of pain is denied to the modern self owing to the excesses of the will which will never allow the mind to remain in a balanced and harmonious relation to the "good-and-evil" present in culture. To an age which has relinquished the "unified sensibility" and "negative capability" the possibility of "tragic salvation" through affirmation, must remain as a truth, if only in the imagination.

In Keats, Trilling finds a harmonious resolution of the two principles that, according to Freud, are the driving force behind all literary works. The pleasure principle is the quality of mind that seeks escape from distressing social reality in day-dreams or mere hedonism. The reality principle connects the mind to the inescapable facts of life, its sorrow and evil. When Keats declares that beauty is truth he means actually that the "pleasure principle is at the root of existence, and of knowledge and of moral life" (Trilling 1965: 98). When he says that truth is beauty he means that in the intensity of the poetic experience the very painful facts of life are perceived with a kind of pleasure. Trilling has brought out Keats's capacity to withstand a dialectic of pleasure and reality and hence has invested him with "the reverential stature of an ideally developed mind and soul, rendered largely unrecognized by the contemporary world" (Robinson 1979: 218). To those who feel that Keats is irrelevant to the modern context because he offered a justification of life by the heroic definition of the self, Trilling reveals the tradition that he followed: the tradition of humanism contained in such great poets as Shakespeare and Wordsworth. They viewed the self as developing and maturing into perfection when pitted against hostile natural laws. It is only by struggling against adversity that the soul gains in beauty. The human condition is in one way superior to the divine, it can exercise its power of freedom either to choose what is ultimate good, or to submit to the "specious good" of civilization. The choice involves a moral struggle and the dignity of man rests upon it. Trilling maintains the relevance and truth of this struggle and offers his concept of the opposing self in literature that will rejuvenate the moral imagination and make for a more authentic existence in the modern world.

Modernity views culture as a prison and seeks to escape from it in alienation or in an aesthetic vision of negative transcendence that derives from the religious ideal of self abnegation. Trilling praises this attitude in Hegel even as he condemns its extreme forms in modern poetry generally. But it exists in another form in Wordsworth's and Rousseau's "sentiment of being", and Trilling points this out to modern readers as a surer means of discovering one's identity. Like Keats, Wordsworth is not attractive to us because he was not a rationalist. He believed in a mystical unknown and was more preoccupied with the authenticity of his experiences than with abstract problems of freedom, rights, political ideologies that attract the modern liberal mind. Trilling observes that for "modern taste he is too Christian a poet", which is meant as a criticism of modern taste in its repudiation of human values. Wordsworth's "concern for the life of humbleness and quiet, his search for peace, his sense of the burden of this life, those which are inherent in the flesh and spirit of man", are the simple human values that the modern writer does not think to be fit subjects for poetry. But they did once form the subjects of great poetry, of high art.

The essay "Wordsworth and the Rabbis" shows Trilling as a man who is unmoved by Christian doctrines as propagated by the Church but adheres strongly to Christian values: "He certainly did not . . . accept as adequate what the Church taught about the nature of man. But he was one of the few poets who really discovered something about the nature of man" (Trilling 1955: 122). His poems are humanistic representations that evade dogmatic religious interpretation and hence encourage remarks like Professor Fairchild's, that as a poet, Wordsworth is actually dangerous to the Christian faith. Trilling thinks that his poems are sublime examples of the moral imagination at work in literature. Commenting upon Wordsworth's vision of life, Trilling goes on to say that the Wordsworthian moral essence comprised in ."the interplay between individualism and the sense of community, between an awareness of the self that must be saved and developed, and an awareness that the self is yet fulfilled only in community" (*ibid.*: 127). It is not a rebellion by the fierce assertion of the self in the true liberal modern tradition that Wordsworth exhibits, but a "certain insouciant acquiescence in the anomalies of the moral order of the Universe, or a respectful indifference to, or a grateful surrender before the mysteries of the moral relation of God to Man" (*ibid.*: 128).

Much of what is contained in Wordsworth's poems may be taken as old fashioned by the modern temper: "the passionate contemplation and experience of the great object which is proximate to Deity; then the plain living that goes with the high thinking, the desire for the humble life and the discharge of duty . . ." (*ibid.*). What the modern world has forgotten is that there are certain values, emotions, passions that continue in the human spirit and constitute the "naked and native dignity of man". Writers like Emerson and Thoreau believed that supra-rational faculties are the best source of wisdom and that the moral vision is superior to logic and intellect. Thoreau retreated from society which was mechanistic and utilitarian. *Walden* expresses his experience of "living" as distinguished from "existence". Wordsworth's most primitive characters, the old cumberland beggar, the idiot boy, the leech gatherer, have escaped conditioned existence experiencing flashes of momentary intensity. They achieve selfhood, not through any exertion of the will, but through dumb faith which according to Trilling is not less than human, even though it is "nearly an animal or vegetable faith" (Trilling 1955: 130). The will-lessness of Wordsworth's characters does not hinge upon the poet's inability to feel passionately. There are many instances in his poems that depict this capacity to feel strongly. For instance in Book V of *The Prelude* Wordsworth defends the violence and fearfulness of literature from the "progressive" ideas of his day. This celebration of movement and speed in *The Prelude* may connect him with the modern writers who believe in depicting the intensity of being without the sanity of meaningful insentience that contradicts it and gives it true significance. Trilling, while comparing the "dizzy raptures" of some of Wordsworth's verses and the "militancy of spirit" in modern literature, gives Wordsworth more credit for "Much as he loved to affirm the dizzy raptures of sentience, of the ear and the eye and the mind, he also loved to move down the scale of being, to say that when the sentient spirit was sealed by slumber, when it was without motion and force, when it was like a rock or stone or a tree . . . passive in the cosmic motion—that even then, perhaps especially then, existence was blessed" (*ibid.*: 131). Trilling's adverse comments on Eliot's parody of Wordsworth's line "the still sad music of infirmity" to depict the lack of force and motion in his poems, are illuminating. They make us realise that our "hostile uneasiness" about Wordsworth's poetry rests on a very flimsy reason, and shows our inability to empathize with his experiences. Trilling's essay on Wordsworth aims to reinstate the modern faith in traditional values of morality and to hold for scrutiny, our belief in radical militancy of spirit, embodied in certain aspects of the work of

Romantic poets like Blake and Byron or modern poets like Yeats and Lawrence.

Trilling is careful to distinguish between the "sentiment of being" that Wordsworth's poetry reveals and the "seduction of non-being" present in post-modern literature. The first is a conscious negation of the personal will to achieve unity with the universal principle, while the latter denotes a life of hypocrisy, loss of self and inauthenticity, through a negative transcendence and refutation of the moral law.

In his essay "The Immortality Ode", Trilling states explicitly his case for Wordsworth, attesting to his relevance to the modern situation. It strives to remove many errors of judgment that critics have perpetrated regarding Wordsworth's poetic genius. First it removes all doubts from our minds that Wordsworth's poetic inspiration declined due to certain biographical factors and that the "Ode" is a dirge upon the poet's departing powers. Second, it is not a poem about growing old, but about growing up and third, Wordsworth's poetic powers were not dependent upon extraneous factors, but integral to his personality, which could hence never die.

Trilling believes Wordsworth to be a great poet because his "finest passages are moral, emotional, subjective". The reality which he portrays is the reality of experience, the kind of responses that is evoked when the mind confronts objects of the natural world. Trilling gives a brilliant exposition of Wordsworth's technique and theme in the "Ode". We then understand that the poem is complex and difficult and the reason why it does not readily unfold to our understanding is because we have lost touch with those sentiments that have been expressed in it. Critics end to simplify the meaning of this great Ode by applying biographical facts from the poet's life and by mistaking the significance of some key words and sentences. "Gleam" is a word which does not mean poetic inspiration, but moments of enlightenment. Similarly, when Wordsworth says that "A power is gone, which nothing can restore", it does not mean poetic power, but the power to unite oneself with the divine which the child Wordsworth possessed, but the mature poet has lost; by being involved more in the human situation of misery: "A deep distress hath humanized my soul".

The 'Ode' is a great poem because it reveals different states of being and different apprehensions of reality. The first is a quasimystical response to nature expressed in dizzy raptures. The child enjoys the "visionary gleam" attendant upon the perfect union of the self and universe. His maturing years are marked by the disappearance of this gleam but he is compensated amply by developing moral insight into the sorrowful human condition and establishing links in the mortal world. Trilling detects that the process of humanization undergone by the soul has increased the intensity of feelings and endowed Wordsworth with philosophical knowledge, whereby his poetic sensibilities are sharpened. This leads to the final stage in the poet's mind that assures him of the beauty and serenity of life, in the face of old age, suffering and death. Trilling remarks with grave composure that ". . . to a man who is aware of man's mortality the world becomes significant and precious" (Trilling 1950: 152).

Trilling views this double vision of reality as an example of secular humanism. He does not regard Wordsworth's sentiment of being as a mystical experience as Wordsworth naturalizes it. The child's sense of union with the universal he feels does not prove Wordsworth's belief in a pre-existence and quotes him as saying that "it is too shadowy a notion to be recommended to faith as an evidence of immortality" (1950: 143). He tries to give a scientific explanation of the feeling of oneness with the universe which is supposed to be the source of all religious emotions. He refers to *Civilization and Its Discontents* in which Freud "conjectures that there is a vestige of the infant's state of feeling before he has learned to distinguish between the stimuli of his own sensations and those of the world outside" (*ibid.*: 144). It is due to this that Robinson remarks: "Trilling brings Wordsworth into the century of Freud" (Robinson 1979: 219).

Through the discussion of Wordsworth's 'Ode' he wants to establish for modern readers what true selfhood consists in, and how it should relate to modern reality. Trilling's association with Hegel helps us to understand the sentiment of being as a personal state devoid of material hankerings, and concerned with the entire condition of the soul and a general sense of enjoyment. A life lived in the light of the sentiment of being involves joy at the perception of unity of the self with the universe and a moral significance that one's self is in union with something larger than itself. Trilling, as a critic, realizes the importance and validity of this vision of reality and supports its inclusion in literature as leading to the reconstitution of the original wholeness of the human spirit.

Trilling is of the view that "religion and poetry have too much in common to permit us to set up any simple opposition between them" (Trilling 1967: 56). He is referring here to Wordsworth's poems which are religious in the sense that they teach simple human virtues. To the readers of the twentieth century, who are unfamiliar with moral struggle in literature, it means the harnessing of the inherent energies of the spirit to confirm to some ultimate good, or the sacrifice of one's selfish tendencies for the achievement of serenity, poise and tranquillity. Trilling reminds us of Wordsworth's moral position in his poems. Disciplining of the spirit by practicing virtues that ennoble and preserve the dignity of man is to be lauded.

In "Resolution and Independence" Trilling finds Wordsworth contrasting two different kinds of selfhood: the poetic self releasing self-destructive energies and the sentient self, preserving its identity in the face of sorrow and poverty. Wordsworth thinks about the disastrous fate that generally befalls poets and which may also be his lot. The poets suffer due to their capacity of feeling intensely and for long periods: "despondency" and "madness" seem to be their common lot. Wordsworth fears that he too may succumb to this fate. When he sees the resolute leech gatherer, old but firm in purpose, and unmoved by real suffering, he is ashamed of his distressed condition produced by the mere imagination of disaster. He is relieved of his burden of sorrow and decides to make the leech gatherer a model to follow.

To the image of the hare in its rapid movements, symbolizing the "poetic temperament which is characterised by its quick responsiveness" is contrasted the image of the leech gatherer, who is like a rock, suggesting in Trilling's words "immobility and lack of sentience, but also endurance". Hence Trilling remarks, "what stands here in contrast to the poetic temperament is the temperament that finds its fulfilment in strictness of control, in what we have come to call 'character' (Trilling 1967: 56-57). The poetic self stands in danger of being exterminated by the energies that the self releases. Sensitivity and responsiveness being qualities of the poetic power, it is ironical, that some degrees of it must be surrendered, to preserve it from being destroyed. One way for the poet to save the self from the forces inherent in it, one way to escape "despondency and madness" is to cultivate values like perceptiveness, honourableness and resoluteness—to be rock-like in endurance. Although this entails negation of the energies of the self, it does not lessen, the dignity of man, it heightens and enriches it, for it fully takes into account the tragic destiny to which the self is subjected.

Trilling finds that even in the most primitive of Wordsworth's characters in *Lyrical Ballads* there is a residue of humanity that gives them dignity and strength. There is in them a force of emotion that makes them "elemental, magical and perhaps a little divine" (Trilling 1955: 137-38).

The emotional barrenness of modern life is very well exemplified in Eliot's poem *The Wasteland*, where the failure of human passions, like love is symbolized in the title. The characters in this poem, Trilling feels, are devoid of humanity and they themselves realise that they have lost their original glory. Trilling sees a distinct similarity between Arnold's "Dover Beach" and Eliot's *The Wasteland*, and concludes:

> Eliot too is primarily concerned with the cultural circumstances that are the cause and the result—of man's loss of belief in his old organic relation to the world. The connection is made by the imagination rather than by the intellect and provides a basis for the ability to experience life immediately and intensely, and, as we say, with meaning.
>
> — Trilling 1967: 131

Thus in Trilling's literary criticism of poetry, we find a deep humanistic impulse. His critical essays make it clear that Trilling regards the idea of the self as central to literature. But in modern literature there is an intense and adverse apprehension of the culture that Trilling realises could prove harmful to the corporate life. He feels that somehow modern poets and novelists like Yeats, Eliot, Joyce, Proust, Kafka, Mann and Gide, articulate some of the discontent with the culture to which readers may respond in a fatal way.

Trilling's criticism invites readers to new perspectives and new ideas and emphasizes the importance of participating in the life of the community. It deplores the rejection of our inherited value systems, and critically examines the institutionalised and apparently progressive ideas of our industrial age. It posits the danger that in the quarrel of the self with culture, culture may lose "much of its facilitative and developmental powers" along with some of its nay-saying oppressiveness" (Shoben 1981: 62). He realises the necessity of a richly defined self, but also maintains that it cannot be achieved without culture, and defended culture as a repository of traditional values, great ideas and a shaping force. Although very much a modern writer, he stuck to classical ideas: in "the middle way" and "nothing in excess" as "entailing a measure of self-restraint . . ." (*ibid.*: 62).

The problem of the artist Trilling avers is to both acknowledge and tame his Dionysiac rage. Irving Howe has rightly described Trilling: "Utterly civilized, he kept looking beneath civilization" (Robinson 1979: 221). Trilling went to the past to figure out models for our modern selves, for he finds in the "archaic centre of older literature his essential humanism. The primary features of the archaic are simplicity and unity, and it is precisely these which bring the comfort to us" (*ibid.*: 234). He looked for signs by which "pleasure", the experience that should be a vital part of the self's experiences could once again be integrated into modern souls, alienated from themselves.

Trilling's criticism of poetry and his choice of poets like Wordsworth, Keats and Arnold, are evidences of his longing to travel beyond the modern "wasteland" which only evokes a panorama of futility and anarchy, and to recover common values and beliefs that can engender cohesiveness, community-living and will connect individuals in a society and impress upon them the importance of acquiring a decent humane living.

WORKS CITED

Arnold, M., 1960. *Essays in Criticism: Second Series*, London Macmillan, New York: St. Martin's.

Chace, W.H., 1980. *Lionel Trilling: Criticism and Politics*, Stanford University Press.

Donoghue, D., 1955. "The Critic in Reaction", *Twentieth Century*,158 No. 944: 379-420.

Goodheart, E., 1973. *Culture and the Radical Conscience*,Cambridge: Harvard University Press.

Leary, L., 1976. "The State of Letters: Lionel Trilling 1905-1975", *Sewance Review*, 84: 302-4.

Robinson, J.C., 1979, "Lionel Trilling and The Romantic Tradition", *Massachusetts'*

Shoben, E.J., 1981. *Lionel Trilling*, New York: Ungar.

Tanner, S.L., 1988. *Lionel Trilling*, Boston: Birmingham Young. University Press.

Trilling, L., 1943. *E. M. Forster*, Connecticut: New Directions.

———, 1950. *The Liberal Imagination*, London: Secker and Warburg.

———, 1955. *The Opposing Self*, New York: Viking.

———, 1957. *A Gathering of Fugitives*, London: Secker and Warburg.

———, 1965. *Beyond Culture*, New York: Viking.

———, 1972. *Sincerity and Authenticity*, London:Oxford, University Press.

———, 1982. *Matthew Arnold*, Oxford, Melbourne: Oxford, University Press.

Wellek, R., 1979. "The Literary Criticism of Lionel Trilling", *New England Review*, 2: 26-49.

6

LIONEL TRILLING'S CRITICISM OF THE NOVEL

> No themes are so human as those that reflect for us, out of the confusion of life, the close connection of bliss and bale, of the things that help with the things that hurt, so dangling before us forever that bright hard metal, of so strange an alloy, one face of which is somebody's right and ease and the other somebody's pain and wrong.
>
> — Henry James (Preface to *What Maisie Knew*)

The objective of this chapter is to maintain that Trilling's analysis of literature, particularly of the novel, is influenced by his belief that literature is a manifestation of culture, and hence it should be viewed as such by critics. It purports to find out from his analysis of the novels, his attitude to modernism in literature, his views of the self in culture and his opinions of the function of literature and criticism in a democratic, progressive, industrial and technological milieu.

Lionel Trilling's criticism of the novel as in the case of literature as a whole, is based upon a great humanistic ideal. He was deeply concerned with the role of literature in society and was aware of its capacity to mould the minds of men. He saw literature as embodying the struggle of the human being against cultural constraints and socio-cultural issues.

Trilling's themes are relatively few and they occur again and again in his works. His main preoccupation is with the ideas that literature as in Arnold, is a criticism of life, that the relationship between the self and culture is always problematic but vital; that the artist must guard against the tendency to oversimplify human experience and human nature, and that the concept of "moral realism", which he explains as the complexity and pain of living the moral life, be amply demonstrated in literature.

In all his important essays, we find Trilling giving a great deal of importance to culture and exhorting modern writers to put up with moral or cultural conventions that can bring about a harmonious relationship between the individual and the society, causing him to exist in a spirit of affirmation. He does not encourage modern writers to alienate themselves from culture's necessities, even though they may rise from gross materialism and prove uncongenial to the freedom of the spirit. It can be inferred, therefore, that in Trilling's works, the emphasis is not upon individual consciousness, but upon social consequence. In modern writings the individual consciousness is extolled and elevated beyond the precints of culture, in the name of liberation, and abstracted into a political idea, and found to be existing in a world which is in Diana Trilling's words, "non-dimensional" (Trilling 1978: 91). Although Trilling does not refrain from according due merit to the individual consciousness as an opponent of cultural repression, he regards it to be inseparable from the community and an agent of change and social amelioration.

Trilling views contemporary American fiction with some scepticism, and contrasts it with nineteenth century European fiction to bring out its deficiencies. He also gives his highest praise to the great realistic novels of the nineteenth century and appreciates them for being a literary form, fully open to the variousness of life, and referring to a moral order that prescribes norms and values in a cultural context. Compared to the richness and moral significance of these novels, Trilling finds modern American fiction lifeless and insipid. Lacking in vitality and social commitment, it is only tangential to reality and bereft of substantial cultural elements in its presentation of life. As such, it lacks the strength of purpose to understand the deeply human and complex nature of life in culture. George Steiner holds a similar view in *Language and Silence.* Richard Chase too, in *The American Novel and Its Tradition* finds that the American writers have tended towards "a more or less formal abstractness", "a tendency to plunge into the underside of consciousness", and "a willingness to abandon moral questions or to ignore the spectacle of man in society . . ." (Chase 1957: IX). As the essays contained in his book *The Liberal Imagination* show, Trilling derived examples of moral and spiritual rectitude from novelists such as Jane Austen, Tolstoi, Henry James, Howells and Orwell. On the whole, these novelists have created characters who can be judged by measuring them against universal values of secular humanism under which moral conflict arises from a deep social purpose. In his critical essays, Trilling resists the tendency in modern literature to conceive of the ideal posture of the self in relation to the conditioned being as one of opposition, so radical as to entail an essentially 'angelic' aspiration. This 'angelism' is the modern mentality which considers the high abstraction, the clear and distinct idea, to be the great thing deserving pursuit by literary men, rather than the concrete objects of life: its manners, morals and everyday common place activities and complex human relationships. As Malcolm Bradbury and James McFarlane point out, "a new era of high aesthetic self-consciousness and non-representationalism" has arrived, "in which art turns from realism and humanistic representation towards style, technique, and spatial form . . ." (1978: 25).

We find Trilling declaring that modern American fiction "has nothing to show like the huge, swarming, substantial population of the European novel" (Trilling 1950: 262). Trilling goes on to point out the deficiencies of some of the leading modern novelists of his day. He finds Dreiser unable to report social facts with the kind of accuracy it needs. Sinclair Lewis lacks social understanding, while John Dos Passos "can never use social fact as more than either backdrop or condition". Among the American novelists, William Faulkner stands out as one "who deals with society as the field of tragic reality", but he finds that Faulkner "has the disadvantage of being limited to a provincial scene" (*ibid.*: 213). In his discussion of Sherwood Anderson, Trilling has pointed out the lack of real sensory experience and the neglect of real social experience, in his novels. He deplores the American writer's attitude to minimize social references in his work and his tendency to depict not real men and women, but embodiments of certain political ideas. Referring to Anderson's novel, he states that his characters have become abstractions, bereft of human emotions. Anderson looks for their "essence" and "the more he does it, the less they are human beings" (*ibid.*: 30). His world is "gray, empty and devoid of meaning" (*ibid.*: 28). These remarks are apt descriptions of Anderson's works, particularly if we take his novel, *Winesburg Ohio,* into consideration. Raymond Williams (1961) in his essay "Realism and the Contemporary Novel" thinks in terms of Trilling's conception of social realism when he writes that in the contemporary novel there is:

> a society, a general way of living . . . but [it] is in fact often a highly personalised landscape, to clarify or frame an individual portrait, rather than a country within which individuals are actually contained.
>
> — Lodge 1972: 586

What gives cogency to Trilling's ideas on criticism is his formulation of what the novel should contain, in order that it is not reduced to mere social document, a history of ideas, or a mythic representation of a social or political reality. Some of the factors that give the novel its realities are social in nature such as class distinctions and manners; emotions of love, duty and brotherhood; suffering sorrow and evil and the manner in which they are resolved. Together with these human factors, there should be an artistic representation of ideas which are intellectual, by integrating them with the thematic content.

Trilling corroborates his statement that "contemporary American prose literature in general lacks emotional power" due to its inherent "intellectual weakness" (Trilling, 1950: 294) by taking into consideration the works of Dos Passos, O'Neil and Wolfe. He finds them lacking in complexity of ideas. They deal in a very limited way with formulated ideas, and their work impresses us as being merely in superficial touch with the philosophical, sociological, political and psychological ideas of their time. On the other hand, Trilling accords a measure of respect to Faulkner despite his provincialism, and to Hemingway. Their greatness lies in their having achieved their effects "by means of the working of the unconscious minds that play upon the recalcitrance of life's material to see the full force and complexity of their subject matter through abdication of intellectual activity" (*ibid.*: 296).

From the above statement, it may be inferred that mental processes form for Trilling, an essential point of the culture the novel tries to reflect. The mind of the artist has to apprehend reality, without the self-deception that the reality he sees is the only valid one. He has to acknowledge that reality is complex and varied in nature, and not merely the sum of social, political and economic matters. In this connection, Dreiser's treatment of reality in his novels, is according to Trilling, inadequate. It trivialises ideas. In his novels Trilling finds that "ideas are held to be mere details", and what is more "details which if attended to have the effect of diminishing reality" (*ibid.*: 21). Trilling also feels that the social responsibility of the writer is not only to resemble reality as much as possible, but also to bring ideas into focus" (*ibid.*: 285). In this observation Trilling is acutely pointing out the limitation of naturalism which regards man as a set of processes, biological, sociological and political to the exclusion of his inner moral and spiritual life. The criticism of life that informs modern American novels therefore becomes limited. Faulkner is surely more penetrating than the other American novelists that Trilling has dealt with but even that penetration is circumscribed by naturalism as in the fiction of Zola. Faulkner's Yoknapatawpha county is populated by freaks, deviants, criminals and there is little evidence in it of man's capacity to transcend such limitations. The novels of Dostoievsky when placed against those of Faulkner make this point clear.

Trilling's social realism is suitably complicated by his emphasis upon ideas. But the most, important element in his criticism of the novel is "moral realism" which he defines in his book *E.M. Forster* as a "quality provided by the dialectical intelligence with its avoidance of oversimplification and absolutes". The human intellect has the tendency to search for absolute values to determine human motivation and to establish rules of conduct. Trilling's moral realism necessitates the development of the dialectical intelligence which avoids rigidities in the journey through the human realm; it fosters the life of acceptant clam, or the life of simple instinct, and goes a long way in humanising man in society by releasing him from the clutches of the deadly reductiveness of modern ideologies. Such a bent of mind is shaped by historical and social elements, and becomes more refined, more capacious and supple than the liberal political intelligence that modern literature and modern criticism are suffused with.

Contrary to popular critical opinion of liberal ideology, Trilling assesses Henry James as a gifted novelist relevant to the American literary culture. His remarkable essay, "The Princes Cassamassima" places James in the line of the great nineteenth century European novelists, Stendhal, Balzac, Dickens and Flaubert. He even goes to the extent of including Tolstoi and Dostoievsky as writers with whom James has certain similarities. Although the novel has suffered at the hands of critics like Rebecca West, who saw in its presentation of romance elements, a repudiation of naturalism, and an archaic reliance on contrivance and possibility, Trilling recognises its striking literary accuracy. Romance and realism have been fused together with such artistic success in this novel that it seems James has gone into the root of the social and political matters depicted in the novel and given them aesthetic significance. Confirming the realism in the novel *The Princess Cassamassima*, Trilling asserts "there is not a political event of *The Princes Cassamassima*, not a detail of oath or mystery or danger, which is not confirmed by multitudinous records" (Trilling 1950: 68).

Trilling's appreciation of the novel, *The Princess Cassamassima*, rests upon its 'moral realism'. "The novel is an incomparable representation" of the "spiritual circumstances of our civilisation" (Trilling 1950: 92). The moral realism in the novel is brought out in the characterisation where each significant character is shown to be having virtues as well as vices. Rosy has "courage, pride and intellect", but we also have to take account of her "cruelty". Millicent Henning possesses "strength, affectionateness and warm sensuality" but she is also a snob. Paul Muniment is a genuine idealist but has a secret desire for "personal power". The Princess is "the very embodiment of the modern will which masks itself in virtue, making itself appear harmless, the will that hates itself and finds its manifestations guilty and is able to exist only if it operates in the name of virtue . . ." (*ibid.*: 91). James, as Trilling sums him up, "had the imagination of disaster" and "the imagination of love" (*ibid.*: 92). This ambivalence allowed him to represent his characters in their "ambiguity and error" as well as their "pride and beauty". The realism of Henry James is superior to the realism of an Anderson or a Dreiser, as it gives us a multi-dimensional view of reality and is nearer to the wholeness of vision that a writer should possess.

In *The Liberal Imagination* Trilling gives us two more American writers, Mark Twain of *Huckleberry Finn* and F. Scott Fitzgerald who like Henry James, have shown their openness to the "density of human contrariety out of which alone good writing can come" (Chace 1980: 95). Trilling considers *Huckleberry Finn* as a classic because it has "the truth of moral passion; it deals directly with the virtue and depravity of man's heart" (Trilling 1955: 106). It portrays the moral responsibility of the protagonist towards the society from which it has escaped. The novel is a unique example in American fiction for in it, the personal and the social are fused. The novel is as much a reflection of a whole way of life of Americans in the period of the Civil War as a narrative of the personal, moral tensions faced by Huck. Trilling finds in Huck an intense and complex moral quality. Huck "has a great sense of the sadness of human life" (*ibid.*: 109) although he is deeply conscious of the wickedness and dangerousness of his fellow men. Trilling focusses our attention on the climatic point in the narrative, when Huck subverts the moral code which he has acquired from the society, in favour of a more personalised and humane ethic that gives precedence to human affection and personal devotion. Trilling makes us realise the difficulty of the moral choice that Huck faces. His Southern temperament that supports slavery and his personal attachment to Jim, are involved in a conflict that amounts to a grave moral crisis for Huck. His final choice to help Jim escape from slavery proceeds not from any sentimentality or ideals but from "the clear dictates of moral reason" (*ibid.*: 113). Reising's remarks on Trilling's analysis of *Huckleberry Finn* are true to some extent:

> . . . he places the novel in a social context and argues against a universalising interpretation. . . . It is more the privatistic importance of this tragic fall from innocence that concerns Trilling, not Mark Twain's human drama of humans enslaving and exploiting other human beings under a system of economic degradation.
>
> — Reising 1986: 152

It may be argued, however, that Trilling's emphasis upon Huck's reliance on "the clear dictates of moral reason" is enough to give the novel a large moral significance. It definitely offers a means of action when the self in its search for "sincerity" faces similar situations of extreme moral crisis. It brings out the importance of "reason" as a reliable source from which solutions to such problems may be derived.

Trilling speaks of the moral and intellectual energy of Fitzgerald. In his book *Speaking of Literature and Society* Trilling feels that Fitzgerald exaggerated the idea of society and his dependence upon it "to provide a field for the activity of his conscience". His "notion of America involved the idea of deterioration, of old virtues coming to an end. He set great store by the belief in good manners and right instincts . . ." (Trilling 1980: 258). These remarks connect Fitzgerald with tradition that transforms the feeling for moral interests and issues into works of literary value. The continued interest in the novel *The Great Gatsby* is proof of the fact that it has a significant moral intention that sets it apart from being merely a novel of manners. Trilling's comments upon the form and style of the novel, provide interesting insights into literary theory. "Its form . . .", he remarks, "is not the result of careful plotting . . . but it is rather the result of the necessities of the story's informing idea, which require the sharpness of radical foreshortening" (Trilling 1950: 252). The success of the novel is due to the "voice of his prose", "the tenderness toward human desire that modifies a true firmness of moral judgement" which he ventures to add, "is the normal or ideal voice of the novelist" (*ibid.*: 253).

The novelists dealt with in the *The Liberal Imagination* are chiefly American. After this, he rarely concerned himself with modern American writers, instead he studied the history and fate of English literature and culture. The reason why he did this was because he found Americans liking to produce and read fictions about the death of the concept of personality embodied in great figures of the literature of an earlier epoch and the disintegration of the old social order in which they had their roots. He found the modern tendency to be based on the idea of a new self-hood existing in a world which had broken all its links with the past. According to Daniel T. O'Hara, Trilling "projects back, beyond the ever-present scene of steady decline to a more sublime realm of legendary figures, whose heroic resistance to modernity stands in judgement of all . . ." (O'Hara 1988: 152). In *The Opposing Self* Trilling seeks to "deal with episodes of the literature of the last century and a half" and the connecting link in the essays contained in the book is "the idea that preoccupies this literature and is central to it and makes its principle and its unity—the idea of self" (Trilling 1955: i). The novelists whom he puts up for emulation and correction of modern taste are Dickens, Tolstoy, Howells, Henry James, Orwell, Flaubert and Jane Austen. These novelists provide for Trilling, a radically anti-apocalyptic vision of harmony with existing cultural conditions.

Trilling is actually reacting against the treatment of the theme of alienation by twentieth century writers. Although alienation could be a means for the fulfilment of the self's destiny, and could lead to self-realisation and harmony with external reality, it was being increasingly utilised as a device to project the horror and evil pervading modern culture, and the despair of the self imprisoned in it. The habitual stance illustrated in modern novels is one of radical opposition of the self to culture, a repudiation of all established values, norms and morals, in the quest for full autonomy of the individual will. Trilling, in his essays, laid the ground for the formation of a fiction standing in consistent opposition to the rules of modernity in all its political and aesthetic forms. He found it disastrous that the writer should deliberately give free reign to his adversary intention and that the readers should cherish the author's deviation from the inherited wisdom of the race. Such a falling away from the centrality of a humanistic tradition that prescribes moral and spiritual values in a secular mould, has led to the "decline in realistic techniques, the death of public themes . . . a recrudescence of the naturalistic and picaresque novel" (Hassan 1961: 103).

Little Dorrit has been correctly assessed as a social novel by critics. The realism in the novel is shown to be in the "cruelty and stupidity of institutions and functionaries", "the general rightness of the people as a whole and of the general wrongness of those who are put in authority over them" and in the description of the Circumlocution Office (Trilling 1955: 55). Yet, Trilling maintains such criticism has not taken due note of "the degree of complexity with which Dickens views society in *Little Dorrit*". The central theme of the novel is not just a simplistic opposition of the self to culture but the validity of the "internal life" and "personal responsibility" (*ibid.*). Trilling mentions Mr. Meagles who despite virtuousness fulfils his responsibility of running such an evil social institution as the Circumlocution Office.

Trilling also exhibits particular skill in presenting Blandois as an "embodiment of evil". He grants him "aesthetic actuality" and "moral actuality", something previous readers would not do, for they could not comprehend the social causes that could produce such extreme wickedness in any man. It would be easier to take Blandois as a 'flat character', personifying evil, than a figure which can ever have any social reality. To Trilling, Blandois is not a social impossibility: "there really are people who seem entirely wicked, and almost unaccountably so; the social causes of their badness lie so far back that they can scarcely be reached" (*ibid.*: 56). It becomes irrelevant to judge the causes of their actions because their effects themselves are so devastating. Hence, the prison in the novel, which may well be taken to be an institution perpetrating social injustice, is in fact a great necessity when there are such evil characters. We are apt to be jolted out of our "comfortable philanthropic thought" about the injustice of prisons for society, in the face of such evil as is represented in Blandois.

The central symbolism in the novel of Dickens is the prison. Trilling takes due note of it and brings out all its moral significances. Another dimension is added to the prison image when Trilling uses it to depict the nature of the mind as juridical. Mrs. Clennam's long illness confines her to her room. The illness may be attributed to guilt feelings as she holds herself responsible for Mr. Dorrit's captivity. The psychological representation of Mrs. Clennam is authentic, Trilling discovers, as it anticipates the Freudian concept of the mind:

> One way of describing Freud's conception of the mind is to say that it is based upon the primacy of the will, and that the organisation of the internal life is in the form, often fantastically periodic, of a criminal process in which the mind is at once the criminal, the victim, the police, the judge, and the executioner. And this is a fair description of Dickens's own view of the mind, as, having received the social impress, it becomes in turn the matrix of society.
>
> — Trilling 1955: 55

In emphasizing the psychological aspects of the representation of society Trilling has demonstrated the relevance of the inner life of individuals to determine their social actions, and the inseparability of the self from culture. The focus on the mind as a cultural phenomenon as well as a distinct entity, has revealed the inadequacy of Marxian theories that interpret man as but the sum total of social and economic effects. The writer has to contend not only with the socio-economic-political constraints, but also with the inner reality which is a complex of moral and spiritual values accumulated from the culture of the past as well as of the present. Together with this there is the residual human element that has its source in the "biological given", and evades critical inquiry of the formalistic kind. Hence, the "Radical Innocence" theory (Hassan 1961) in modern American novels is discredited by the moral stance of the protagonist. His journey through life is not merely a progression from innocence to experience but it involves the making of choices that proceed from his own moral self.

The last part of Trilling's essay illustrates the moral imagination of Dickens that gives a social basis to a great moral idea. It is an example of what Trilling calls a 'literary idea' given social validity. In the figure of Doyce, an engineer who invents gadgets, but who would never take credit for it on the affirmation that "the Divine artificer had made it, and he had happened to find it", Trilling sees the creative mind of the artist. Doyce's power of self-negation represents the novelist's heroic negation of the unmitigated social will. As Trilling comments, "the whole energy of the imagination of *Little Dorrit* is directed to the transcending of the personal will to the search of the Will in which shall be our peace" (*ibid.*: 64).

From a realistic social document, the novel, moves to a great height of aesthetic abstraction to show us Dorrit as a Beatrice-like figure and "Paraclete in female form" (*ibid.*: 65). Trilling claims that it is easy to read in the novel, its partly religious intentions and its deep aesthetic meanings, if only "we do not permit critical cliche to interfere" (*ibid.*: 64). Thus, Trilling is standing beyond the culture of his times, to discover fresh meanings and attitudes in literature. He claims: "The imagination of *Little Dorrit* is . . . under the dominion of a great . . . moral idea which tends to find its full development in a religious experience. It is an imagination akin to that which created *Piers Plowman* and *Pilgrim's Progress*. And indeed it is akin to *The Divine Comedy*" (*ibid.*: 64). The estimate inspite of its exaggeration makes the reader aware of fresh insights into the novel and demolishes some of the adverse criticism of Dickens that he is sentimental in his treatment of Dorrit. One may think of the entire critical perspective on Dickens beginning with his revaluation after his centenary and refer to the critical opinions of critics like

F.R. Leavis and Santayana who have redeemed Dickens from being considered only as a great entertainer, or a chronicler of Victorian social life, lacking in high seriousness.

In his essay "Anna Karenina" Trilling points out how literary criticism based on the "psychological analysis of language" is inadequate to deal with a novel of great epic proportions like Tolstoi's *Anna Karenina*. He is referring here to the New Critical methods that had become so prevalent in his time. The moral imagination that informs the novel makes it "a piece of life" itself (Arnold 1960: 152). The novel exerts a kind of power and fascination over us; "the power does not depend on language but on the moral imagination" (Trilling 1955: 72). In the novel there are situations poignant with meaning that elude formal critical analysis. They are "mostly quiet moments, prosaic, circumstantial" (*ibid.*: 73) and unlikely to appeal to a mind founded on modernist conceptions of what reality in a novel should consist of. It would be difficult for modern readers to appreciate Tolstoi's superior moral imagination which envisions the human spirit amidst life's "inescapable conditions" and vicissitudes. Trilling refers to the modern imagination as Henry James does as "the imagination of disaster", and points out the way it kills our appreciation of literature which is conceived by the "imagination of love". In the words of Chace: "The imagination of disaster displaces and devalues all other forms of imagination" (Chace 1980: 103). It is a bent of mind that assumes that "evil is equivalent to reality and . . . to honour it as such" (Trilling 1955: 71).

Modern literature emphasizes the pain and evil in human life without a corresponding view of its possible joys. Trilling's appreciation of Tolstoi proceeds from the fact that he had a "low pitch" of the "imagination of disaster" and "reminds us of what life in its normal actuality is". Both the trivial and the uncommon constitute real human life. Human beings are a mixture of both good and evil. Human relationships are both satisfying and a source of great agony. In contrast, Trilling avers that "although many writers have been able to tell us of the pain of life" and "represented the attenuation or distortion of human relationships" they have not been able to "make actual the normalities" of life (*ibid.*: 72). Tolstoi like Henry James represents the totality of life. His characters are not "wholly good and not wholly bad, not heroic yet not without moments of light, not to be comprehended by any formula" yet having their "principle of being . . ." (*ibid.*: 70). Like Wordsworth's characters, they attain "an unexpected dignity" (*ibid.*: 70), despite or because of their common human traits.

According to Trilling, Tolstoi "is the most central of novelists" as he prescribes the norms or standards of reality for art. He teaches us that moments of crisis can be resolved by relying upon the "materials of peace" like "piety, work, tradition, and the continuity of family" (*ibid.*: 71) which are social and cultural virtues. These virtues emphasize the moral intent in a novel, and it is because Tolstoi realises their importance to human life that it has led Leavis to remark that Tolstoi is "transcendentally great", he is "pre-eminent in getting the spirit of life itself" (Leavis 1977: 146). Like the tragic sense of Keats, Tolstoi possessed the rare knowledge and understanding of the human spirit existing in a conditioned state.

Trilling finds Howells' novels to be of great cultural and moral interest. Like the nineteenth century novelists of social realism Howells' conception of reality is based on the firm terrain of human experiences, or what Trilling refers to as "the common place of the conditioned" or "the oppressive assurances of civil life" (*ibid.*: 92). The reality of Howells' novels comprises the family life of the middle class. Trilling is of the view that the family represents an important aspect of the human condition made up of "those material circumstances in which spirit exists" (*ibid.*: 90). Therefore, the place of the family in literature, has to be given due recognition and substantial representation. Contrary to popular critical opinion, Howells being able to do so, attains the stature of a true artist. Howells' criticism of Zola's art as "romanticism", meaning venturing away from the family of the middle class, defines his quality as a novelist. Trilling supports Howells' "theory of the common place" which emphasizes his family piety, as much as he disapproves of the "much attenuated" familial theme in the most representative novelists of the modern age: Joyce, Faulkner, Proust and Kafka.

Trilling contends that the family is excluded from American reality because the modern temper regards it as a culture-surrogate beyond which the self should travel, to exist in a realm of pure spirit. Trilling's affirmation of the conditioned state of spirit is, however, not total. He conceives of "man's tragic fate" as a "dialectic that goes on between spirit and the conditioned" (Trilling 1955: 93) and hence gives Howells credit for representing spirit in terms of the actuality of the conditioned.

However, Trilling regards Howells' denigration of form with distrust. According to him presentation of literal reality in art does not automatically connote literary formlessness. On the plea that life seldom has a well-defined shape, and events do not reach toward a steady and purposeful resolution, many modern realists are apt to devalue the importance of form. Hence, Howells' hatred of a story, suggests impatience with order and coherence in art and is aimed at removing the barriers between life and art.

Joyce's experiment in *Ulysses* shows the truth of the statement that the formlessness of reality cannot be captured by art and depicted in a literal manner. Joyce tried to do so, that is, to capture reality for twentyfour hours and hardly succeeded. That panorama of "futility and anarchy" (Eliot) was sought to be given a form by borrowing the form from Homer. Hence, Trilling subscribes to the view of a critic like Mark Schorer who in his essay "Technique as Discovery" remarks that it is the novelist's use of technique that helps him discover some order, some meaning from the chaos of life and that "technique contains intellectual and moral implications" (Lodge 1972: 391). Trilling's advocacy of form in art may be further substantiated by psychological evidences which support the thesis that Kermode puts so succinctly in his essay "Objects, Jokes and Art", that "the act of the mind" (which is art) is a "form-creating act and the form it creates provides satisfactions of the rage for order that cannot be had in life . . ." (Lodge 1972: 662). Trilling brings out the inadequacy of the impersonality theory as understood and practised by modern realistic writers by stating that the artist's personality impinges upon his material, however objective he may try to appear. Whatever the artist perceives as real or "literal reality", "is in some sense conceived or created, it is controlled by intention and indicates intention . . ." (Trilling 1955: 94). If intention is a determining factor in the artistic creation, then it proves that literature cannot be evaluated by positivist and reductive methods, for as Wimsatt and Beardsley have pointed out in their essay "Intentional Fallacy" one can only assume an intention, never know it.

Even so, Trilling supports Howells' naturalistic treatment of social reality, even as he admits that complete objectivity in a form of art "that makes its effects by the accumulation of the details of literal reality" is unattainable (*ibid.*: 94). Finally, Trilling defends Howells on moral grounds. His "intense imagination of pleasure" made him invite American novelists to deal with the "more smiling aspects of life" (*ibid.*: 100) and to refrain from making evil the object of aesthetic contemplation. Trilling's understanding of psychology makes him contend that the domination of the reality principle in man, over the pleasure principle is the cause of the modern dissatisfaction with the joys of every day life from the simplest to the highest. Howells' "smiling aspects" of reality can serve a moral purpose, by binding us to the earth, to prevent our being seduced by the charismatic evil of disintegration (*ibid.*: 103).

In "George Orwell and the Politics of Truth", Trilling refers to some representational writings of the novelist to explain the force of his moral imagination. He, like Howells, took delight in the common place duties and activities in life. His novel *Keep The Aspidistra Flying* is, according to Trilling, "a remarkable novel". It demonstrates the heroism that marks the life of a man belonging to the lower middle-class when he is faced with social and natural compulsions. The heroism is implicit in the quality of life lived: a progression from "the depths of splenetic negation to the acknowledgements of the happiness of fatherhood, thence to an awareness of the pleasures of marriage, and of an existence which, while it does not gratify his ideal conception of himself, is nevertheless his own" (*ibid.*: 162). The protagonist's affirmation of life is a kind of self-discovery, and is a means by which he attains spiritual stasis and human dignity. It is Trilling's conviction that the individual becomes heroic through the recovery of an organic social life of which the family is the unit. Orwell has succeeded in presenting the dialectic between the spirit and the biological and social 'givens' which as Trilling believes constitute man's tragic plight. In the essay Trilling seeks to impress upon us that Orwell is a genuinely interesting and seminal literary mind in line with the writers of the European humanistic tradition. They have resisted the final disintegration of a decaying religious tradition by significantly drawing upon the old virtues, while refusing to compromise their contemporary worldly insights.

Trilling talks about Orwell's "natural piety" and belief in "such things as responsibility, and orderliness in the personal life and fair play and physical courage" as "they sometimes help to shore up the crumbling ramparts of the moral life" (*ibid.*: 159). These are qualities which also find a place in Wordsworth's poetry. It is clear from the above remarks on Orwell, that Trilling aims to project him as an inspiring figure like Wordsworth for liberal academicians in post World War II America. Trilling attacks the liberal's attitude to politics, which is analogous to "a nightmare abstraction" and "pointing to the fearfulness of the nightmare as evidence of their sense of reality" (*ibid.*: 164). On the other hand, Orwell's view of politics was founded upon truth and reality, as *Homage to Catalonia* makes evident. Being conscious of the nightmarish quality of war and revolution and the repressiveness of a communist government and administration, Orwell clung to the British political and cultural order in which he had his roots. His acceptance of the conditioned was based on the "possibility of a social hope" that "the old British order" was "one of the still beneficent things in the world" (*ibid.*: 164). In Trilling's view, therefore, Orwell stands as the opposing self to the liberal political culture of his times as one who urges upon his liberal counterparts to eschew their craze for Stalinism and to turn to the "other" culture of England to derive an understanding of the conditioned nature of life.

Trilling's comments on Flaubert's *Bouvard and Pecuchet* again project a disapproval of alienation. The lives of the principal characters in the book represent the possibility of remaining beyond culture, yet retaining one's humanness. Their friendship which Trilling is certain is a virtue, redeems them from being 'imbeciles'. They live a life of "innocence and a pleasant sufficiency" (*ibid.*: 185) and become comical because they are so simple and unfitted to take up the intellectual life. Flaubert's novel is satirical, its intention being to expose the "inadequacy of all the disciplines", that Bouvard and Pecuchet take up for study. Like Faust they are disillusioned and give up their studies of philosophy, science, medicine and literature. The reason for their failure which Trilling gives is in itself satirical of the intellectual life: "They are perhaps too thoroughly Whole Men; they lack the degree of benign limitation which permits an intense preoccupation, making a single subject seem the satisfaction of the demands of a whole temperament" (*ibid.*: 186).

Bouvard and Pecuchet stand beyond their bourgeois culture of mediocre democracy. Although ideas are "life and death" for them, they learn about the vanity of human thought and creation, embodied in various disciplines. They attain a vision that is enunciated in the *Ecclesiastes*—the purposelessness and fruitlessness of seeking after knowledge. Hence, Flaubert's book which is generally understood to be an attack on the culture of the nineteenth century, begins to have a larger moral significance for us. The book is an attack on culture itself: "it rejects culture" (*ibid.*: 195), and finds felicity in a way of life antithetical to the conventional mode, still linked to the general culture, yet in opposition to it. The characters in Flaubert's novel form a small unit of themselves and live amidst minimal cultural entailments, fulfilling themselves in a simple and unobtrusive way. Trilling contrasts Melville's Bartleby the Scrivener with Bouvard and Pecuchet. The former, when he sees the nothingness of society, "simply curls up and wills to die, and dies". The latter give up their meaningless research but continue to live the life of the mind by recording human "absurdities they have learned to recognise". They do not lose "their love of mind, to which they testify by recording the mind's failures" (*ibid.*: 197). Their pessimism has arisen from culture and has led to an almost spiritual perception.

The concluding part of the essay deals with the *Three Tales* which is a collection of three stories of Falubert. They share the same theme of nihilism which is a state of mind, engendered by contemplating the human condition. Flaubert shows in each of these tales how it is possible to transcend culture and retain self-hood. The protagonists exist beyond the life in culture and finally reach "that moment of charity which is the surrender" of what Flaubert believed to be, "the richest luxury of culture", the self "in the separateness of sensibility and pride that define it" (*ibid.*: 204). Flaubert's moral vision affirms that selfhood can be maintained by denying primacy to the human will, and a life of sacrifice or self-denial is the highest that deserves pursuit.

"Flaubert's Last Testament", traces the novelist's moral vision, that progresses from complete despair of culture, through a hope of selfhood, to a final self-affirmation through self-denial, as in *Bouvard and Pecuchet* and the *Three Tales*. Trilling as a cultural critic, prescribes the old values of self-sacrifice as a means to counter disintegration and de-humanisation, that despair and nihilism are bound to produce. This vision of the spirit, expressed not as a diabolically opposing force in culture, but as grace, as manner and style, is present as a cogent but unavailable moral truth in literary history. Trilling recalls that vision "and in recalling it condemns the culture for which it must remain lost" (O'Hara 1988: 173).

In "Mansfield Park", Trilling emphasizes the deep importance of the conventional virtues, of grace, decorum, and sound religious feelings that characterise civilisation. The heroine Fanny Price's strict adherence to these virtues, and submissive alliance with the virtuous people in the story, make her a conventional character. This is one of the aspects of the novel that "scandalises the modern assumptions about social relations, about virtue, about religion, sex and art" (*ibid.*: 210). The novel condemns the freedom of the spirit from cultural ties. Hence it is anti-modernistic in its affirmation of the material circumstances that surround the spirit.

Trilling finds that in the novel Jane Austen has dealt with the issues of sincerity and authenticity. She shapes the contrast between characters on the basis of their propensity to act either on firm moral values that are of perennial importance (sincerity) or to adopt a convenient social attitude in keeping with the needs of the occasion (authenticity). Trilling concludes that Jane Austen has made effective use of the debate over the influence of amateur theatricals to depict the conflict between having to commit oneself permanently to a social role and the willingness to play any role or many different roles in the theatre. Impersonation implies insincerity to the self, and destroys its integrity. It contrasts with the centrality and wholeness that commitment to one social role entails. In the novel Austen uphold the old moral tradition that views the theatre with suspicion as it is a profession that corrupts culture. For Trilling then, Austen is a novelist who builds upon a moral foundation and deals with essential human issues.

Unlike Austen's more popular novel *Pride and Prejudice* which celebrates energetic participation in the activities of the social sphere, *Mansfield Park* displays the anti-vital element and withdrawal from the world as the ideal of the opposing self. Trilling appreciates this novel because the author does not endorse total nihilism. She does not think that it is a way of countering social conditioning; on the other hand, she opposes the tendency and lays down the rules of the good life which Trilling deduces to be living "the round of one's days in stasis and peace by "making one's mode and principles of life the very center of existence" (*ibid.*: 211). Trilling approves of this kind of individualism for it reposes faith in the archaic values of virtue and happiness arising not from social freedom, but "social stasis". In his opinion, Fanny Price, with her retiring ways, is a more authentic figure than Mary Crawford. The latter "impersonates the woman she thinks she ought to be", in order to live up to the social demands. Trilling remarks, "In Mary Crawford we have the first brilliant example of a distinctively modern type, the person who cultivates the style of sensitivity, virtue and intelligence . . . style, which expresses the innermost truth of any creation or action, can also hide the truth . . . *Mansfield Park* proposes to us the possibility of this deception" (*ibid.*: 220, 223).

The theme of the authentic self as envisaged in Fanny Price's and Mary Crawford's attitude to life, is paralleled in the problem of choosing a profession. The choice of a profession means commitment to a social role that one has selected for oneself. It also means "the open avowal of principles and beliefs" (*ibid.*: 214) which exerts a certain moral force. Trilling brings out the moral intent of Austen, by suggesting that she advocates a profession which shall not merely be the medium through which personality, power or prestige, or autonomy of the will may be expressed. In short, it should not cater to "an impersonation and an insincerity" (*ibid.*: 221).

Trilling is of the view that Jane Austen was the first novelist who revealed to us the ways in which moral choice tended to be influenced not by the norm most applicable to the situation but by the kind of selfhood that the character wished to assume or to project. According to Trilling, "it is the peculiarly modern bad quality which Jane Austen was the first to represent—insincerity" (*ibid.*: 220). Trilling goes on to say that insincerity is not the "hypocrisy of the earlier novelists". Mary Crawford is insincere because her aim is "not to deceive the world, but to comfort herself". She impersonates the woman that she would like to be but is not. She assumes or projects a virtuous image which masks her true self. In the same way her brother Henry Crawford, while still courting Fanny, impersonates the role of Maria Bertram's lover, in a downright cold and insincere manner. In the end, his role requires him to carry Maria off "from a dull marriage to a life of boring concupiscence". To Mary Crawford, this situation is of no moral significance whatsoever and therefore it shows her "deficiency of seriousness". Fanny Price, on the other hand, is full of sincerity. Jane Austen's mode of judgement of the authenticity of the self lies in our comprehension of Fanny as a character in the novel. The response to life in culture is based on the philosophy that "the path to the wholeness of the self which is peace" does not entail skill in impersonation or the cultivation of a personal style of behaviour, but in following the sanctions of a traditional morality, and adhering to virtues of duty, sentience and commitment to family and community.

Jane Austen's novel clearly brings out the irony behind civilisation. Lack of moral earnestness, and absence of a sturdy character, are not deterrents to social respectability. Rather, the skill with which role playing can be undertaken or the self-diversified, and a convincing display of an assumed role can be projected would assure us of success in our personal life. Moral choice which had once proceeded out of the fixed values that religion had prescribed is replaced by a set of fluid, personal value judgements. This personal code has its source in an amalgam of historical, cultural, moral, biological and psychological compulsions that inhabit the unconscious and determine the quality of being, and the moral worth of a certain choice made by the individual. Trilling, who draws upon Hegel, Dewey and Nietzsche, conceives of the secularisation of spirituality that has given rise to concepts of "sincerity" and "vulgarity" that mark the behaviour of men in the modern ethos: "The secularization of spirituality . . . requires of us that we judge not merely the moral act itself but also, and even more searchingly, the quality of the agent" (*ibid.*: 229). The new mode of judgement is based on the kind of selfhood one wishes to assume.

While the essays in *The Opposing Self* find out ways in which the adversary position to culture may be transcended in order to forge a sturdy, well-balanced attachment to reality, the essays in *Beyond Culture* establish a sense of disenchantment and disharmony with culture itself. The "Fate of Pleasure" may be taken as the initial point of reference for it connects all the other essays in the book as well as the work that went before. Wordsworth's statements in the preface to the *Lyrical Ballads* are central to Trilling's discussion of modern literature. It is "the grand elementary principle of pleasure" which constitutes "the naked and native dignity of man", that it is a principle by which man "knows, and feels, and lives, and moves" (quoted in Trilling 1965: 58). Our present sense of life stands at a great remove from this Wordsworthian vision. Trilling takes the example of Dostoievsky's *Notes from Underground* to confirm that modern literature is based upon the "repudiation of pleasure in favour of the gratification which may be found in unpleasure" (*ibid.*: 72). The protagonist of the novel (an anti-hero) voices his resentment against practically all forms of pleasure that life in culture provides: "To know and feel and live and move at the behest of the principle of pleasure—this for the Underground Man, so far from constituting his native and naked dignity, constitutes his humiliation in bondage" (*ibid.*: 74).

The Underground Man's resentment is directed against persons less disadvantaged than himself and takes a savage character expressed as contempt for men who have managed to win happiness by discovering the purposefulness of life. But this Trilling asserts, does not constitute the whole truth of the Underground Man. His repudiation of pleasure is a way of protesting against a "society organised in the service of pleasure" (*ibid.*: 76). It is also a way of escaping from the conditioned nature of man who is habituated to work in the interest of pleasure. He chooses the savage life as a mark of his sense of spiritual freedom. He deliberately cultivates an "exigent, violently subersive spirituality" (*ibid.*: 80) which is aimed at destroying all that which is but speciously good.

In Dostoievsky, Kafka, Proust, Lawrence and others, Trilling detects this tendency to invalidate pleasure as a legitimate factor of spiritual affirmation. Destructive violence of the specious good and "insistence upon the sordid and the disgusting" are the chief literary enterprises of our age, according to Trilling, and they represent the adversarial position to culture in our age.

How far away from the belief and acquiescence in genuine pleasure the modern mind has travelled can be deduced from Trilling's idea that pain and evil have a markedly larger place in contemporary aesthetic culture than the impulse towards pleasure, thus propagating and legitimising a culture of alienation and bitterness. Since family, manners, human relationship are aspects of civilisation that affirm culture, the modern tendency to isolate these themes from literature is hardly surprising.

Trilling's analysis of *Emma* gives a contrasting picture of reality. Jane Austen's characters and situations evolve out of the social and cultural background of nineteenth century society. Manners and morals are depicted in a perceptive way. Realism and romance mingle to create aesthetic depth. Emma grows by shedding assumptions and fallacies, trying to grapple with changing social concepts about men and society, fast progressing towards democracy. Jane Austen has focussed upon the different nuances of Emma's mind in its progress towards reality. Her "modern consciousness" that cannot appreciate Miss Bates is perceptive enough to gauze her own shortcomings. "A consciousness is always at work in her, a sense of what she ought to be and do", Trilling says of her. So we cannot ever accuse her of insincerity or vulgarity even though we can call her a snob, her "hubris" being self-love. Although self-assured, "she never takes the high self-defensive line" (*ibid.*: 44). Unlike the protagonists of modern literature, she believes in the idea of community, her aim being to raise other people to her status of social superiority. This is to be seen in her relationship with Harriet. There is very little doubt that Emma is the most lively of all the characters in the novel and yet her energies are not directed upon self-assertion but upon her struggle to attain harmony with her universe. In the figures of Mr. Woodhouse, Mr. Knightly, Miss Bates and Mrs. Weston, Jane Austen depicts a highly anti-modern belief that "man may actually live in harmony and peace with himself and the external world" (*ibid.*: 53).

Modern readers find Kafka's depiction of reality to be more valid than the idyllic representation of it in Jane Austen's novels. Readers have hence mistaken her for being a gentle, conventional and charming chronicler of manners and morals of a particular period in English history. But taking into consideration the complexity of *Emma*, Trilling rightly points that the novel is more difficult than any of the hard modern books we admire: "The difficulty of Proust arises from the sheer amount and complexity of thought, the difficulty of Joyce from the brilliantly contrived devices of representation, the difficulty of Kafka from a combination of doctrine and mode of communication" (*ibid.*: 35-36). In all these authors, Trilling finds either an intellectual or technical complexity, where the focus is upon ideas and contrivance and literary skill. These difficulties for the reader are overcome on repeated readings of the text. But, as he correctly states "the difficulty of *Emma* is never overcome" (*ibid.*: 36). It is a novel about person seen by Jane Austen as possessing an infinite variety of human characteristics and possibilities issuing out of her energy, style, intelligence and moral commitment.

"Hawthorne in our Time" discusses the modern critic's response to the works of this great nineteenth century American novelist. Trilling cites Professor Agnes Donohue's views on Hawthorne in her preface to the volume, *A Case Book On The Hawthorne Question*. She traces the ambiguity in his works which arises out of a complex weaving of romance and realistic elements an ambivalent attitude to the human being seen as depraved and as living in the innocent dreams of a Adamic hero, and as instinctively good as well as foul and wicked. She concludes that Hawthorne tells us about "man's dark odyssey in an alien world" (*ibid.*: 184).

Such an interpretation of Hawthorne is a typically modern one. The modern vision of spiritual fulfilment in unpleasure and its acquiescence in that which speaks of the darker aspects of life, make it increasingly difficult to regain the moral vision of Henry James. James' monograph on Hawthorne celebrates the beauty of his work, "its textures and hues", of which he speaks, according to Trilling, "not so much with critical admiration as with personal delight" (*ibid.*: 192).

The modern critical tradition, of which T.S. Eliot is a seminal force, gives credence to complete objectivity to be derived by a thoroughly scientific and technical method of analysis and interpretation directed at the text. While giving such a method its due recognition, Trilling opens up the possibilities of an approach to literary texts, based on reason, taste and good sense. He shows how Henry James reads into Hawthorne's works, an imaginative transmutation of the moral vision into an artistic creation with an "ironical" concern with conscience (*ibid.*: 181). He considers Hawthorne to be neither cynical nor tragical. Between Kafka and Hawthorne, Trilling sees some affinities. Both these novelists are preoccupied by ideas of man's destiny in an alienated world. Both negate the world of concrete reality to focus on "agencies of human destiny which are not of this world" (*ibid.*: 198). But the main difference between them lies in the fact that while Hawthorne grants his characters an autonomy of spirit, he is also aware of the material reality of life. Sin for example, is seen in a cultural context. Trilling finds that Hawthorne's 'romances' project the moral problem in dramatic terms, effecting a dialectical approach suffused with irony. He is important for Trilling as he stands between the nineteenth century world of idyllic vision, and the twentieth century ethos of apocalyptic despair of culture and the resultant aggressive assertion of the will.

Trilling's admiration for Hawthorne originates from the novelist's concern with human centrality and an avoidance of positivistic extremes. A preference for the mimetic mode moderated by the didactic intent is very much in evidence in Trilling's literary criticism. He decries the modernist tendency in Kafka's novels and remarks that our modern writers are "preoccupied by the ideal of the autonomous self as it seeks autonomy in its tortured dream of metaphysical freedom" (*ibid.*: 205). Whereas, Trilling detects the necessity of society and culture in Hawthorne who felt that "to be removed from one's fellow beings was to commit a mortal sin" (*ibid.*: 191), Kafka's hero "was still the center but the center of complete indifference" (*ibid.*: 197). His position in the world appears to be pointless, he exists in a void. His commitment is to his own conscience, not to human beings. From the moral world of premodern literature we have travelled to the metaphysical realm of the modern.

Running counter to the modernistic craze for active self-assertion and passionate volition, is Trilling's theory of "the morality of inertia"—"the not making of moral decisions" which "constitutes a large part of the moral life of humanity" (Trilling 1957: 37). Although he does not praise moral inertia, he bids us to take note of it, as it governs the moral life of the majority in the society. In his discussion of the novel *Ethan Frome* he is critical of the modern sensibility that considers this kind of morality as dull and hence endeavours to "qualify its dullness by endowing it with a certain high grace" (*ibid.*: 38). Trilling feels that morality that is inherent in the performance of duty or doing good through force of habit or acting on biological compulsion, should be presented in a realistic way, instead of adding a halo around the character to idealise him beyond all actuality.

The characters in *Ethan Frome*, Ethan and Zeena are given no heroic stature by the novelist Edith Wharton, although they live out their lives, doing the right things at the right time. In the end, Zeena nurses her husband Ethan, and his mistress Matty after they are crippled for life in a failed suicide pact. Although compared to many modern novels of suffering and intense moral preoccupations, *Ethan Frome* is not a great work, yet it is a novel which must be taken note of to realise that morality does not only constitute the making of a moral decision through a deliberate choice involving courage but it also proceeds from brute necessity. The novel justifies moral inertia in as much as it separates morality from human destiny. But it gives a realistic picture of the moral life of most men and women where suffering and morality have no visible connection.

Finally, Trilling concludes the essay by contrasting Edith Wharton's novel with the great novels of Dostoievsky and Faulkner. *Ethan Frome* provides a counterpoint to the "great invigorating books" of moral life that obscure "the larger bulking dull mass of moral fact". Morality for Trilling is not only "the high, torturing dilemmas of Ivan Karamazov and Captain Vere. It is also the deeds performed without thought, without choice, perhaps even without love", as in *Ethan Frome* (*ibid.*: 40).

Trilling's sceptical attitude to modern literature arises from the element of negation of life that the writer promotes. Hence, in his critical essays he always goes back to the theme of the self and culture. *Sincerity and Authenticity* contains Trilling's views of the quality of selfhood that culture fosters, and the ways and means by which the self's autonomy becomes authentic. The models of selfhood, Trilling encounters in literature of the past and present exhibit sincerity and authenticity respectively.

The early culture promoted sincerity and the later culture authenticity. Trilling compares the theory of sincerity and authenticity with Hegel's dialectic of master and slave, Nietzsche's Apollo and Dionysus and Freud's Eros and Thanatos. It also reflects the Arnoldian conflict of the conservative instinct and the revolutionary principles. While recognising the validity of a radical stance in regard to the decadent aspects of culture, Trilling gives greater importance to sincerity which necessitates belief in the presence of order and integrity. He depicts this quest for order as integral to culture, but culture in the modern times has rejected it as superficial and hypocritical. In the chapter entitled "The Honest Soul and the Disintegrated Consciousness", Trilling gives his response to three great works: Diderot's *Rameau's Nephew*, Hegel's *Phenomenology of Mind* and Goethe's *Sorrows of Young Werther*. He argues that authenticity has its roots in sincerity, but is more radical in its separateness from culture. The authentic individual's vehement repudiation of society results in cynicism, nihilism and destruction of himself in an attempt to escape universal corruption. Sometimes he goes mad in apocalyptic frenzy. *Rameau's Nephew* illustrates two attitudes to the hypocrisy of society: an urbane acceptance of social hypocrisy in the "honest soul" of the Uncle, and the resentful cynicism of the "disintegrated consciousness" of the nephew. Trilling finds similarities between the nephew and Dostoievsky's Underground Man: "The nephew is the victim of an irresistible impulse to offend those with whom he seeks to ingratiate himself. And stronger than his desire for respect is his appetite for demonstrative self-abasement; his ego, betraying its proper function, turns on itself and finds expression in buffoonery, at once inviting shame and achieving shamelessness in a fashion that Dostoievsky was to make familiar" (Trilling 1972: 29).

Trilling's understanding of the nephew is based upon knowledge of Hegel's *Phenomenology*. Hegel professes the view that selfhood requires the spirit to free itself of cultural constraints, to eschew the 'nobility' of dutifully acceding to society's authority, and to resort to the 'baseness' of rebelling against everything in society that restricts the power of self-expression. Therefore, the free spirit is a newer and higher form of nobility, as it has been achieved by strenuous moral effort. According to Trilling, Diderot endorses the moral significance of sincerity which is associated with the "old visionary norm" of the good life in Shakespeare's later romances and Jane Austen's major novels. He also finds in Diderot a condemnation of the emerging modern ethos that has as its aim, a fierce authenticity culminating in the image of the Underground Man (*ibid.*: 43-44). Howe feels therefore that in the modern and post-modern contexts it is the Uncle, the honest soul or "the whole man" "who is the imagined creature, while the nephew, revelling in chaos approaches a condition of actuality" (Howe 1991: 58).

Trilling's reading of Goethe's novel, *The Sorrows of Young Werther* is influenced by his knowledge of the self derived from Diderot and Hegel. Werther commits suicide when his pastoral paradise is disrupted by the disintegrative forces of modern love. Trilling tries to explain Werther's failure to accommodate himself to the changed circumstances because unlike Rameau "his alienation did not proceed far enough: he was not able to achieve that detachment from himself which for Hegel constitutes Rameau's triumph and significance" (*ibid.*: 52). Werther and Rameau are contrasts: both are alienated but one expresses his sincerity to the self, symbolised in his preferring to dress in a "singular and apparently unchanging mode of dress"; and the other pours "scornful laughter" on the whole of existence and resorts to "wilful impersonations and role-playings". Werther's holding on to the image of himself as a serious and sincere man, possessing "a one true self" is the cause of his ruin, according to Trilling. Further, he asserts, that although Werther is a "disintegrated consciousness, he had persisted in clinging to the simplicity of the honest soul" (*ibid.*: 52).

Although Trilling shows an avowed preference for the "honest soul" his dismissal of the "disintegrated consciousness" is never final. Hence it is always difficult to find out from his book any categorical statement in favour of one or the other. This ambivalent tone is a sign of his maturity. Of Werther, Trilling says that he is "incapable of embodying this desperate cosmic wit", such as Rameau possesses and which makes it easy for him to detach himself completely from his own self, and that "irony is beyond his (Werther's) comprehension" (*ibid.*: 52). Trilling knew that in the modern context it was impossible to regain the archaic vision of sincerity. The individual today lives in a fragmented world where influences from diverse sources intrude upon his mental plane, till he loses sight of his own inner self. At the same time he suggests that the quest for lost sincerity among modern authors is a pointer to its intrinsic value.

Modern literature has alienation as its dominant theme. Society, more often than not, perpetrates insincerities upon the individual who is forced to regress to savagery. Joseph Conrad's novel, *Heart of Darkness*, also posits the theme of sincerity and authenticity. Trilling sees Marlow as a 'sincere' character of the English cultural background, whose commitment to society is complete. "Marlow sees civilisation as fraudulent and shameful", but "at the same time he has a passionate commitment to civilisation . . ." (*ibid.*: 108). Kurtz, chooses the life of savagery, but not out of any romantic illusions. He establishes himself as the chief of a local tribe in the Congo not because he has the illusions of the "noble savage", but "by his regression to savagery, Kurtz has reached as far down beneath the constructs of civilisation as it was possible to go, to the irreducible truth of man, the innermost core of his nature, his heart of darkness" (*ibid.*: 108). In Trilling's interpretation, the novel moves simultaneously toward quite opposite poles" on the one hand to the view that civilisation is of its nature so inauthentic that personal integrity can be wrested only by the inversion of all its avowed principles". On the other hand, it asserts that "civilisation can and does fulfil its announced purposes not universally indeed, but at least in the significant instance of one particular nation" (*ibid.*: 109-10).

Here we have an instance of Trilling's perception of the importance of a faith in some form of culture, and a belief that there are in civilisation, some established principles that foster the dignity of the individual and refine his human qualities. This vision of culture should be complemented by a clear-eyed perception of the dark side and the weaknesses of culture so that the hope of improving it and the quality of human life lived in it may never die. It also reduces the risk of alienation by inculcating faith in some idea, either created by the self or discovered by the rational intellect, one which "you can set up, and bow down before and offer a sacrifice to" (*ibid.*: 109). Such faith is essential to counteract the dehumanising process which is bound to follow when the self opposes society and seeks to live a life away from it.

Viewed from this angle Trilling's book *E.M. Forster* holds the key to his idea of the novel as a document of manners and morals. Against the background of stark realism and grim solemnity of novels written by authors like Kafka, Gide and Proust, one is likely to consider Forster as lacking in seriousness. Trilling feels that it is his comic manner "that prevents a greater response to his work" (Trilling 1943: 8). The modern literary sensibility is apt to dismiss the comic manner as a technique belonging to the past. But as Leavis comments in his essay "E.M. Forster", the comic mode as used by Forster "is a distancing art" which gives *Where Angels Fear to Tread* and *A Room With A View* "a sure easy poise". In these novels Forster shows exemplary control over his material, the control of a "born novelist" (Leavis 1976: 264). Trilling resembles Leavis in holding similar views of Forster as a novelist.

Trilling situates Forster in the tradition of Fielding, Dickens, Meredith and James, a tradition marked by an "unremitting concern with moral realism" (Trilling 1943: 11). Forster stands at par with Hawthorne for his deep moral intent, although many critics would consider the latter to be a greater novelist.

Trilling tries to draw our attention to the depiction of manners and morals in Forster's work. They are not just documented but act as devices by which moral, social and cultural ideas can be given dialectical emphasis. Moreover, as Trilling contends in his essay "Manners, Morals and the Novel" manners are "a culture's hum and buzz of implication". They are made up of "half-uttered, or unuttered or unutterable expressions of value" (Trilling 1950: 206) and hence a dialectical approach is the only way in which moral ideas can properly be represented. Trilling asserts that *The Longest Journey* quite explicitly depicts the meeting and conflict of diverse social classes and in it Forster takes scrupulous note of the differences of manners. This is executed in a manner which gives evidence of Forster's dialectical understanding of class. Class which determines character and destiny and gives a subject his identity is also regarded as "not fully determining" (Trilling 1943: 18). Forster represents class not by description only but by "struggle and contradictions" and by the "moral struggle in the heart of a single person" (*ibid.*). Hence Forster does not forget to deal with the "subject's essential humanity" (*ibid.*: 19) which transcends class considerations as much as it is determined and controlled by his station in life. To this end Trilling finds that *Howards End* stands with James' *The Princess Cassamassima* as one of the great comments on the class struggle (*ibid.*).

Trilling appreciates Forster's technique of contrasting one culture with another. Mostly it is the liberal culture as depicted in the British society of the pre-war years that is set against another culture, for instance, the Italian culture of *Where Angels Fear to Tread* and the Indian culture of *A Passage to India*. In *Howards End* however it is the business culture of the Wilcoxes that is held out as the opposing force to the liberal English culture of the Schelgels and both these are held out against the plight of Leonard Bast, the insurance clerk who "is under the terrible necessity of being cultured" (*ibid.*: 129) and in whom culture is an external quality, derived from his contact with people like the Schelgels.

The inauthenticity of characters like Cecil in *A Passage to India* for whom "culture is a way of hiding his embarrassment before life" shows how right Trilling really is when he detects the source of Forster's greatness to be lying in his ability to portray the inner life of every character as constituting true reality, not their outer facade. For Trilling as for Forster a truly cultured person is one in whom the head and the heart are equally developed: his intellect and emotions are unified. Trilling gives the example of Herbert Pembroke in *The Longest Journey*, ". . . he has the will to be good, but the underdeveloped heart prevents him". Pembroke's stupidity is regarded as the result of the "failure of connection" between the head and the heart (*ibid.*: 78). Trilling's admiration for Forster lies in the way the latter uses class distinctions to expose insincerities and anomalies in behaviour patterns and moral acts and in the way he upholds values that strengthen the inner life. The importance of the novel *The Longest Journey*, according to Trilling, lies in the portrayal of the truth that the inner life is real. Rickie's loss of the inner life in the above novel is part of its theme. Forster's ability to portray the vital nexus between culture and character is the chief focus of Trilling's attention, and Leavis' view that Forster deals "with the problem of living truly and freshly from a centre" (Leavis 1976: 262) corroborates Trilling's assessment of Forster as a novelist.

To the question posed by a humanistic culture, "How should one live?" Forster's answer as deduced by Trilling after a close examination of his work is not by trying to become better "but by ordering and distributing his native goodness" (1943: 22) a man can live a life as befits him. Hence Trilling's analysis of Forster's novels enables him to detect evidences which point to the latter's dissatisfaction with the liberal progressive culture of his day that conceives man as the product of natural processes, ever in the state of becoming something else, ever proceeding towards a Utopian perfection. Forster's stoic "acceptance of the human fact as we know it now" and his "acceptance of man in the world without the sentimentality of rationalism" or the "sentimentality of cynicism" (*ibid.*: 23) reveal his humanistic concerns which appeal most to Trilling. This attitude we find reflected again in Trilling's novel *The Middle of the Journey*.

Forster's technique of the novel which gives so much importance to manners and morals leads Trilling to remark that it connects him directly with tradition. The sense of the past in Forster is a valuable factor in his art for it invests him with "curious tough insight" (*ibid.*: 21) into the human condition. How necessary it is to cultivate this sense by keeping in touch with the literature of the past is illustrated by Trilling by comparing Forster with the American novelist Sherwood Anderson. Anderson's disaffiliation from tradition weakened his insight into human nature and made him less aware of human beings as human beings. Anderson imbibed the American literary sensibility which alienated him from the central humanistic tradition. Forster's connection with this tradition made him avoid oversimplifications and absolutes in judging moral acts and gave strength and significance to his novels.

What emerges from Trilling's discussion of Forster's novels is that they directly belong to the tradition of the novel which gives prominence to "the difficulties and complications of the moral fact" (*ibid.*: 12) and which depict the "contradictions, paradoxes and dangers of living the moral life" (*ibid.*: 11). Like James and Tolstoi, Forster does not give us good and bad characters, heroes and villains, but real human beings. He represents them as both good and evil, effecting a full interplay of human emotions, passions, intellect and culture that really go towards the formation of the whole personality.

Lawrence with whom, Trilling holds, Forster has some affinities, gives equal emphasis to this function of the novel. In his essay "Why the Novel Matters" Lawrence points to the importance of the novel as a genre that allows the depiction of human feelings in an exhaustive manner, so as to project before us the image of man in his totality. Forster's own assertion in *Aspects of the Novel* is that "round" characters behave in a contradictory manner and continually surprise us, and that "the test of a round character is whether it is capable of surprising us in a convincing way" (Lodge 1972: 143). These remarks justify Trilling's view that moral realism is one of the most outstanding qualities of Forster's novels, for his characters act not according to an external moral code of right and wrong, but act instinctively with the force of their consciousness.

Trilling defends Forster's use of surprise and melodrama and his "addiction to sudden death" against the charge of incongruence to material reality levelled against them. Trilling sees these facts not as easy technical devices adopted by the novelist to get out of a difficult situation, but as an inevitable part of life's probabilities. Their presence in the novel opens our minds to the incalculability of life. As instances of life's incalculability we have Miss Bartlett the scheming relative in *A Room with a View* who is redeemed in our eyes when it is found that far from intending to cause ruin to the heroine she had actually desired her happiness and her union with the man she loved. On the other hand Mr. Beebe the clergyman whom we had come to regard as "an angel of light", lets us down by opposing the wedding. A casual statement at the beginning of a chapter like "Gerald died that afternoon" (*The Longest Journey*) reminds us that death in real life can come to someone just as suddenly without any warning and therefore sudden deaths in a novel do not make it less realistic. Gerald's death, according to Trilling is given a kind of "primitive dignity" (*ibid.*: 17) when the maidservants weep although they had not liked him. Their weeping is given no other motivation other than that (Trilling quotes from the novel) "he was a man, they were women, he had died" (*ibid.*). Therefore Trilling's comment that Forster refuses to be conclusive actually indicates Forster's negative capability. Forster's novels surprise us, just as life does, and makes it nearly impossible for us to be complacent about the fate of any one of his characters. As Trilling puts it he removes "the heroism of his heroes and heroines" like Tolstoi (*ibid.*: 17).

Such sudden twists complicate the plot and show Forster's art and ingenuity in plot contrivance. He produces an effect that for example, naturalistic novelists like Zola cannot. The Forsterian novel becomes, in Trilling's words "our friendly opponent pleasing us by outwitting us" (*ibid.*: 64).

Forster's novels make clear the necessity of establishing connections between people of different cultures, classes and nations through sincerity of feelings. In *Howards End* Trilling finds that despite culture differences between the Schelgel sisters and Leonard Bast they are able to connect with him on the basis of his "solid grain of honesty" which they cannot help cherishing. Similarly Turton the collector of a district in *A Passage to India* has "contemptuous affection" for the subject race of Indians. His commitment to them is inadequate for the Indians want to be well and truly liked.

Hence, Trilling argues that the theme which runs through Forster's novels is that of the separateness that underlies every relationship. In *Howards End* the theme is "only connect the prose and the passion" (*ibid.*: 118) and the difficulty of making such a connection is clearly indicated. Only by connecting the reason and the imagination, the emotions and the intellect can one achieve a state of equilibrium, an inner poise and a detachment by which one can come to a proper understanding of human nature. Only then is our connection with people validated. We may say that Trilling's study of Forster makes us realise that connectedness is the true sign of culture and forms the real basis of every genuine civilisation.

Thus, we may infer from the critical works of Lionel Trilling that in his criticism of the novel, he has dealt with many aspects of cultural, moral, social and political life. He discusses the great novels of the nineteenth century and the twentieth century and raises questions that are of immense value to the literary theory of the modern and postmodern ages. He sees literary texts not as "rhetorical constructs" or as "figural combinations", but as a reflection of society, having a moral aim in view. The novel, he maintains, "is a perpetual quest for reality the field of its research being always the social world, the material of its analysis being always manners as the indication of the direction of man's soul" (Trilling 1950: 212).

Consequently, he finds the American novelists of the modern age deficient in their perception of reality, and content in projecting a world that is unlike the thickly-textured world of the nineteenth century English novels of realism. He studies the sense of complexity and dialectical vitality and gleans lessons of simple acquiescence for the modern intellectual. R.W.B. Lewis makes the same point about modernism: "Ours is an age of containment (Lewis 1955: 190) in which complex moral and cultural dilemmas are settled by "one-dimensional answers". Lewis condemns the modern trend of simple minded positivistic thinking just as Trilling condemns "ideological thinking". The nineteenth century literature provided him with literary models that upheld human relationships and attempted to see life steadily and to see it whole. It focussed on the social fabric in which human relationships are established, and in which the self is given shape.

In most modern novels written by Kafka, Joyce, Dostoievsky, Gide and Mann for example, Trilling finds that instead of a position of acquiescence attained after a critical surveillance of society, the self reaches for ethical norms through underground journeys. According to Irving Howe, "modernism declares itself as an inflation of the self, a transcendental and orgiastic aggrandizement of matter and event in behalf of personal vitality" (Howe 1970: 5). Trilling deplores this disintegration of traditional moral norms in literature and the installation of the code of authenticity as a legitimate subjective expression of the self. As Howe remarks, "in modernist literature there is a turn from truth to sincerity, from the search for objective law to a desire for authentic response" (*ibid.*: 9). Elsewhere Howe states: The idea of self becomes a force within public life, almost taking an institutional shape" (1991: 57) thus posing a great danger to life in community.

Trilling again and again, shows his eagerness to establish the writer's responsibility to society in the context of values that are life-giving.

In the post-modern age to evaluate Trilling as a cultural critic we have to be aware of the structure of feelings that Raymond Williams discusses in *The Country and the City* (1973). This structure when referred back to the Age of Enlightenment with its firm belief in the capacity of reason to unravel truth and its failure to achieve that end with the discoveries of modern science and other branches of knowledge like psycho-analysis in our times, becomes a pointer to the predicament of culture that James Clifford (1988) has so ably discussed in his book of that title. With the advent of phenomenalism, structuralism and post-structuralism, the interpretation of literature becomes a difficult task. When we take into account such phenomena as alienation, violence, cruelty and widening permissiveness with the gradual erosion in the age-old sanctions that held society together, we need not be surprised at the emergence of a hippie or Yuppie culture which are the inevitable outcome of a fragmented society. As Clifford points out the beginning of this predicament goes back to the 1920's the date that Trilling has taken into account. The modern man's cosmopolitanism requires a perpetual veering between local attachments and general possibilities and creates problems of life and living for him. This problem is in the final analysis a moral one: it is a problem of choice between sincerity and authenticity. This choice finally stems from the trained human intelligence. In his study of fiction, therefore, Trilling exhibits the same kind of intelligence, the exposition of a critic who subscribes to a liberal humanistic culture which embraces diverse disciplines to throw light on the novel as a human document. Hence, his stress is on the themes and their social relevance. This relevance in a wider context becomes an issue of culture: literature from that view-point is both culture-forming and culture-ridden as has been shown by authors like Ruth Benedict and Susanne Langer.

WORKS CITED

Arnold, M., 1960. *Essays in Criticism: Second Series*, London: Macmillan, New York: St. Martin's.

Bradbury, M. and McFarlane, J., 1978, ed. *Modernism: 1890-1930*, Sussex: Harvester, New Jersey: Humanities.

Chace, W.M., 1980. *Lionel Trilling: Criticism and Politics*, Stanford: Stanford University Press.

Chase, R., 1957. *The American Novel and Its Tradition*, Garden City: Doubleday.

Clifford, J., 1988. *The Predicament of Culture*, Harvard University Press.

Hassan, I., 1961. *Radical Innocence: The Contemporary American Novel*, Princeton University Press.

Howe, I., 1970. *The Decline of the New*, New York: Horizon.

————, 1991. "The Self in Literature", *Salmagundi*, 90-91: 56-77.

Leavis, F.R., 1976. *The Common Pursuit*, Penguin.

————, 1977. *The Great Tradition*, Penguin.

Lewis, R.W.B., 1955. *The American Adam*, Chicago: University of Chicago Press.

Lodge, D., 1970, ed. *20th Century Literary Criticism: A Reader*, London and New York: Longman.

O'Hara, D.T., 1988. *Lionel Trilling: The Work of Liberation*. Madison, Wisconsin: University of Wisconsin Press.

Reising, R.J., 1986. *The Unusable Past: Theory and Study of American Literature*, New York and London: Methuen.

Trilling, D., 1978. *Reviewing the Forties*, New York and London: Harcourt.

Trilling, L., 1943. *E.M. Forster*, Connecticut: New Directions.

————, 1950. *The Liberal Imagination*, London: Secker and Warburg.

————, 1955. *The Opposing Self*, New York: Viking.

————, 1957. *A Gathering of Fugitives*, London: Secker and Warburg.

————, 1965. *Beyond Culture*, New York: Viking.

————, 1972. *Sincerity and Authenticity*, London: Oxford University Press.

————, 1980. *Speaking of Literature and Society*, New York: Harcourt.

7

LITERATURE, SOCIETY AND CULTURE WITH SPECIAL REFERENCE TO *THE MIDDLE OF THE JOURNEY*

> There are thus Gods of light and idols of mind. But it is essential to find the middle path leading to the faces of men. . . . We merely lack man's pride which is fidelity to his limits, lucid love of his condition.
>
> — Albert Camus (*The Myth of Sisyphus*)

This chapter deals with Lionel Trilling's treatment of literature, society and culture in his novel *The Middle of the Journey*.

Lionel Trilling's critical work as has been shown in the preceding chapters has found its leading focus in a complex dialectical pattern of the self and the moral life, of literature and culture. In his one and only novel *The Middle of the Journey* we find a full representation of this particular endeavour. It is a novel which deals with the difficulties that the mind encounters when faced with the exigencies of culture. It depicts persuasively and cogently the effect of suffering, illness and death upon the intellectual and the strange inaptitude of rational-minded men and women to understand the human being in all his weakness and strength. It also makes a plea for the cultivation of genuineness and sincerity in dealing with complex social and political issues, for in the final analysis, they are to be judged not by the force of the ideologies on which they are grounded, but by highly complicated moral and human values.

It is fruitful to take up Trilling's treatment of literature, society and culture in his novel as sub-texts, the text being the story of John Laskell's journey into life. As such it is the sub-texts which have a greater critical importance than the text. The text is the story in the literal sense. But Trilling has not written the novel to tell a story merely, he has sought to bring out the moral and allegorical meanings through sub-texts. While the moral meaning is involved in the complex relationship between literature and society, the allegorical meaning is brought out in the relationship of literature and culture as in Dante. That literature plays a definite role in forming the selfhood of man and reveals to him "images of personal being" has been Trilling's contention. The modern intellectual thrives on ideas which are propagated by the written word. They form his mind and personality. In the novel, there are many references to literature and an inter-relatedness between literary culture and general culture is made evident. In regarding the socio-cultural atmosphere of the novel, we find Trilling dealing with a small group of literary and political intelligentsia of the mid-century American with whom characters of lesser intellectual ability come into contact. The novel deals with political issues, but in a large way. The main focus is upon the selfhood of these characters and how they stand in relation to the ideas they follow. It is relevant here to point out that Trilling's ideas on literature, society and culture are all directed towards the study of human nature and the prospect and place of man in society.

The Middle of the Journey is a novel which assimilates literary, social and cultural ideas to show their inter-relatedness. The central character John Laskell, has a mind shaped by literary influences. He has definite ideas about literature, gleaned from the modern culture. He believes that literature makes one "sentient and free", and that it was the craze for "freedom and experience" that urges a young man to write. His early desire to oppose the impositions of his class and to revolt against his own cultural roots were inspired by the adversarial nature of literary culture. The "freedom" and "experience" he sought after were the freedom from the conditioning effects of culture—in his case the comfort and security of his station in life, and the experience of his own unique selfhood, cut off from society and general culture. Till the age of twentyfour, literature was for him a means of making inroads into the realities of his own consciousness and of negating the objective reality of the world outside. But at twentyfour, he did not encourage this kind of individualism; ". . . a kind of modesty . . . kept Laskell from writing, a diffidence about imposing himself or about looking into himself" (Trilling 1975: 32). Therefore, he took up the study of philosophy and found that it was not such a great change, for literature itself dealt with ideas. But when he engaged himself in more practical affairs having public utility, such as serving on semi-political committees or writing a book, *Theories of Housing,* he found, that there was a vast difference between the modern literary temperament and the socio-political temperament. Although the activities to which he later devoted himself were less romantic than the literary career he had forsaken, they gave him greater satisfaction for having embarked upon a more useful occupation.

The sense of the meaninglessness of life and a consequent withdrawal from society into a privatised, autonomous and imaginary world was one on which his literary temperament had nourished itself. It was in every way different from the public oriented spirit of enterprise that Laskell's active participation in social and political life demanded. For Laskell, it was a journey from the edges of consciousness to the vast human arena where the struggle for existence took place with such great force. Where once he had viewed the world as a "great sea of misery" and was intermittently depressed, he now showed more vitality to contend with those "forces" which were always "in struggle" (*ibid.*: 34). What he once considered tragic and heroic was the life of the mind, cut off from the conditions imposed by culture. But now he begins to think that the life based on reasonableness, moderateness and usefulness was of greater moral significance than the life of extreme radicalism and individualism that his literary temperament had afforded. Through his profession he became completely involved in his culture. He was satisfied that "every aspect of culture bore upon it [his writings], economics, sociology, history, technics, art" (*ibid.*).

While Laskell's political and social essays carried the flavour of realism and were quite popular Gifford Maxim's article entitled "Spirit and Law" transcended all material considerations and became incomprehensible to the clear, optimistic, rational world of modern people, the Crooms and Laskell. The article purports to defend a highly dialectical Christian theology, and is a rejection of Maxim's former Marxist ideas. The article is a review of Melville's book *Billy Budd* which appears in *The New Era* and which triggers off a whole lot of critical comments from the liberal intelligentsia that the Crooms in the novel represent.

The article argues that Claggart represents the principle of Evil and that Billy is Christ incarnate or "spirit". The world of Necessity or Law is represented by Captain Vere. It shows how spirit must conform to Law of Necessity in this world and not take a solitary course all its own. The reality of Evil makes Law all the more necessary. Melville's parable depicts the destruction of Claggart (Evil) by Billy Budd (Spirit), and Captain Vere's (Law's) condemnation of Billy by hanging. Maxim's interpretation of the story is quite beyond the comprehension of modern liberalism, "that loose body of middle-class opinion which includes such ideas as progress, collectivism and humanitarianism" (Trilling 1943: 13). They feel that "spirit should find its complete expression at once" and that:

> . . . Captain Vere is culpable because he does not acquit Billy in defiance of all Law. To them, Vere's suffering at being unable to do so is a mere sentimentality. It is even an hypocrisy.
>
> — Trilling 1975: 156

Maxim adopts an adversarial position to the liberal culture by giving equal importance to Vere and to Billy Budd: "Vere must rule the world of Necessity because Claggart—Evil—exists". Modern liberals have simplistic notions of Good and Evil and refuse to acknowledge the reality of cultural and social processes that condition moral choice. The main thrust of Maxim's article is to maintain that Spirit is not fully perfect. It is limited by Necessity and natural and social laws. Melville's perception, says Maxim, is that, as long as there is evil in the World, "Law must exist, and it—not spirit—must have the rule" (*ibid.*: 156). His essay goes on to speak of Billy Budd's role in Melville's design as Christ-like and Vere's tragic choice of condemning Billy Budd to death by hanging as akin to that of "God the Father, who must condemn his own son", though "not as in the familiar transaction of Christian theology, as a sacrifice and an atonement, but for the sake of the son himself, for the sake of spirit in humanity" (*ibid.*: 156-157). Perhaps the most insightful statement in the article is that ". . . we cannot understand Vere's suffering choice because we do not understand tragedy. And we do not understand tragedy because we do not understand love" (*ibid.*: 157). Vere's moral choice seems all the more tragic because of his great love for Billy Budd. Billy Budd himself goes willingly to his death. His acquiescence of Vere's decision is also tragic.

The modern literary temperament is incapable of understanding tragedy because the tragic vision is a highly refined sensibility that is able to resolve opposite view points and gain sentience by discarding an extremist position. Moreover, it is a vision that considers conditions necessary for the process of self-realisation. For the spirit to realise itself, Law is necessary and Law ought to change and modify itself in accordance with the changing needs of the spirit. The modern intellectual sensibility which is either radical or liberal, takes a highly extremist position regarding moral issues and either condemns Law for curbing the freedom of the spirit, or condemns the spirit if it is not reactionary enough.

In the novel, literature is not only a means of understanding great metaphysical questions and a reflector of political, social and moral processes, but is also a determinant in the cultural process. Emily Caldwell who has literary inclinations is sarcastically referred to by Nancy as "Our Emily Dickinson Caldwell, our Emile Brontë Caldwell, above all our Emily Bovary Caldwell" (*ibid.*: 77). Intellectually she is inferior to the Crooms, as her foolish articulations of snatches of poetry and lines of prose indicate. Her appreciation of Spengler's book *Decline of the West* further illustrates her lack of objective reflection and awareness of the new critical opinion that denounces his view of history. Nevertheless, through her knowledge of literature and art she wishes to have an identity other than the one of a housewife and mother, something with which she can establish comradeship with the real intellectuals and academicians. It is Laskell's insight into human nature that allows him the ability to see her in her essential womanhood. Inspite of her inaptitude for being either an intellectual like the Crooms or a rebel like her husband Duck, she retains a womanly dignity that does not depend upon intellect, but upon "a kind of biological intelligence" (*ibid.*: 189). A literary education has not been able to corrupt, or in the modern sense, "civilise" her natural instincts. Hence, she behaves with great propriety and faces every crisis in her life with calmness and fortitude, qualities rare in liberal intellectuals and revolutionary politicians whose connection with reality is minimal. Foster's novel *Howards End* also contains a similar idea of literature and culture.

Emily's failure to live upto the modern adversarial strategy of decrying Spengler's book is met with critical wariness. Nancy and Arthur Croom who are continually exposed to new ideas are sceptical about Spengler's book which they feel negates the future and offers a dark picture of human nature. Their doctrinaire liberalism makes them judge the book as "entirely reactionary because it cut off all hope of the future" (*ibid.*: 82). Emily Caldwell's appreciation of the book, in comparison, rises out of her own inner needs, her personal anxieties and fears about the future of her daughter who suffers from a weak heart. Although the liberal outlook regards the future with optimism since "history shows that man is dialectically developing and improving himself all the time", and that "there is no limitation to his potentialities" (*ibid.*: 83), Emily's own personal world has a bleak future. Incapable of being optimistic of the future, her motto she declares is *Carpe diem*. "Snatch the day" she says, "and put very little trust in tomorrow" (*ibid.*: 84). It is because of her sense of inevitable doom that she finds Spengler interesting.

Emily's experience of literature is only a limited one. She chooses such passages and recites such lines of poetry that suit her individual wants and sustain her spirit. She has not given much thought to Spengler's view of human fate as preordained and human beings as conditioned by historical processes, and that "all civilisations rise only to reach decay". But it may be argued that inspite of her lack of large sightedness in disregarding the future of the entire mankind, and inspite of her lack of concern for the larger political and social issues, she does not suffer from loss of integrity and good sense. This is because of her cultural background and a classical training that have endowed her with ideals. Her playful outburst of Latin phrases may seem archaic to the modern temperament of Nancy Croom, but it betrays her innate sense of tradition. Nancy refers to it as "dated, foolish hedonism" and in doing so voices her own cynicism of the past and of traditional culture, a phenomenon common to university-trained men and women of today.

In the novel, it is apparent that literature occupies an important place in defining and forming selfhood of different characters. Trilling deplores the weakness of the literary imagination in the modern society. In modern literature virtues like peace and brotherhood are represented as dull. On the other hand, modern literature has laid bare "the world's imagination of strife" (*ibid.*: 187). It has given a romantic halo to evil, to the autonomous will and to the self detached from culture. Men in society deem it heroic to live an alienated life on the strength of conflicting religious, social and political ideologies. Their passionate attachment to ideas leaves them no inclination to link up with their fellow men on the basis of the essential humanness that they share with each other. Literature has the power to unite the hearts of men, as Laskell realises, when it offers "the true emotion of reconciliation" as an heroic one (*ibid.*). To the modern mind, it must be again made clear that "Hamlet never appears in fuller virility than when he offers Laertes his hand, and nothing he says rings with a sweeter and graver note of masculinity than his 'Give me your pardon, Sir. I have done you wrong'" (*ibid.*). Literature must influence social life by teaching us moral values and establishing norms of behaviour, thought and feelings by which our actions can be measured and corrected.

In the novel, the text deals with the American socio-cultural background of the nineteen thirties and forties. The main events in the text take place in a small rural setting of the Connecticut countryside. But the central characters have an urban background. They belong to the intellectual middle-class with a comfortable source of income. They draw their literary and political awareness from their own cultural climate. They are conversant with every form of ideological differences that govern political activities: the liberal mode and the radical intention. Trilling's initial objective in the novel was "to draw out some of the moral and intellectual implications of the powerful attraction to Communism felt by a considerable part of the American intellectual class during the Thirties and Forties" (from the introduction to the novel). The novel also reaches out to larger issues of the reactions of men to universal problems like death, disease and suffering. These are the sub-texts which relate to the perennial question of the human condition. They relate to the cultural milieu with moral and intellectual adumbrations.

As the story opens we are sufficiently apprised of the disintegration to which the modern society is subjected. Gifford Maxim's anxiety that he be not recognised, his paranoid condition, his fears of being assassinated by the Communist Party from which he has broken, all point to the inescapable fact that he is the symbol of the anxiety-ridden, fearful modern man, suffering from a bitter crisis of conscience. Maxim's presence in the book is also symbolic of the "world's sickness" (*ibid.*: 3). Along with the violence, treachery, secrecy and incertitude that leftist politics perpetrates upon its followers, it also generates psychological disturbances. These social conditions eventually cause people to live a life of inauthenticity, here illustrated by Maxim's change of political ideology, his need to prove his existence, his search for a new public identity; and his later resort to Christianity is after all no progress made by the spirit because it is only a change from one kind of extreme idealism to another with the difference that one is concerned with man's outer behaviour and the other with the inner one.

John Laskell's moments of terror at the station when the Crooms do not turn up to receive him point to a deep psychological disorientation also within him. He admits the irrationality of his mind which associates his own feelings of loneliness and despair at not finding the Crooms on the platform, with images of horror that war, cruelty and illness foster in the psyche. It is but natural that Laskell's neurosis in this "empty new world" (*ibid.*: 24) should become manifest and provide him with a feeling of security in the experience of death. He nurtures nostalgic memories of his illness and contrasts the "beauty and truth of that life" (*ibid.*: 24) with the present world of "grief and injustice" (*ibid.*: 28).

Laskell's mind receding into a private world of beauty where the will has no function is actually a state of nothingness, that negates the real world of human beings and the moral responsibility he ought to feel as a member of the society. For some time after his illness he has no desire to connect with the world of living men and women, performing their tasks, involved in affairs of daily living, contending with joy and sorrow in their heroic struggle for existence. We can contrast this predicament of alienation with Forster's injunction "only connect" as the means of personal relationships which are frustrated by the distractions of the life of "telegrams and anger". This mental state of Laskell is described as one in which "all the adverse conditions of the self" are held in abeyance, and the personality lives in "nothing but delight in itself" (*ibid.*: 26). It is only when he lives in the country that the realisation dawns on him that "life was really a matter of routine" (*ibid.*: 28). His previous condition was really an escape mechanism designed to stave off the tediousness of life in society, for a fully matured individual must eventually come to terms with his cultural environment. Laskell renews his connection with the world but in a detached way.

For Trilling, to live in the modern world and to function as a mature individual means to be perceptive about the human condition and to be alive to the social and cultural and psychological pressures that determine human character and activities. In the ultimate analysis, human beings cannot be judged only by rational criteria, nor can their actions be simplified as either good or evil. To avoid philistinism, to base one's ideas not on the processes of the reason or the imagination alone, but upon both and to recognise the variousness, complexity and difficulty of the human situations are the true marks of a cultured individual in a society. Hence the novel makes the point that Trilling most admires in Forster: "only connect. . . ." that is to connect the reason and the imagination the head and the heart the "prose and the passion" (Trilling 1943: 78).

Laskell loses the vague rebelliousness towards social life when he lives in the close communal atmosphere in the village. He feels rested at seeing the domestic harmony of Nancy and Arthur Croom and the easy mother-daughter relationship between Emily Caldwell and Susan. Marriage brings responsibility and imposes conditions which one should gladly accept. This idea is contrasted with Laskell's own relationship with Elizabeth whom he had loved but could not marry due to his inherent fear of taking up responsibilities. Elizabeth's death which is untimely and swift is an irony of fate and it reveals to him that social ties strengthen and fortify emotional ties. It was in the fitness of things that love should have led to marriage despite anti-traditional opinions to the contrary. Legally he could not claim any relationship with her. Neither could he publicly give vent to his sorrow nor could he keep any of her belongings as a keep-sake. He feels that he has no moral right over her after her death and that the rights of her parents and sister are more legitimate. The full implications of what he has lost are very well brought out by the fact that during her illness Elizabeth herself does not call for his help, although they were very intimate, but calls her sister to attend to her needs. That Laskell's illness and his subsequent pleasure in the negation of the will involve a denial of guilt and responsibility cannot finally be dismissed. He is separated from his judging, willing self and is invested with a strange quietude.

The Crooms are the closest associates of Laskell. Arthur is a young university economist who has gained public recognition by publishing a book on business cycles. Like Laskell he writes for liberal magazines and is attracted to radical politics. In fact, the novel is an attack on the pieties of middle-class radicalism. The Crooms' Marxist ideas are reflected in their "passionate expectation of the future" (*ibid.*: 13) in their unwavering commitment to social justice, human welfare and decent living conditions and in their advocating reason in the true humanistic tradition as a means to judge, analyse and promote the larger affairs of public life. For all their avowed interest in social and political issues, they fail to live up to truly humane standards of behaviour. They refuse to talk about Laskell's illness and possible death because illness and death are beyond their powers of thought. Such an attitude to illness is exhibited by Thomas Mann in the *Magic Mountain*. They even regard Laskell's pre-occupation with the idea of death as politically reactionary like Joseph Conrad in *The Secret Agent*. For them death is an idea, not a concrete fact of existence. As an idea, death negates the future and hence can have no place in the rational, optimistic, modern world which they inhabit. They show Laskell a lot of tenderness and solicitude and talk on a variety of subjects of common interest, but whenever Laskell desires to speak about what it means to be seriously ill and dying, they withdraw themselves. They behave "in a polite, intelligent, concerted way . . . as if they were the parents of a little boy and were following the line of giving no heed to the obscenities their son picked up on the street and insisted on bringing to the dinner table. . . . They simply, in a sensible modern way, paid no attention at all" (*ibid.*: 75). The subject of death in western literature has a complex development as has been shown by Leslie Fiedler in *Love and Death in the American Novel.* Here Trilling's treatment of the subject resembles that of Forster in whose works, death comes suddenly and that is an abrupt end in contrast to Thomas Mann's where it is a lingering process.

The quality of personal relationship enjoyed by the Crooms and Laskell suffers a setback by their respective ways of dealing with ideas, people and moral issues. Laskell is resentful of the Crooms' failure to respond to his experience of death and the Crooms regard with great consternation Laskell's appreciation of Emily and condemnation of Duck, her husband. Emily is as "unreal" as Duck is "real". This is the comment made by Nancy in her prejudice against the woman whose foolish attempts to refine her literary sensibilities are met with malice. The Crooms' partiality to Duck is based upon his coarseness, his alcoholic conduct, his vulgar speech and occupation as handy man. They take these qualities to be the signs of authenticity. They admire his freedom from social norms of behaviour and for having the courage to disown his cultural heritage expressed by civilised men through good manners, virtuous conduct, politeness and decorum. He represents for them "a high manifestation of ordinary life". Their Marxist theory commits them to the cause of the workers and their repudiation of the realities of class distinction makes them sympathise with Duck. They tell Laskell that Duck "has his own way of doing things and . . . can't be hurried" (*ibid.*: 95). In Laskell's eyes Duck is not exactly an agent of "evil" (*ibid.*: 96), but he is also not what the Crooms take him to be, a symbol of something noble and good. Laskell comes to realise, moreover, that Emily as a woman and as a human being has a certain dignity. She is a good mother and housewife and carries on her social duties unperturbed by her poverty or by her uncultured husband. Nancy's failure to see Emily in her essential womanhood is a measure of the inadequacy of the liberal attitude to fathom the depths of a human being's whole personality.

Laskell reaches such an impasse in his relationship with the Crooms that he withholds for some time the news that Maxim has broken with the Communist Party. When he does tell them what Maxim had done they are angry with him for being the bearer of such news. They are strangely resistant to any discussion of what it means for a human being to discard the political affiliations of his own choice, to which he has dedicated nearly half his life. They are unmoved by his fears of being assassinated, and the strange horror of the situation that drives an individual to prove that he exists as a public figure. They can only see the utter irrationality of the deed and declare him to be mad. For them, the Party, the Communist movement and Marxist ideas are above reproach for they are certain that in the "far future" the Utopia for which everyone longs, will be built upon these new and advanced ideas. Maxim had always been for them the symbol of youthful revolutionary power which would usher in a new era, a new social organisation with economic, military, diplomatic and political development as was already present in a foreign country like the Soviet Union. That Communism may have its dark and evil side and that Maxim's fears are not unfounded are hardly acceptable to them. They refer to his fears and anxieties as reactionary fantasies.

Trilling's critique of the liberal intelligentsia's lack of imagination is very well brought out in Laskell's words:

> We do have sympathies with the Party and even, in a way, with its revolutionary aims. But may be, sympathetic as we are, we prefer not to think about what the realities of such a party are.
>
> — *Ibid.*: 144

Later, when Maxim reappears in the novel, his mind has undergone a complete reversal. His religiosity is another form of extremism that Laskell cannot favour. He develops an altogether different approach to human nature and to moral issues like guilt and responsibility. Once influenced by sociological theories, he had considered along with the liberal intellectuals, that human beings are without any moral responsibility, conditioned as they are to think and act in a certain way. Now he endorses the theological view of man as linked to the universal order so that, "His every act . . . involves the whole universe"; for the individual there is "never-ending responsibility" and a personal God ultimately shows him according "forgiveness for his sins" (*ibid.*: 299-300). In his new system there is "ultimate absolute responsibility for the individual, but mercy" (*ibid.*: 300).

To Laskell Maxim's new posture is an endorsement of the complete autonomy of the individual and a denial of conditioned human reality. The incident of Duck striking Susan who falls dead becomes the occasion for a metaphysical discussion which is a sub-text. Maxim puts the blame for Susan's death squarely on Duck, while Laskell and the Crooms cannot do so. For Kermit Simpson, the editor of *The New Era* and to the Crooms Duck is only an agent of fate. They project a deterministic view of human nature that absolves the individual from all guilt and responsibility:

> . . . social causes, environment, education or lack of education, economic pressure, the character-pattern imposed by society, in this case a disorganised society, all go to account for any given individual's action.
>
> — *ibid.*: 298

The cultural differences as envisaged by Trilling in this novel are comparable to the difference between Sawston and Cambridge in *E.M. Forster*. Of these two cultures, one is external, the other internal. The Crooms' snobbish philistinism shows them as lacking in inwardness. For the Crooms, there can be no moral choice and hence no moral responsibility.

Between these extreme view points of the autonomous will and the radical innocence of man is the middle position from which actions are judged as neither good nor evil, but as good-and-evil. What Maxim and the Crooms forget is man in his essential humanness who is neither beast nor angel, who is both conditioned and responsible. As Laskell puts it, "An absolute freedom from responsibility—that much of a child none of us can be. An absolute responsibility—that much of a divine . . . none of us is" (*ibid.*: 301).

For people who demand ideas "on which to build their lives" (*ibid.*: 300). Trilling offers the wisdom to hold "an idea in modulation" and evade the attraction of slipping into some form of absolutism or the other. This kind of dialectical intelligence is the means to the sanity of spirit and composure for a modern individual exposed to the cultural, social and political ideas, the twists of fate, conflicts of opinion and clashes of will. This is not so much an attitude of compromise as an intelligent awareness of the complexities, bitternesses and confusions of an age riven with ideological differences, utilitarian motives and materialistic designs. Trilling stresses the moral significance of maintaining an independent life of the mind amid such disturbing and disorienting conditions of culture.

The independence of mind that is advocated in the novel is actually a critical spirit that weighs and analyses any modern idea before giving it due credence. The liberal attitude which distrusts the past and looks forward to the new and the original assumes always that the new is best only because it is new. This assumption stems merely from a simplistic idea of progress—progress in terms of a past stage in the development of technology. The Crooms' admiration for the Movement is a result of their seeking after new ideas that invalidate their decaying bourgeois culture and hold the promise of a possible golden age in the distant future. This is a technocratic approach to society, to history and to culture. A true historical perspective is central to tradition and culture, but the American intellectual is incapable of conceiving the past as essential to the present owing to the shortness of the American history.

Laskell's sudden realisation is that the future and the present are one, they are connected and that this idea of history and the nature of time "brought its own heroism" . . . "at this very moment he had the full measure of existence. . . . If at this moment he did not have the simplicity of character he wanted, he would never have it; if he was not now answerable for himself, he would never answer" (*ibid.*: 140). The notion that man develops and changes and becomes something else, unconnected to what he was before, is a cultural phenomenon of the modern times where discontinuity has become a major experience of life. The Crooms' idea of history is based upon the evolutionary principle by which they deduce, that human beings have immense capabilities and can progress infinitely. The far future holds for them the vision of the unconditioned spirit reigning supreme, unhampered by historical and cultural necessity.

Trilling's centrist position countervails the relativistic philosophy that shows human nature changing in relation to historical forces and the positivistic ideas that relate human progress to scientific and technological advances. Laskell's invocation of Pascal's philosophy points to the fact that the "here and the now" when man is neither beast nor angel, but a human being possessing "the full measure of existence", is the proper sphere for observation. Trilling goes back to the ideas of the Enlightenment to maintain continuity with the past culture and to stress the need for countervailing ideas as distinct and powerful as Marxism. There is no place in the views of Laskell for the future which middle class liberals believe is full of the promise that society, human nature and culture would "grow and change for the better" (*ibid.*: 139).

Trilling's criticism of the pieties to which the liberal minded submitted themselves is clearly brought out in the following lines:

> The promise of the future might have its uses as a way of seducing the child to maturity, but maturity itself meant that the future and the present are brought together, that you lived your life *now* instead of preparing and committing yourself to some better day to come.
>
> — *ibid.*: 139

Laskell realises that sincerity requires a man to have "simplicity of character" (*ibid.*: 140), that is to mould his imagination and intellect to function together. Culture is the development of reason and imagination so that one's response to social situations follows from a unified sensibility and a well developed moral sense. Such a task must be undertaken now. To develop internally is the first duty and responsibility for any man of any time, much more so in the present age.

The liberal intellectual culture of the middle class Americans, draws them to the "ideational aspects" of the Communist Movement, "to the emotional superstructure of the movement". Nancy and Arthur Croom cannot reconcile themselves to the violence, secrecy and loss of personal identity which they entail. Arthur and John Laskell refuse to work for Maxim although they espouse his cause. This reveals their lack of sincerity. Nancy's "self-deceiving pose of maturity" is also evident in her "desire to refuse knowledge of the evil and hardness of the world" (*ibid.*: 104). Her optimism about society, about the future, are not founded upon reality. Therefore, the Crooms represent for Maxim a certain group of people who make "revolution serve their individualistic aspirations for romantic action and utopian morality" (*ibid.*: 217).

Maturity of personality means accommodation to the twin visions of the disaster and joy that culture involves. Maxim's experience of life has invested him only with the imagination of disaster. Laskell's appraisal of him in the last part of the novel is true in every way. He says, "It seems to me Giff, that you have lost your sense of community with men in their suffering and goodness and found it only in their cruelty and evil" (*ibid.*: 220). The Crooms as well as Maxim live a life disconnected from their particular class and political group and whereas Maxim veers towards a spiritual communion with men in their cruelty and suffering, the Crooms' extreme rationalism, makes them unable to do so. They can connect neither on the human level as their attitude of intellectual superiority to Emily shows nor on the spiritual level as their disgust for Maxim's religiosity shows. They live only on the mental plane and can establish connection with people abstracted into ideas. This comes out most tellingly when Nancy becomes convinced that Duck is not a murderer, but refrains from all human contact with him.

The Middle of the Journey unfolds with perfect cogency the ideas that regulate life and culture. They focus upon the intellectual middle class and their attempts to form opinions by which they can conduct their lives. Particularly, the novel projects radical politics as a cultural and sociological phenomenon and the relation of educated men and women to the world of culture. Laskell represents the true critical spirit, at once oppositional and reconciliatory, analysing, judging and contemplating the complex moral issues that a highly developed society is faced with. We see him struggling to come to an understanding of his experiences of life and people, not by the accepted ideals and mores of topical cultural theories, but by a standard of values ingrained in the consciousness by a rich traditional past which sharpens the perceptual powers and moulds the critical spirit. He bears the burden of the conscious modern individual who has travelled from the abyss of darkness and insentience towards the surface, only to encounter ideological conflicts, disintegration of values, disorientation and rigid philistinism that threaten the existence of men as human beings. As the title of the novel indicates, the middle phase of the journey of the soul from Inferno to Paradiso is Purgatario where the self is surrounded by difficulties, and only where he has the freedom and feels the urgency to exercise his moral choice. It is also the stage where the self is endowed with the capacity to suffer and feel pain and joy simultaneously and takes pleasure in winning felicity in spite of his conditioned nature.

Trilling's use of the model of the *Divine Comedy* gives his novel the same enduring emotive power. The journey motif has been used with remarkable effect in great works of literature as for instance in *The Pilgrim's Progress* and *The Ancient Mariner*. *The Middle of the Journey* is not so different in form from these works. Laskell's journey becomes an allegory of the intellectual's predicament in modern culture, his exploration of the self and his struggle with difficult and paradoxical moral issues to give life meaning. In a way, the novel links us to the tradition of humanism that such works in the past have projected and seeks to revive the traditional Western concept of art and literature as our most valuable repository of moral and spiritual wisdom.

Viewed in this way, Laskell's journey into life and his total involvement in human existence conditioned by culture is a literary mode which subverts the modern trend of alienation. It also inverts the solipsistic withdrawal of the modern self from external reality into the dark abyss of one's own consciousness, a regression that is anti-cultural and anti-humanistic as well. The reference to Dante makes it easier for Trilling to reconstruct the hierarchy of values relating to life, literature and culture which modern methods have sought to deconstruct and demystify. The title of the novel which is taken from the opening lines of the "Inferno" ("In the middle of the journey of our life. . . .") imparts seriousness to the novel by summoning up for us the tragic grandeur of a journey whose middle phase between the dark hopeless void of bestial existence and the paradise of pure essences and sublime insentience is the second realm where the human spirit is purged. The reference to the "middle of the way" in Eliot's *Four Quartets* and Aristotle's "golden mean" and Buddha's "middle path" can all be recalled in this context.

Trilling partly avoids the modern literary conventions that reduce the narrative content and minimise reality. The sub-texts deal effectively with the complex relationship of individual, society, literature and culture while the text maintains its link with social reality. Life is seen whole: the material, the intellectual, the cultural and the moral spheres find adequate representation in the interweaving of the text and the sub-texts. All of them together form the structure of reality in the novel. Each character as well as each idea is examined against a social, political, intellectual and moral background. The novel gains in density as each major incident evokes a serious intellectual or moral reaction which contributes to the amplification and illumination of the nature of reality and intensification of the moral effect.

The novel serves Trilling's purpose of pointing out the liberal unimaginativeness of ideas as reflected in modern literature. Modernism has become a quest for eager and advanced views in art. Its repudiation of the human element in literature and loss of thematic centrality leads it into underground journeys to a void or to a beyond where concrete human reality is nullified and pure consciousness exists in perfect autonomy. That vital human existence is a valid literary reality is an idea which it violently subverts. The novels of Sartre, for example, show this trend most effectively. Here the protest of the protagonist against culture is an empty gesture expressing nausea. In Kafka, we are exposed to a vision of the world dominated by angst and of man at the mercy of incomprehensible terrors. Post-modernism's elimination of literature's referential nature and functions and assertion of literary autonomy have strengthened the mood of nihilism as the theories of Derrida and Lacan have done.

In *The Middle of the Journey*, we find the novelist as thinker and critic. He is primarily concerned with the meaning and value of life and this moral purpose aids him in the selection and ordering of human experiences in the novel. Hence the incidents in the text assume serious proportions for us. The authenticity of the novel is to be deduced from the way it relates to Trilling's concept of actual reality. The allegorical meaning, the use of Dante's model as a means of understanding and ordering human experiences, the text and the sub-texts, all cohere to present a vision of reality, a geist that governs in Trilling's view, the life outside as well as the life in the novel. Trilling's novel offers a notion of reality antithetical to the "authentic" theories of literary autonomy of Derrida and Foucault who believe in the fabrication of the forms of order, meaning and value which external nature is bereft of. Trilling gains in authenticity by authenticating the belief that human existence has meaning only in relation to other human beings and literature too has authenticity if it is a criticism of life meant to instil respect for common truth and a sense of responsibility for the artist to his community.

The attitude to life and literature which informs the novel has a grand literary past. The literary talent of Trilling connects it to contemporary issues of art and life and endeavours to see man in the broader perspective of history. The novel moves us intellectually but not merely as a self-contained literary work. The social and moral implications are so strong that it cannot be taken as a mere political novel or even as a comedy of manners. It is a criticism of life, in the fullest sense of the term. In this way, Trilling goes beyond the modern ethos of literary autonomy, nihilism, dehumanisation, loss of self and obfuscation of reality, to interpret and illuminate those aspects of life and art that the present culture has repudiated.

WORKS CITED

Trilling, L., 1943. *E.M. Forster,* Connecticut: New Directions Books.
Trilling, L., 1975. *The Middle of the Journey*, London: Secker and Warburg.

CONCLUSION

Lionel Trilling's literary criticism is directed at raising the general cultural level of the society. Such a literary enterprise involves the necessity of shaping the discriminatory powers of the individual by making available to him ideas pertaining to human values, moral purposes and spiritual truths, ideas which will help him understand himself and his place in the universe. Trilling's concept of literature as a moulder of taste has power to direct the energies of men, to organise their emotions and to correct their mistakes. The humanist in Trilling reasserts for us the traditional claims of literature to truth and human value, ideals which modern and postmodern writers have since repudiated. Moreover, his support of the view that literature is a repository of human values and a standard of reference for moral choices made by the individual links us to the high ideals of Western humanism. Its resuscitating effect on the fragmented modern mind is to be devoutly hoped for. Thus, Trilling's literary criticism acts as a deterrent to the soulless positivism of much modern literature, its decadent romanticism and its nihilistic conception of reality.

The focus on human nature as an independent reality, not as a product of natural, social, and political forces, shows his independent critical spirit. His attempt to redefine the human being as a complex entity, both conditioned by external forces and internal necessities, and ever striving to break through to a beyond by asserting his inner freedom, has invested him with dignity and nobility. Keeping in view Protagoras' statement that "Man is the measure of all things", we may evaluate Trilling as a literary humanist critic who has increased our understanding of literature as an imaginative record of man's life in and through culture and as the deepest resource of the human spirit.

The ethical intent of Trilling's literary criticism broadens the field of literary enquiry in the modern age. As Martha Nussbaum puts it, "The sense that we are social beings puzzling out in times of great moral difficulty, what might be for us the best way to live . . . always animated much of great literature", but "is absent from the writings of many of our leading literary theorists" (Nussbaum 1989: 60-61). Cleanth Brooks' assertion (1992: 28) that great literature offers us insights into human behaviour and the knowledge how human beings "justify their lives or how they fail to do so", whereby we can enrich our own lives, has a strong resemblance to Trilling's views on literature and its affectivist powers.

Critically surveying the contemporary literary scenario, Trilling concludes that modern literature by projecting and promoting literary autonomy as an oppositional stand to the industrial, technological and commercial social order, has divested literature of its social, moral and cultural contexts.

The most sophisticated theories of twentieth century criticism treat language, knowledge and experience as fictitious, to be studied without regard to their correspondence to extra-textual reality. The New Critical method of literary analysis was initially a powerful alternative to the impressionistic mode which laid stress on the process of the creative imagination and which conceived reality to be inseparable from the operations of the poet's own mind. However, the impersonality and detachment sought after by the New Critics and their emphasis upon the study of intrinsic elements like form, language and content, anticipated structuralism, which finally did away entirely with the human subject. J. Hillis Miller in "The Fiction of Realism" defines literature as a structure of words and distinguishes between "referent" and "meaning" and invalidates the notion that a literary text corresponds to some social, historical or psychological reality. This view of a literary work as a verbal artifact expounded earlier by the New Critics has been taken to the level of epistemology by the structuralists and post-structuralists who have gone to the extreme limit of questioning the validity of knowledge accruing from any literary work. In pursuance of this concept a whole gamut of critical opinions has been evolved by post-structural theorists. They have propounded the theory of literature as an autonomous verbal structure to be evaluated on its own terms; not by any extra-literary concerns such as biography, intentionalism, historicism and social realism or philosophical and moral propositions which critics may abstract from the text or impose on it. The work of literature then becomes a self-reflexive aesthetic reality. The modern critic's distaste for the utilitarian function of literature and criticism has helped to valorise the autonomous, experiential and non-rational elements that literature today is suffused with.

The implication of the self-reflexive model is to isolate not only the texts but the self as well from social existence. Theories of the autonomy of literature and literary language in a broader perspective are theories which uphold the autonomy of the individual human being, the existential self. The extreme forms of the de-centred self are to be found in the theories of Lacan and Foucault. They intensify the alienated understanding of the individual by validating the fragmented human consciousness. Their conception of the human consciousness finds its way into modern poetry and novels which are written with the notion that human consciousness is the only reality, and that the writer constantly builds new worlds out of his own creativity.

Another manifestation of the modern critical spirit is the problem of textuality: whether the real text is a structure of words, whether it is "writerly" or whether it is "readerly". By severing the text from any reality outside its textual borders, and by defining the intra-textual world ahistorically, critics like Fredric Jameson seem to be making out a case for themselves by referring to the "systematized and disembodied nightmare which is our culture today" (Jameson 1972: IX). It is interesting to note how for instance, linguists like Ferdinand de Saussure have added to the disruption of the total experience of literature by harping upon the differences between the reader's knowledge and experience and articulation of words (his individual speech-act) and the system of language ('langue', a collection of conventions and norms in a literary work) that all readers may not be fully conversant with (Wellek and Warren 1963: 152).

The various systems of modern literary analyses are concomitants of the academisation of literary studies, a fact noted by T.S. Eliot in "The Frontiers of Criticism". This phenomenon makes it apparent that literary criticism has become the specialised study of a coterie guided by a compulsion to employ the tools of scientific research and to give an objective and rational basis to their critical canons. Criticism which is at bottom an enquiry into the elusive human nature, and an appraisal of the human condition, has become the hand-maid of a few contentious and contending writers who resort to ingenious strategies to purge literature of the dehumanising and destructive ideas which the modern technological society is committed to. Their strategical debunking methods are aimed at breaking conventions and thereby popularising "flights of stylistic freedom" that "radically disrupt our expectations about reality and literature" (Reising 1986: 189).

The idea that modern and postmodern theories are derivations of the art for art's sake theories cannot finally be overlooked. Just as Edgar Allen Poe favoured art that produced "an elevating excitement of the soul . . . independent of . . . the intoxication of the Heart . . . or of that of Truth which is the satisfaction of the Reason", (quoted in Wimsatt and Brooks 1957: 479) the modernist writer elevates the intellect and negates the life of emotions and feelings and turns away from moral truths. What Baudelaire said of the art for art's sake model is equally true for modern literature: "a flagrant defiance of human nature", a repudiation of the "higher and universal principles of life itself. . . " (*ibid.*: 480).

Trilling's criticism when viewed against the background of recent critical theories posits the dangers of an over-specialised literary activity that does not ratify the wholeness concept of the human being. That his concern for morals was inseparable from his concern for artistic excellence is a fact that gives cogency to his ideas and methods. He is different from literary critics who use texts to reveal political, historical and sociological information. His pre-occupation with literature is to find out what it can contribute to the advancement of culture in the way of defining purposes, values and ends. The focus of Trilling's criticism is upon the powers of literature to strengthen and rehabilitate the individual's inner life which an exclusive adherence to reason and the intellect has impoverished. He realises the serious importance of good literature and its educational value for living life meaningful in a mass society continuously under the threat of the technological imperative which negates the categorical imperative. The importance of classical education that refined the taste of a gentleman in the past serves as a reminder that a similar task could be performed by English studies a kind of attitude that prevailed with the Kenyon College critics or F.R. Leavis in his English school at Droning College after the Second World War. Trilling points to the good effects upon "the general intelligence and general moral tone" of a person if "the other culture", that of the Greek and English tradition is made available to him (Trilling 1980: 353, 355).

Trilling's position as a teacher makes him an anxious spectator of a radical literary culture oblivious to the tradition of good sense and moral fervour. A valueless, materialistic, technological and anarchical social environment is uncongenial to the spiritual growth of individuals whose connection with the rich literary heritage of the past has been cut off, steadily but surely. If the violent student unrest at Columbia University in the late 60's is an indication of the distrust and mental ill-health of a good number of citizens of a modern society, then most assuredly Trilling's anxiety for the future of mankind is not unfounded. Trilling feels that the modern mind is crumbling under the impact of anti-cultural ideas and is in the grip of forces of disintegration that are tearing away at the cultural fabric.

Under these circumstances we may turn to Cleanth Brooks' statement that vivifies the plight of university academics. He argues that universities today are preoccupied with teaching students the means of getting a good job, whereas the primary aim of education should be "not how to make a living but how to live" (Brooks 1992: 33). Referring to the technological studies which are flourishing vigorously, he says that as a result education based on the studies of the humanities is on the decline. Literature today is taken to be "just rhetoric meaning nothing" and that "any one interpretation of a poem or a story is just as good as another" (*ibid.*). At the hands of post-modernist critics literature has been reduced to a meaningless exercise, a strenuous word play, that teachers and students find difficult to understand or explicate. In this way "sweetness and light" and "high seriousness" which it was the function of literature to incorporate and disseminate are replaced by the study of semantics and literary concepts derived from epistemology and metaphysics.

Trilling's dissatisfaction with the academic humanities which are over-specialised and chaotic is founded upon their failure to transmit a common ground of humanistic values and cultural traditions and their contribution to the debasement of intellectual standards. Trilling strove to raise ethical and social issues that give literature its crucial importance in our lives. His criticism is then of major interest today as it encourages the diverse and excellent analyses of human social experience which should be taken to have an interesting bearing on the activity of the theorist. The modern critic, in the manner of Trilling, should transform critical enquiry into a search for choice and emotions and should value the human being in all the totality of his connections and relationships.

How best to live in a modern dehumanised cultural environment is a problem that demands the immediate attention of literary criticism and any theory that does not give a full, cogent analysis of the human condition falls short of its aim. The distinction Trilling makes between living sincerely and living authentically is a pointer to his anxiety that man, through the help of great literature may be induced to live a life of moral responsibility and genuine human concerns, measuring each thought, each act of his by standards and values illustrated in high literary culture.

The great classics in which man is depicted neither as an angel nor as a brute, but as a tragic protagonist engaged in an inevitable struggle with forces of necessity and heroically proceeding towards self-knowledge should be reinstated. The tragic spirit of sublime acquiescence to the course of fate forms an important part of Trilling's cultural theory. The death of the tragic vision in modern literature does not denote the disappearance of tragedy altogether from our lives. Trilling's study of nineteenth century English novelists and poets is of great importance to the sceptic. It sets a standard of judgement which emphasizes a proper understanding of man and his place in the universe. The fundamental spiritual obligation of literary criticism is to recommend values essential for the good life and to uphold the dignity of man as a moral being whose powers of will and judgement harmonise with his feelings and emotions and make life worth living. Literature, as Trilling has amply demonstrated in his criticism can be an antidote to the pervasive sense of cynicism and nihilism that characterizes modern life in a bewildering world.

The urgency of such a humanistic approach to the study of literature can be realised from the widespread confusion that characterises literary criticism at present. It has been described as a 'wilderness' by Geoffrey. Hartman. But the remedy suggested by him, a philosophical or metaphysical approach is not satisfactory either in view of the lack of clarity in any Western philosophical perspective in the postmodern age. If by a philosophical approach Hartman means the often obfuscating perspective of the deconstructonists, then literary criticism is not likely to help the reader in finding his way out of the wilderness.

This mental confusion causes a multi-dimensional crisis to the extremely penetrating analysis of the contemporary situation by Fritzof Capra in *The Turning Point* (1982) supplemented by the emerging 'Weltenschaung' that has been presented by Stephen W. Hawking in *A Brief History of Time* (1988). As we move into the twenty-first century the problem of human communication is likely to create problems of the type that have been envisaged by Jürgen Habermas in *Communication and the Evolution of Society* (1979). To regain the ground lost by the fragmentation of the human mind by the extreme specialisation in a technological civilisation, it is necessary to steer clear of concepts like "one-dimensional man", "organisational man", "dangling man", "hollow man", "mass man" in order to strive to grasp the image of the whole man. How this specialisation and fragmentation and other factors have contributed to the growing up of the absurd man has been very well analysed and explicated by Paul Goodman in *Growing up Absurd* (1956). If that frightening image of life as a rat race has to be pushed back and human dignity and sanity recovered, literary criticism has to move on the path explored by critics like Trilling. This path leads the reader to explore, understand and appreciate the life of the mind on his own. Without participation and involvement in that life man is hardly *homo sapiens*.

WORKS CITED

Brooks, C., 1992. "In Defense of the Canon", *Dialogue*, 96: 28-33.

Capra, F., 1983. *The Turning Point*, New York: Fontana.

Goodman, P., 1956. *Growing Up Absurd*, New York: Vintage.

Jameson, F., 1972. *The Prison-House of Language: A Critical Account of Structuralism and Russian Formalism*, Princeton: Princeton University Press.

Hartman, G.H., 1980. *Criticism in the Wilderness: The Study of Literature Today*, New Haven and London: Yale University Press.

Hawking, S.W., 1988. *A Brief History of Time*, New York: Bantam.

Nussbaum, M., 1989. "Perceptive Equilibrium: Literary Theory and Ethical Theory", in *The Future of Literary Theory*, ed. R. Cohen, New York and London: Routledge, 1986.

Reising, R.J., 1986. *The Unusable Past: Theory and the Study of American Literature*, New York and London: Methuen.

Trilling, L., 1980. *Speaking of Literature and Society*, New York and London: Harcourt.

Wellek, R. and Warren, A., 1963. *The Theory of Literature*, Penguin.

Wimsatt, W.K. and Brooks, C., 1957. *Literary Criticism: A Short History*, Calcutta: Oxford and IBH.

BIBLIOGRAPHY

Primary Sources

Trilling, L., *Matthew Arnold*, Oxford, Melbourne: Oxford University Press, 1982, 1st Published 1939.

————, *E.M. Forster*, Norfolk, Connecticut: New Directions, 1943.

————, *The Middle of the Journey*, London: Secker and Warburg, 1975, 1st Published 1948.

————, ed., *The Essential Matthew Arnold*, London: Chatto and Windus, Viking, 1949.

————, *The Liberal Imagination: Essays in Literature and Society*, London: Secker and Warburg, 1950.

————, *The Opposing Self*, New York: Viking, 1955.

————, *A Gathering of Fugitives*, London: Secker and Warburg, 1957.

————, *Beyond Culture: Essays in Literature and Learning*, New York: Viking, 1965.

————, *The Experience of Literature*, New York, Chicago, San Francisco, Toronto: Holt, Rinehart and Winston, 1967.

————, ed., *Literary Criticism: An Introductory Reader*, New York: Holt, 1970.

————, *Sincerity and Authenticity*, London: Oxford University Press, 1972.

Trilling, D., ed., *Speaking of Literature and Society*, New York, London: Harcourt, 1980.

————, ed., *The Last Decade, Essays and Reviews*, 1965-75, London: Oxford University Press, 1982.

Secondary Sources: Books

Aaron, D. ed., *Paul Elmer More's Shelburne Essays on American Literature*, New York: Harcourt, 1963.

Alkon, P.K., *Samuel Johnson and Moral Discipline*, Evanston: Northwestern University Press, 1967.

Anderson, Q., *Art, Politics and Will*, New York: Basic, 1977.

Arnold, M., *Culture and Anarchy*, ed., J. Dover Wilson Cambridge: Press Syndicate of University of Cambridge, rep. 1986, 1st published 1932.

————, *Essays in Criticism: First Series*, New York: St. Martin's, 1924.

————, *Essays in Criticism: Second Series*, New York: St. Martin's, 1960, 1st published 1935.

Babbitt, I., *Literature and the American College*, Boston: Houghton, 1908.

————, *The New Loakoon*, Boston: Houghton, 1910.

————, *Rousseau and Romanticism*, Boston and New York: Houghton, 1919.

————, *Spanish Character and Other Essays*, Boston: Houghton, 1940.

————, *Democracy and Leadership*, Boston: Houghton, 1962.

Barnes, H.E., *The Literature of Possibility: A Study in Humanistic Existentialism*, London: Tavistock, 1961.

Barrett, W., *Irrational Man: A Study in Existential Philosophy*, London, Melbourne, Toronto: Heinemann, 1961.

————, *The Illusion of Technique: A Search in the Meaning of Life in a Technological Age*, London: William Kimber, 1979.

————, *The Truants: Adventures Among the Intellectuals*, New York: Anchor, 1982.

Bell, D., *The Cultural Contradictions of Capitalism*, New York: Basic, 1976.

Blackmur, R.P., "The Politics of Human Power" in *The Lion and the Honeycomb*, New York: Harcourt, 1950.

Bownan, J., ed., *Contemporary American Criticism*, New York: Henry Holt, 1926.

Boyers, R., *Lionel Trilling: Negative Capability and the Wisdom of Avoidance*, Columbia: University of Missouri Press, 1977.

Bradbury, M. and McFarlane, J., *Modernism: 1890-1930*, Sussex: Harvester, New Jersey: Humanities, 1978.

Brown, J.E., ed. *The Critical Opinions of Johnson*, Princeton, 1926.

Buckley, V., *Poetry and Morality*, London: Chatto and Windus, 1980.

Bullock, A., *The Humanistic Tradition in the West*, London: Thames and Hudson, 1985.

Bush, D., *The Renaissance and English Humanism*, Toronto: University of Toronto Press, 1968.

Cain, W.E., *English in America Reconsidered: Theory, Criticism, Marxism and Social Change*, Baltimore: John Hopkins University Press, 1980.

Camus, A., *The Myth of Sisyphus*, London: Penguin, 1977.

Capra, F., *The Turning Point*, New York: Fontana, 1983.

Chace, W.M., *Lionel Trilling: Criticism and Politics*, California: Stanford University Press, 1980.

Chandra, N., *New Criticism: An Appraisal*, New Delhi: Doaba, 1988.

Chase, R., *The American Novel and Its Tradition*, Garden City: Doubleday, 1957.

Clifford, J., *The Predicament of Culture*, Cambridge: Harvard University Press, 1988.

Cohen, R., ed. *The Future of Literary Theory*, New York and London: Routledge, 1989.

Commanger, H.S., *The American Mind: An Interpretation of American Thought and Character since the 1880's*, Bombay: Popular Prakashan.

Dale, A., *The Victorian Critic and the Idea of History*, Cambridge: Harvard University Press, 1977.

Davis, R.C. and Schleifer, R., *Criticism and Culture: The Role of Critique in Modern Literary Theory*, Singapore: Longman, 1991.

Duggan, F.X., *Paul Elmer More*, New York: Twayne, 1966.

Durant, W., *The Story of Philosophy*, New York: Washington Press, 1967.

Eagleton, T., *The Function of Criticism: From the Spectator to Post-structuralism*, Norfolk: Thetford, 1984.

Eliot, T.S., *After Strange Gods: A Primer of Modern Heresy*, London: Faber, 1934.

————, *Selected Essays*, London: Faber, 1951.

————, *The Sacred Wood*, London: Methuen, 1960.

————, *The Selected Prose of T.S. Eliot*, London: Penguin, 1965.

————, *To Criticise the Critic*, London: Faber, 1965.

————, *Notes Towards a Definition of Culture*, London: Faber, 1967.

————, *The Use of Poetry and the Use of Criticism*, London: Faber, 1975.

Ellman, R. and Fiedleson, C.J., Jr., ed., *The Modern Tradition*, New York: Oxford University Press, 1965.

Fekete, J., *The Critical Twilight: Exploration in the Ideology of Anglo-American Literature Theory from Eliot to McLuhan*, London, Henley and Boston: Routledge, 1978.

Fekete, ed., *Life after Post Modernism: Essays on Values and Culture*, Macmillan Education, 1988.

Fiedler, L.A., *Love and Death in the American Novel*, New York: Stein and Day, 1960.

Fiedler, L.A., *What was Literature? Class, Culture and Mass Society*, New York: Simon and Schuster, 1982.

Foerster, N., *Towards Standards*, New York: Farrar, 1930.

————, ed., *Humanism and America*, New York: Farrar, 1930.

————, ed., *American Critical Essays*, London: Oxford University Press, 1930.

Fraiberg, L., *Psychoanalysis and the American Literary Criticism*, Detroit: Wayne State University Press, 1960.

Frank, J., *The Widening Gyre: Crisis and Mastery in Modern Literature*, New Brunswick: New Jersey, 1963.

French, P., ed., *Three Honest Men: A Critical Mosaic*, Manchester: Carcanet New Press, 1980.

Ford, B., ed., *The Pelican Guide to English Literature*, 7 Vols., Penguin, 1970.

Garvin, S., *Science and Literature*, London: Bucknell University Press, 1985.

Glicksberg, C.I., ed., *American Literary Criticism*, New York: Hendricks, 1951.

Goodheart, E., *Culture and the Radical Conscience*, Cambridge, Massachusetts: Harvard University Press, 1973.

Goodman, P., *Growing Up Absurd*, New York: Vintage, 1956.

Goubsblom, J., *Nihilism and Culture*, Oxford: Basil Blackwell, 1980.

Graff, G., *Literature Against Itself: Literary Ideas in Modern Society*, Chicago and London: The University of Chicago Press, 1979.

Grattan, C.H. ed., *The Critique of Humanism*, New York: Brewer and Warren, 1930.

Hamphshire, S., *The Age of Reason: 17th Century Philosophers* (Selected, introd. comment), New York: New American Library, 1961.

Harland, R., *The Philosophy of Structuralism and Post-structuralism*, London, New York: Methuen, 1987.

Hartman, G.H., *Criticism in the Wilderness: The Study of Literature Today*, New Haven and London: Yale University Press, 1980.

Hassan, I., *Radical Innocence: The Contemporary American Novel*, Princeton: Princeton University Press, 1961.

————, *The Dismemberment of Orpheus: Towards a Post-modern Literature*, New York: Oxford University Press, 1971.

Hassan, I., *Contemporary American Literature 1945-1972: An Introduction*, New York: Fredrick Ungar, 1973.

Hawking, S.W., *A Brief History of Time*, New York: Bantam, 1988.

Hirsch, E.D., *The Aims of Interpretation*, Chicago and London: University of Chicago Press, 1976.

Hirsch, D.H., *Reality and Idea in the Early American Novel*, The Hague: Mouton, 1971.

Hoeveler, J.D., *The New Humanism: Critique of Modern America 1900-1940*, Charlottesville: University Press of Virginia, 1977.

Howe, I., *The Decline of the New*, New York: Horizon, 1970.

————, *A Margin of Hope*, San Diego: Harcourt.

Hulme, T.E., *Speculations: Essays in Humanism and the Philosophy of Art*, ed., Herbert Read, London, New York: Routledge, 1924, rep. 1977.

Jameson, F., *The Prison-House of Language: A Critical Account of Structuralism and Russian Formalism*, Princeton: Princeton University Press, 1972.

Johnson, S., *Lives of the English Poets*, ed. G.B. Hill, 3 Vols., Oxford, 1905, rep. New York: Octagon, 1967.

————, *Works*, ed., A. Murphy, 2 Vols., London, 1823.

Kazin, A., *On Native Grounds: An Interpretation of Modern American Prose Literature*, New York: Harcourt, 1942.

Krojecky, R., *T.S. Eliot's Social Criticism*, New York: Farrar, 1972.

Krupnick, M., *Lionel Trilling and the Fate of Cultural Criticism*, Evanston: Northwestern University Press, 1986.

Krutch, J.W., *The Modern Temper*, New York: Random, 1929.

————, *Samuel Johnson*, New York: Henry Holt, 1944.

————, *The Measure of Man: On Freedom, Human Values, Survival and the Modern Temper*, New York: Bobbs, 1954.

————, *Human Nature and the Human Condition*, New York: Random, 1959.

Krutz, P. ed., *American Philosophy in the Twentieth Century: From Pragmatism to Philosophical Analysis*, London: Macmillan, 1969.

Lambert, B.C., ed., *The Essential Paul Elmer More: A Selection of his Writings*, New York: Arlington, 1972.

Leavis, F.R., *Two Cultures?*, London: Chatto and Windus, 1962.

————, *English Literature in Our Time and the University*, London: Chatto and Windus, 1969.

————, *Revaluation*, London: Penguin, 1972.

————, *Education and the University: A Sketch for An 'English School'*, London: Chatto and Windus, 1972.

Leavis, F.R., *The Common Pursuit*, Penguin, 1976.

————, *The Great Tradition*, Penguin, 1977.

Lesley, J., *The Cultural Critics: From Matthew Arnold to Raymond Williams*, London, Boston and Herby: Routledge, 1979.

Lewis, R.W.B., *The American Adam: Innocence, Tragedy and Tradition in the Nineteenth Century*, Chicago: University of Chicago Press, 1955.

Lodge, D., ed., *20th Century Literary Criticism: A Reader*, London and New York: Longman, 1972, 14th Imp., 1990.

Mattheissen, F.O., *American Renaissance: Art and Expression in the Age of Emerson and Whitman*, New York, London: Oxford University Press, 1968.

————, *The Achievement of T.S. Eliot: An Essay on the Nature of Poetry*, 3rd edn. New York: Oxford University Press, 1959.

McKean, K., *The Moral Measure of Literature*, Denver: Allan Swallow, 1961.

Miller, J., *History and Human Existence from Marx to Merleau-Ponty*, Los Angeles: University of California Press, 1982.

Muller, H.J., *Science and Criticism: The Humanistic Tradition in Contemporary Thought*, New Haven: Yale University Press, 1943.

Mumford, L., *The Condition of Man*, London: Mercury, 1963.

Niblett, W.R. ed., *The Sciences, the Humanities and the Technological Threat*, London: University of London Press, 1975.

Norris, C., *The Deconstructive Turn: Essays in the Rhetoric of Philosophy*, London and New York: Methuen, 1984.

O'Hara, D.T., *Lionel Trilling: The Work of Liberation*, University of Wisconsin Press, 1988.

Ortega Y. Gasset, J., *The Dehumanisation of Art,* Transl., H. Weyl, New York: Anchor, 1956.

Peterfreund, S., ed., *Literature and Science: Theory and Practice*, Boston: Northeastern University Press, 1990.

Poirier, R., *A World Elsewhere*, New York: Oxford, University Press, 1966.

Pritchard, J.P., *An Account of the Development of Critical Techniques from the Early Period of the Republic to the Middle Years of the Twentieth Century*, Norman University of Oklahama Press, 1956.

Raleigh, J.H., *Matthew Arnold and American Culture*, Berkeley and Los Angeles: University of California Press, 1957.

Raleigh, W. ed., *Johnson on Shakespeare*, (selected), London, 1908.

Reising, R.J., *The Unusable Past: Theory and the Study of American Literature*, New York and London: Methuen, 1986.

Scott, N.A., *Three American Moralists: Mailer, Bellow Trilling*, Notredam: University of Notingham Press, 1973.

Scott, W., ed., *Five Approaches to Literary Criticism*, New York, Collier: Macmillan, 1962.

Shafer, R., *Paul Elmer More and American Criticism*, New Haven: Yale University Press, 1935.

Shoben, E.J., *Lionel Trilling*, New York: Ungar, 1981.

Shusterman, R., *T.S. Eliot and the Philosophy of Criticism*, New York: Gerald Duckworth, 1988.

Skaff, W., *The Philosophy of T.S. Eliot: From Skepticism to a Surrealist Poetic 1907-1927*, Philadelphia, 1986.

Sypher. W., *Loss of the Self in Modern Literature and Art*, New York: Random, 1961.

Tanner, S.L., *Lionel Trilling*, Boston: Birmingham Young University Press, 1988.

Trilling, D., *Reviewing the Forties*, New York and London: Harcourt, 1978.

Wain, J., ed. *Johnson as Critic*, London and Boston: Routledge, 1973.

Walsh, W., *The Uses of Imagination: Educational Thought and The Literary Mind*, London: Chatto and Windus, 1960.

Wellek, R., *A History of Modern Criticism, 1750-1950: The Late Eighteenth Century*, New Haven: Yale University Press, 1955.

———, *A History of Modern Criticism: American Criticism, 1750-1950*, Jonathan Cape, 1986.

_____, *The Attack on Literature and Other Essays*, Chapel Hill: University of N. California Press, 1982.

Wellek, R. and A. Warren, *Theory of Literature*, 3rd edn., London: Penguin, 1963, rep. 1968.

Willey, B., *The English Moralists*, London: Chatto and Windus, 1964.

———, *The Eighteenth Century Background: Studies in the Idea of Thought in the Period*, London: Chatto and Windus, 1st pub. 1962, rep. 1967.

———, *Nineteenth Century Studies: Coleridge to Matthew Arnold*, London: Chatto and Windus, 1949, Penguin, 1964.

Williams, R., *Culture and Society: 1780-1950*, London: Chatto and Windus, 1967.

———, *The Country and the City*, London: Chatto and Windus, 1973.

———, *Marxism and Literature*, Oxford University Press, 1977.

Wimsatt, W.K. and Brooks, C., *Literature Criticism: A Short History*, Calcutta: Oxford and IBH, 1964.

Articles in Journals

Abel, L., "Lionel Trilling and His Critics", *Commentary 82*, 1986: 56-63.

Adamowski, T.H., "Lionel Trilling: Modern Literature and Its Discontents", *Dalhousie Review 55*, 1975: 83-92.

Barret, W., "The Authentic Lionel Trilling", *Commentary 73*, 1982: 36-47.

Barzun, J. "Remembering Lionel Trilling", *Encounter 47*, 1976: 82-88.

Brooks, C. "In Defense of the Canon", *Dialogue 96*, 1992: 28-33.

Chace, W.M., "Lionel Trilling: The Contrariness of Culture", *American Scholar 48*, 1978-79: 49-59.

Daiches, D., "The Mind of Lionel Trilling", *Commentary*, July, 1957: 66-69.

Dekovan, M., "The Politics of Modernist Form", *New Literary History 23.3*, 1992: 676-690.

Donhogue, D., "Trilling, Mind and Society", *Sewanee Review 86*, 1978: 161-866.

Dickstein, M., "Lionel Trilling and the Liberal Imagination", *Sewanee Review, 94*, 2, 1966: 323-34.

————, "Farewell to the Gilded Age", *Partisan Review, 59*, 3, 1992: 435-443.

Edel, L., "Literature and Life Style: A View of *Beyond Culture*", *Saturday Review 48*, (Nov. 1965): 37-38.

Frank, J., "Lionel Trilling and The Conservative Imagination", *Sewanee Review 64*, 1956: 296-309.

Frohock, W.H., "Lionel Trilling and The American Reality", *South West Review 45*, 1960: 224-32.

Hirsch, D.H., "Reality, Manners and Mr. Trilling", *Sewanee Review 72*, 1964: 420-32.

Hollander, P., "The End of Communism?" *Partisan Review 58*, 1, 1991, 107-15.

Howe, I., "Lionel Trilling: A Word of Remembrance", *Salmagundi* 35 (Fall '76): 43-52.

————, "The Self in Literature", *Salmagundi 90-91*, 1991: 56-77.

Green, M., "Lionel Trilling and the Two Cultures", *Essays in Criticism 13*, 1963: 375-80.

Greenwood, E.B., "The Literary Criticism of Lionel Trilling", *Twentieth Century 163*, 1958: 44-48.

Kubal, D., "Lionel Trilling: The Mind and Its Discontents", *Hudson Review 31*, 1978-79: 279-95.

Langbaum, R., "The Importance of The Liberal Imagination", *Salmagundi 41*, Spring 1978: 55-65.

Lasch, C., "Politics and Culture: The Fragility of Liberalism", *Salmagundi 92*, 1991: 5-18.

Lewis, L., "Lionel Trilling, 1905-75", *Sewanee Review 84*, 1976: 302-4.

Leavis, F.R., "The Literary Mind", *Scrutiny I*, 1932: 32-35.

Lewis, R.W.B., "Lionel Trilling and The New Stoicism", *Hudson Review 3*, 1950-51: 313-17.

Marcus, S., "The Psychoanalytic Self", *Southern Review 22*, 2 April 1986: 308-25.

Norris, C., "Wrestling with Deconstructionists", *Critical Quarterly 22*, 2, 1980: 57-60.

Phillips, W., "The Crisis in Our Culture", *Partisan Review 58*, 2, 1991, Conference on "The Changing Culture of the University", 192-226.

Robinson, J., "Lionel Trilling and The Romantic Tradition", *Massachusetts Review 20*, 1979: 211-36.

Sanet, T., "Lionel Trilling and The Social Imagination", *Centennial Review 23*, 1979: 159-84.

————, "The Modulated Vision: Lionel Trilling's Larger Naturalism", *Critical Inquiry 4*, 1977-78: 539-57.

————, "Trilling, Arnold and The Anxieties of the Modern", *Southern Quarterly 16*, 1977-78: 191-209.

Schwarz, D., "The Duchess' Red Shoes", *Partisan Review 20*, 1, 1953: 55-73.

Sennet, R., "On Lionel Trilling", *New Yorker 5*, Nov. 1979: 204-17.

Shechner, M., "Psychoanalysis and Liberalism: The Case of Lionel Trilling", *Salmagundi 41*. Spring 1978: 3-32.

Symons, J., "Opposites Unresolved", *T.L.S.*, Sep. 5, 1986: 959.

Tanner, T., "Lionel Trilling's Uncertainties", *Encounter 27*. 1966: 72-77.

Trilling, L., "Young in The Thirties", *Commentary 41*. 1966: 43-51.

————, "Literature and Power", *Kenyon Review 11*, 1949: 119-25.

————, "Why We Read Jane Austen", *T.L.S.*, Mar. 5, 1976: 252.

————, "The Liberal Mind: Two Communications and A Reply", *Partisan Review 16*. 1949: 649-65.

————, "The Life of the Novel", *Kenyon Review 8*.

Wellek, R., "The Literary Criticism of Lionel Trilling", *New England Review 2*, 1979: 26-49.

———, "Culture and The Present Time: A Round Table Discussion", *Commentary 56*, 6, 1974: 34-50.

INDEX

Acculturation, 108
Acculturisation, 66
Alexandar Pope, 39
Alkon, Paul Kent, 47
Allegorical meaning, 158
American fiction, 126, 130
Ananda, 106
Anderson, Sherwood, 127, 152
Angelism, 127
Anglo catholic, 64
Antigone, 113
Anti-human, 31
Anti-stalinism, 74
Aristotelian definition, 96
Aristotle, 27
Arnold, Methew, 38, 39, 41, 44, 48, 49, 50, 53, 55, 59, 60, 64, 65, 84, 85, 107, 109, 114, 135
Austen, Jane, 140, 141
Authentic unconscious, 97
Autonomy, 31, 55, 77, 79, 114, 146, 175

Babbitt, Irving, 19, 20, 41, 44, 51, 52, 53, 54
Barrett, William, 33, 100
Bell, Daniel, 96
Benthamite civilisation, 36
Benthan, Jereny, 30
Beyond culture, 90
Billy Budd, 160
Blake protests, 104
Blandeis, 133
Bownan, J., 50
Bradbury, Malcolm, 127
Buddha, 172
Bullock, 24, 32, 33, 36
Bush, Douglas, 27, 28, 71

Cain, William E., 42
Camus, Albert, 157
Capra, Fritzof, 179
Carlyle, 37
Cascardi, A.J., 101
Challenges, 36, 79
Chase, Richard, 126
Christian humanism, 54
Christian values, 28
Clifford, James, 155
Columbia University, 177
Communal atmosphere, 164
Communication, 145
Communist movement, 170
Communist Party, 163, 166
Comradeship, 161
Contemtuous affection, 154
Counter culture, 36
Criticism, 19, 24, 42, 51, 55, 60, 73, 81, 83, 84, 91, 176
    importance of, 97
Croom, Arthur, 158, 159, 160, 161, 164, 165, 170
Croom Nancy, 162, 164
    snobhish philistinism, 168
Crowford, Mary, 141, 142
Cruelty, 130
Cultural constraints, 125
Cultural criticism, 104
Cultural environment, 86, 87, 164
Cultural philistinism, 85
Cultural radicalism, 108
Curiosity, 32

Dadaism, 42, 56
Dangling man, 179
Darwinism, 38
Davis, R.C., 98
Death of literature, 42
De-authenticization, 78
De-christianisation, 34
Dehumanisation, 22, 34, 35, 37, 56, 60, 66, 74
Democratic literalism, 64
Democratisation, 49
Depersonalised societies, 23
Despondency, 122
Deterministic monism, 26

Dickstein, Morris, 84
Disintegrated consciousness, 79, 149
Disintegration, 37
Dizzy raptures, 119
Dostoievsky, 143
Dover Beach, 49
Dramatic contradiction, 72
Durant, Will, 27, 70

Ecclesiastes, 139
Education, 21
Eliot, T.S., 22, 38, 41, 44, 57, 58, 60, 110, 123, 145, 172, 176
Elizabeth, 165
Emily Caldwell, 161, 163
Emma, 144, 145
Empty new world, 163
England, 139
Ethan Frome, 146

Faulkner, William, 127
Figural combination, 154
Fitzgerald, 131
Flaubert, 139, 140
Foerster, E.M., 21, 22, 26, 29, 33, 38, 50, 88, 150, 151, 153, 154
Fragmentation, 37

Gandhian Plan, 129
Gasset, Ortega Y., 32, 100
Gleam, 120
Goodheart, E., 36, 49, 108
Goodman, Paul, 179
Graff, G., 99, 100
Graves. Robert, 109, 110

Hallow Man, 179
Hassan, I., 132, 134
Hawthorne, 145
Hirsch, E.D., 43
Hollender, Paul, 74
Honest soul, 149
Howe, I., 155
Hulme, T.E., 22
Human consciousness, 176
Human language, 46
Human responsibility, 88
Humanism, 22
  stresses, 20
  tradition of, 48
Humanistic tradition, 41-50
Humanitarianism, 160

Ideological thinking, 155
Imbeciles, 139
Immediate perception, 22
Immigration, 43
Immortality ode, 120, 121
Industrial revolution, 95
Industrialisation, 43
Intellectual adumbration, 163
Intellectual weakness, 128
Intentional Fallacy, 137
Irrationalism, 42

James, Henry, 125, 130
Jameson, Fradric, 176
Johnson, Samuel, 45, 46, 47, 48
Joyce, 123
Judeo-Christian tradition, 93
Jungian psychology, 42

Kafka, 172
Kazim, A., 51, 54
Keats, 109, 114, 115
Know Thyself, 34
Krupnick, Mark, 86
Krutich, J.W., 22, 25, 47
Kurtz, 39, 149

Laskell, John, 158, 159, 163, 164, 165, 166, 167, 170
  sudden realisation, 169
Lawrence, D.H., 59
Leavis, F.R., 38, 41, 59, 61, 62, 85, 177
Lewis, R.W.B., 154
Liberal criticism, 51
Liberal intellectual culture, 170
Liberalism, 65
Literary criticism, 19, 24, 25, 27, 37, 47, 48, 50, 53, 59, 60, 62, 73, 101, 104, 105, 109, 179
Literary autonomy, 172, 173
Little Dorrit, 132
Lodge, D., 127, 155

Mann, Thomas, 165, 166
Marcus, Steven, 72
Marx, Leo, 34, 38, 43
Marxism, 61, 72

Maxim, Gifford, 163, 166, 170
Maxim, Laskell, 167
Mecca, 108
Mediocre democracy, 139
Melodrama, 153
Mill, John Stuart, 30
Miller, J. Hillis, 34, 175
Modern American criticism, 42
Modern American fiction, 127
Modern consciousness, 144
Modern culture, 116
Modern dehumanised cultural environment, 178
Modern literary criticism, 41
Modern literary temperament, 159, 160
Modern literature, 23, 36, 149, 150
Moral imagination, 86
Moral obligation, 56
Moral redism, 129
Moralism, 46
Morality, 147
More, Paul Elmer, 41, 44, 54
Muller, H.J., 21
Mumford, Lewis, 23, 30

Negative capability, 116, 117
New anarchy, 42
New critical method, 175
New criticism, 43, 73, 83, 96
New critics, 107, 108, 11
New humanism, 51, 52, 54
New humanistic movement, 57
Newton, 29
Newtonian Science, 44
Nihilism, 33
Nussbaum, Martha, 174

Ode, 120
O'Hara, Daniel T., 97, 100, 132, 140
Old Visionary norm, 148
One-dimensional answers, 154
One-dimensional man, 179
Organisational man, 179
Orwell, George, 138
Oscillation, 71
Owen, Wilfred, 110

Panorama, 137
Parochialism, 21
Phenemenology, 98
Phenomenolism, 42, 155
Political constraints, 134
Political problems, 53
Political propaganda, 74
Post-modern criticism, 42
Post-modernism, 172
Post-modernist critics literature, 178
Pragmatism, 38
Primitive dignity, 153
Pure humanism, 22

Quintessence of dust, 36

Raleigh, J.H., 46
Radical innocence, 143
Rationalism, 32, 33
Renaissance, 19, 26, 44
Renaissance age, 27
Renaissance humanism, 83
Rhetorical constraints, 154
Robinson, 117, 123
Romantic self, 31
Romanticism, 21, 29, 30, 32, 48, 52, 55, 58, 62, 74
Rousseau, 29, 30, 118
Russell, Bertrand, 101

Schleifer, R., 42, 98
Scholar-Gypsy, 49
Schwartz, Delmore, 90
Scornful laughter, 148
Scott, 70
Secularism, 44
Self-confused nihilism, 42
Self-discovery, 138
Self-hood, 146, 147, 148, 158
Sex satisfaction, 25
Shakespeare, 35, 37, 46, 58, 116, 148
Sincerity, 131
Skinner, F., 23
Snobhish philistinism, 168
Social hypocrisy, 148
Socio-political temperament, 159
Spiritual destitution, 39
Spiritual nihilism, 35
Sthitadhiti, 99
Structuralism, 42, 155
Surrealism, 42, 57
Sypher, Wylie, 30

Technological age, 19
Toffler, Alvin, 95
Tolstoi, 126, 135
Tolstoy, 132
Transcendental value system, 54
Trilling, Lionel, 19, 21, 38, 41, 43, 61, 63, 67, 71, 78-80, 104
    admiration, 110, 111, 146, 157
    assessment, 151
    association, 121
    centrist position countervails, 169
    critical attitudes, 95
    critical temperament, 89
    criticism, 82, 83, 84, 169, 177
        of novel, 125-35
    critique of liberal intelligentsia, 167
    cultural criticism, 92
    cultural theory, 179
    ideas on criticism, 127
    interpretation, 149
    literary criticism, 87, 104-120, 123, 146, 174
    strategy, 109
    treatment of literature, 157
Triumphant industrialisation, 36
Trotskyism, 63
Twain, Henry, 130

Ulysses, 137
Uncritical nationalism, 21
Underground man, 143, 148
Unified sensibility, 116-17
Urbanisation, 43
Utilitarianism, 30
Utopia, 167

Victorian ethics, 62
Violence, 110
Visionary gleam, 120
Vulgarity, 142

Walden, 119
Wellek, René, 46, 108
Weltenschaung, 179
Wharton, Edith, 146, 147
Willey, Basil, 29, 34, 35
Williams, Raymond, 127, 155
Wordsworth, 37, 80, 99, 109, 118, 119, 120, 143
World War II, 138, 177

Yeats, 110, 113, 114, 123
Yoknapatawpha county, 128
Yuppie culture, 155

Zola, 155
    criticism of, 136
    fiction of, 128
    nature of, 56